HARD ROCK BASS BIBLE

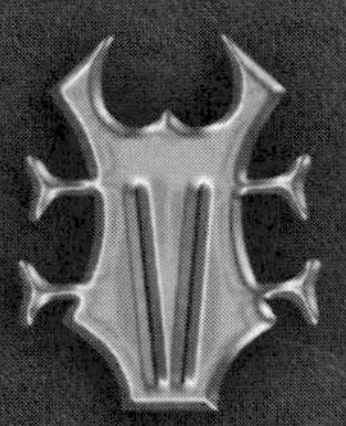

ISBN 0-634-08928-5

7777 W. Bluemound Rd. P.O. Box 13819 Milwaukee, WI 53213

Visit Hal Leonard Online at
www.halleonard.com

TABLE OF CONTENTS

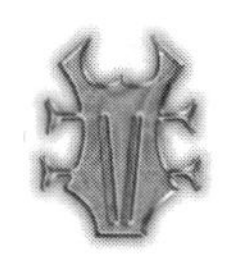

Addicted to That Rush

Words and Music by William Sheehan, Pat Torpey and Paul Gilbert

D5/A
Am7

Verse
Am7
D5/A
1. When I was a young boy, my ma-ma said to me,
2. Look a - round I stop and stare, got to get a taste.

Am7
2nd time, Bass: w/ Bass Fill 1
D5/A
E♭5/A
D5/A
"Once a wom - an gets your soul, you'll nev-er shake her free."
Pret-ty wom - an ev - 'ry - where, we ain't got time to waste.

Bass Fill 1

Am7
D5/A
These are words of wis - dom, it turns out she was right.
Look - in' for a lit - tle thang, to fit in - to my plans.

2nd time, Bass: w/ Bass Fill 2
Am7
Got - ta find a lov - er, 'cause I need a fix to - night.
On the town I'll hunt you down, I'm walk - in' like a man.

Pre-Chorus
C
D5
A5
(Woh!
Watch it touch me deep in - side.
Bass Fig. 2

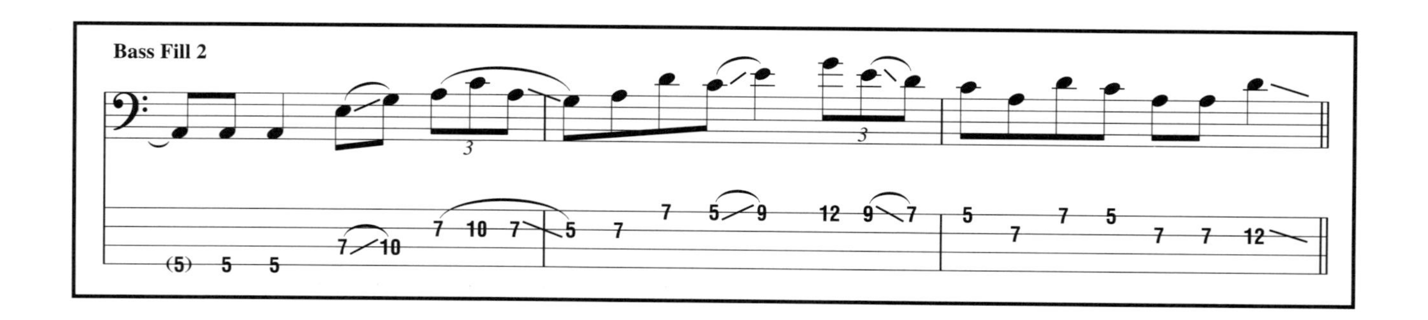
Bass Fill 2

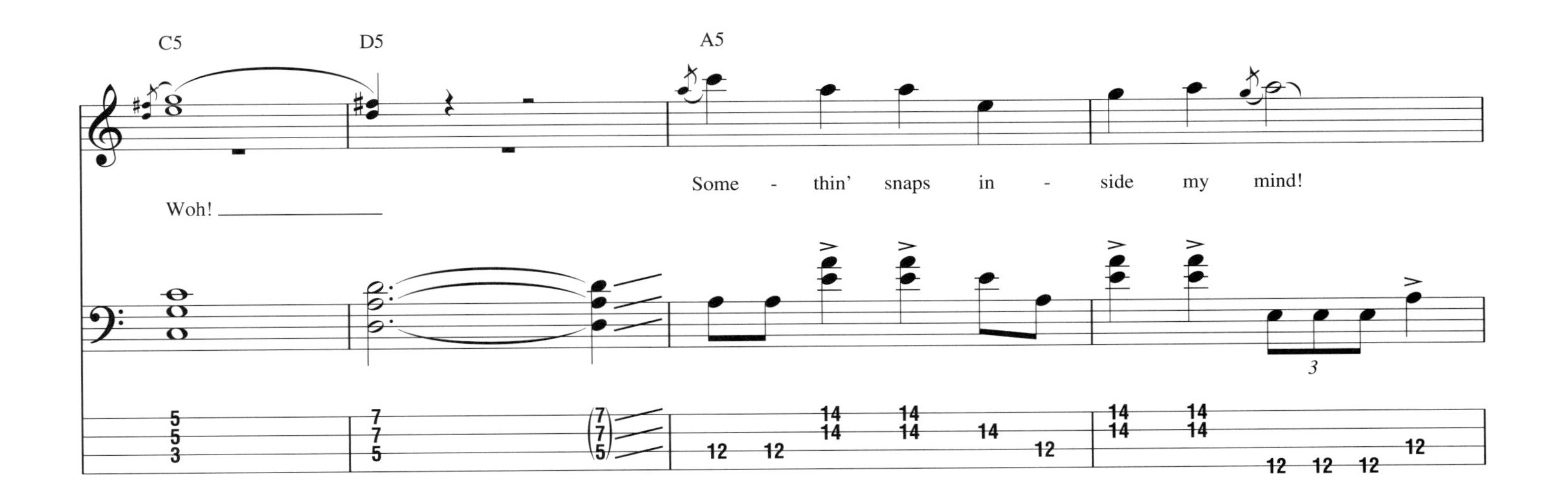
C5
D5
A5
Woh!
Some - thin' snaps in - side my mind!

2nd time, Bass: w/ Bass Fill 3
C5
D5
F5
Em7
Woh!)
When I feel it com - in',

Chorus
F5
G5
A5 N.C.
A5 N.C.
ain't no sense in run - nin'. I'm ad - dict - ed to that rush,

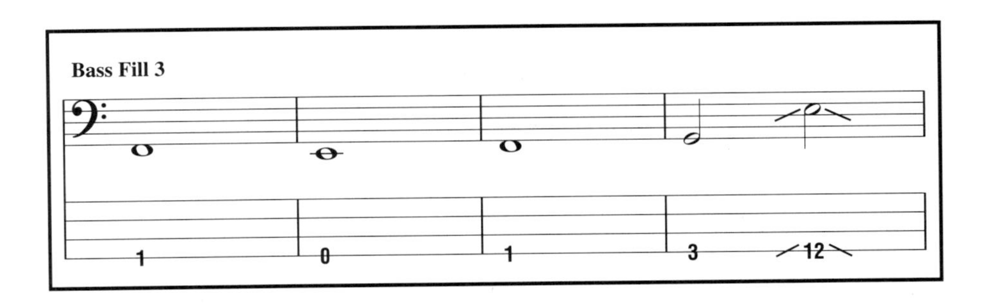
Bass Fill 3

1.
A5
N.C.
ev - 'ry time we touch.
Nev - er get e - nough,
'cause I'm ad -
Am7
dict - ed to that rush?
Ow!
D5/A
C5
A5
G5
E5
2.
Woh no!
I'm ad - dict - ed to that rush,

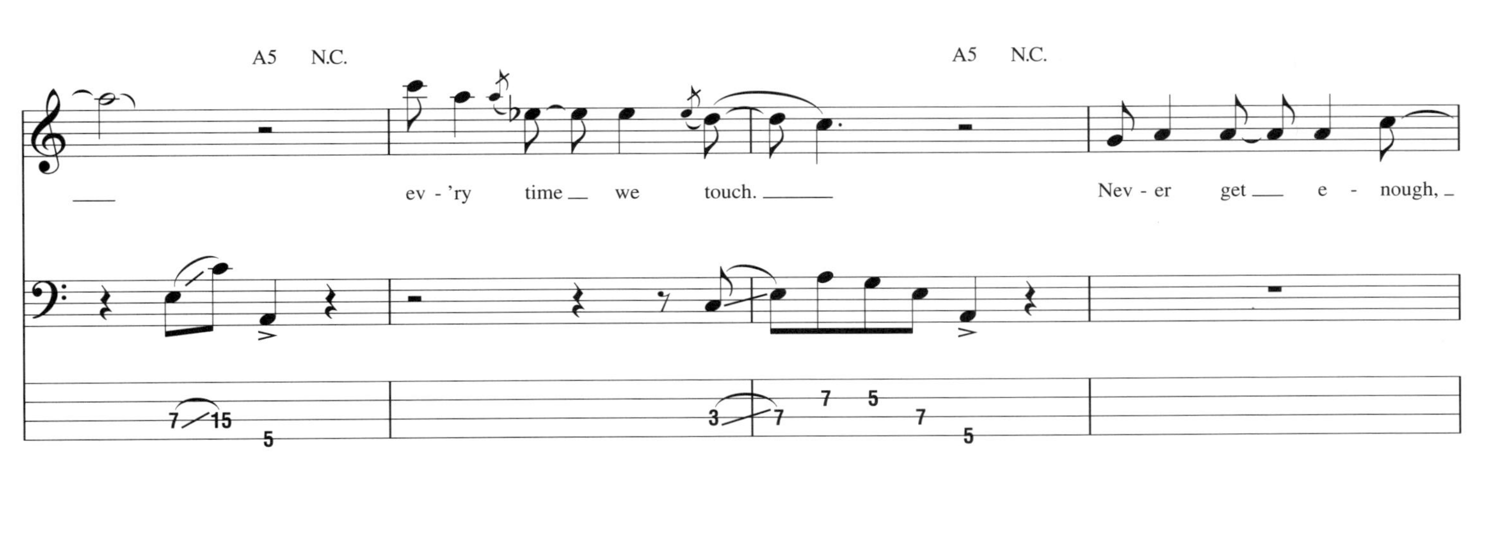

*Vibrato achieved by pushing headstock of bass back and forth.

Guitar Solo

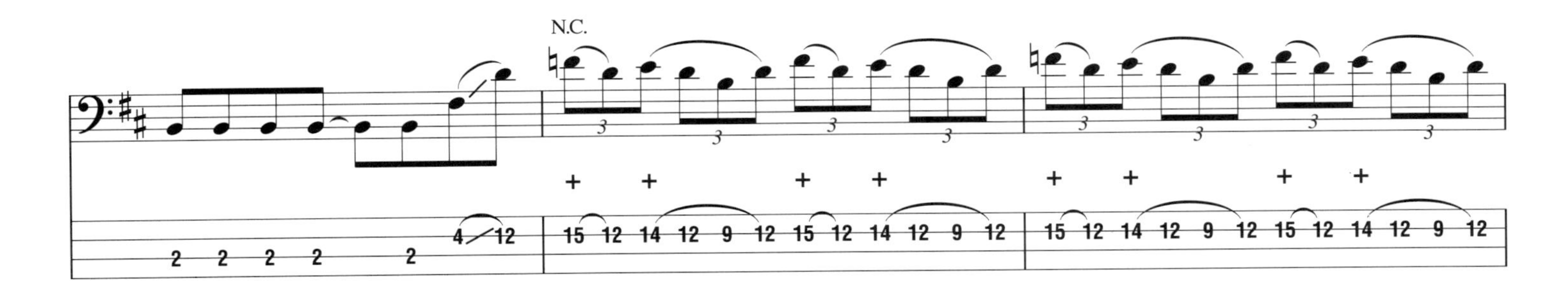

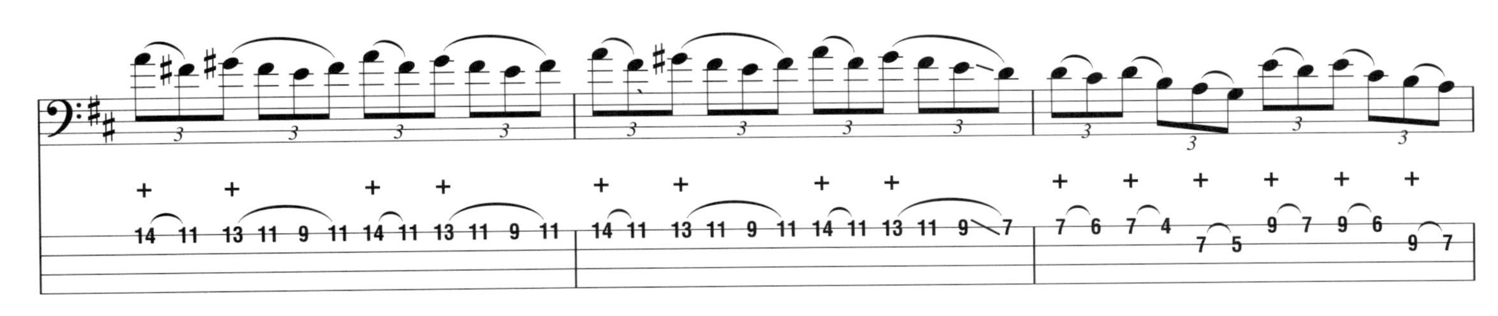

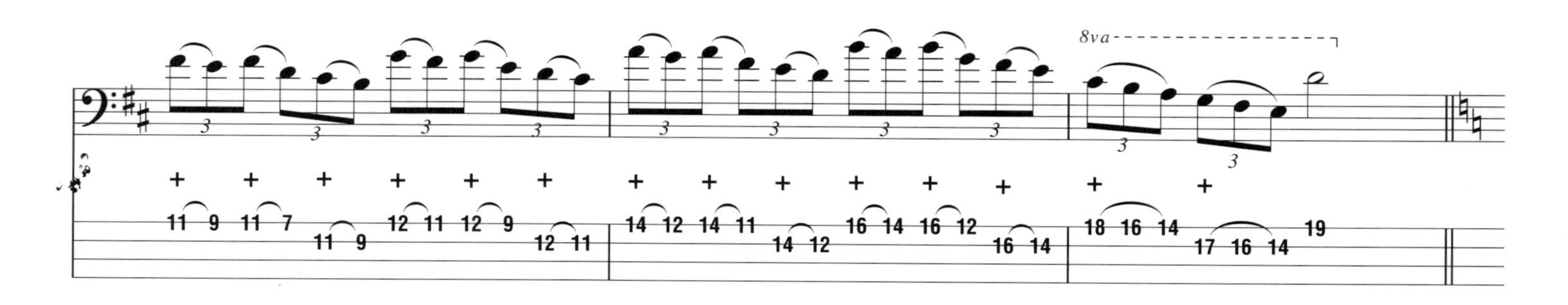
8va
11 9 11 7 11 9 12 11 12 9 12 11
14 12 14 11 14 12 16 14 16 12 16 14
18 16 14 17 16 14 19

Pre-Chorus
C5
D5
(Woh!
Watch it touch me deep in - side.
loco

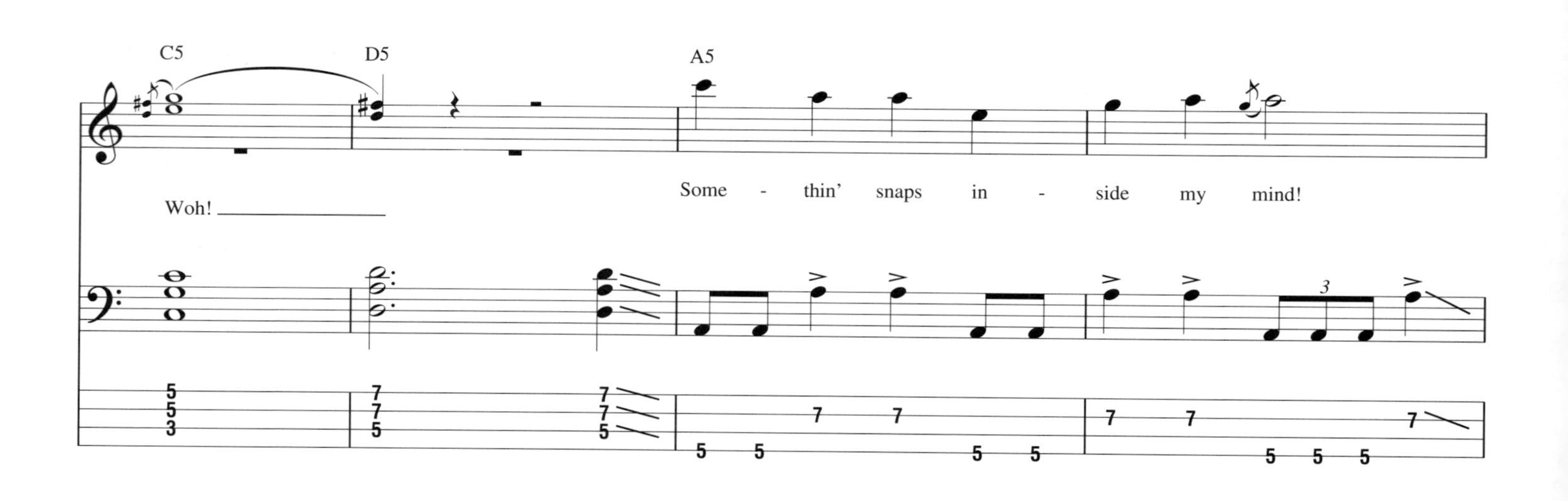
C5
D5
A5
Woh!
Some - thin' snaps in - side my mind!

C5
D5
F5
Em7
Woh!)
Oh!
When I feel it com - in', ain't

F5
G5
A5
no sense in run - nin'.
10
10
8
12
12
10
7
7
5
14 12
14 12
14 12
14
12 14 12
10
7
12
steady gliss.
Bridge
A5
N.C.
Bass tacet
Once I thought her lov - in' was a hab - it I could break!
0
But when I go with - out
it, my bod - y starts to ache.
12 (12) 0 3 0
0 2 0 4 5 0 4 5 0

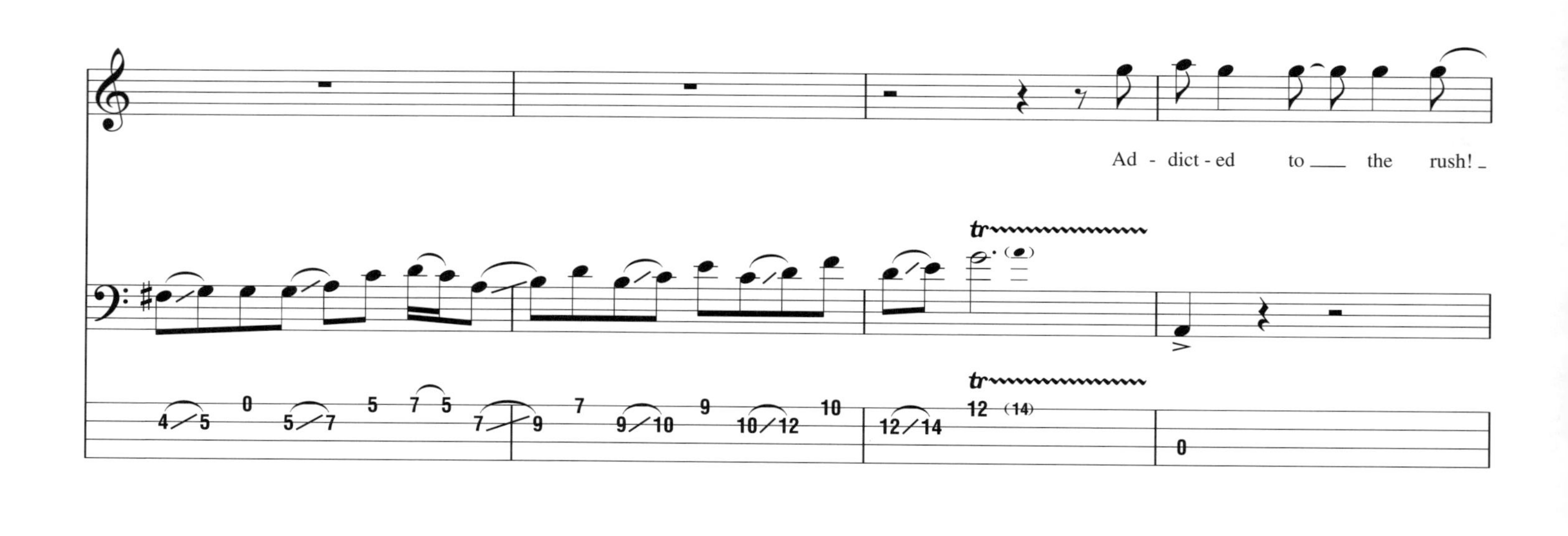

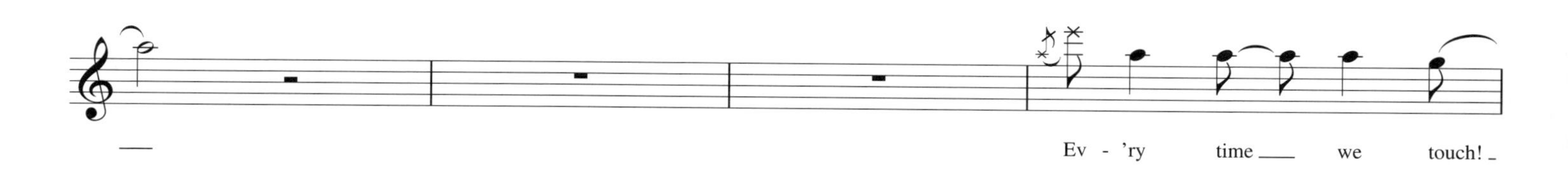

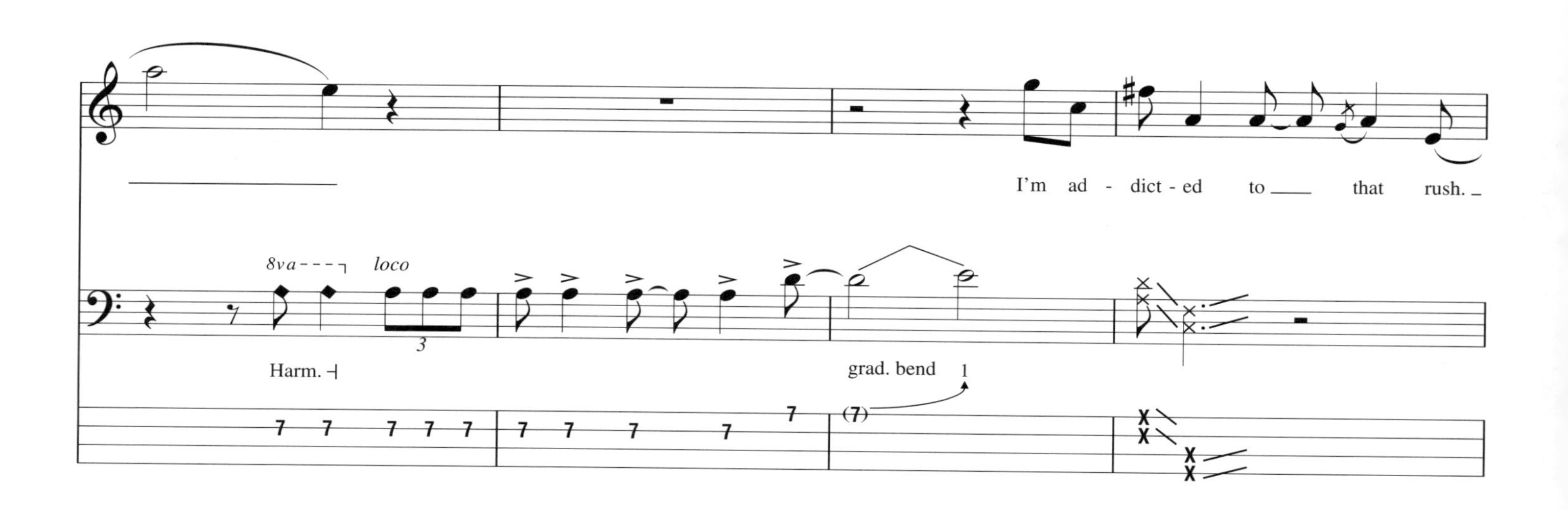

*Hypothetical fret location.

Pre-Chorus
C5
- er, nev - er, nev - er get e - nough!
(Woh!
8va
H.H.
steady gliss.
D5
A5
Watch it touch me deep in - side.
C5
Woh!
D5
A5
Some - thin' snaps in - side my mind!
C5
Woh!)
D5
F5
Em7
F5
Oh! When I feel it com - in', ain't no sense in

Chorus
G5
A5
run - nin'. I'm ad - dict - ed to that rush!
Ad - dict - ed to that rush!
I'm ad - dict - ed to that rush!
Ad - dict - ed to that rush!
I'm ad - dict - ed to that rush!
I'm ad -
dict - ed to that rush!
Ad - dict - ed to that rush!

I'm ad - dict - ed to that rush!
Ow!
Free time
N.C.
*Bend and vibrato achieved by pushing headstock of bass back and forth.
A5

Aqualung

Music by Ian Anderson
Lyrics by Jennie Anderson

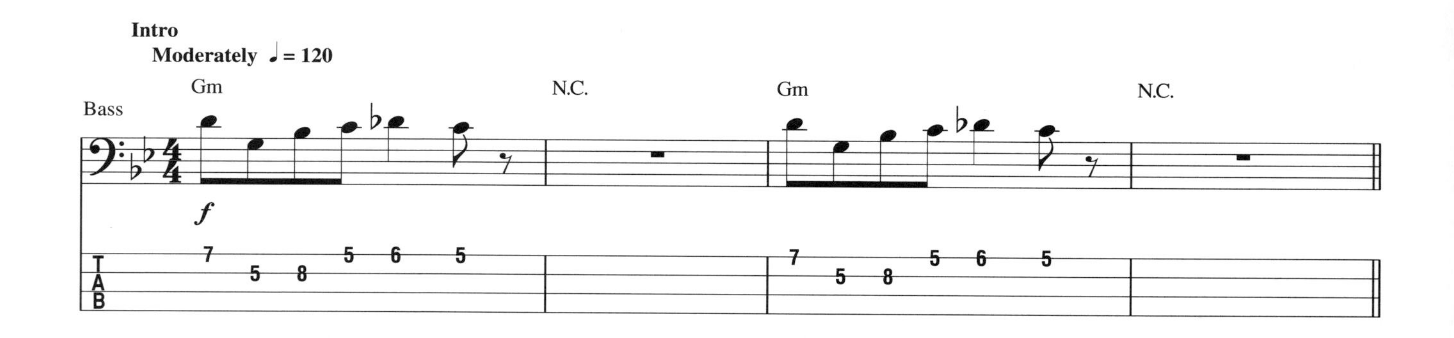

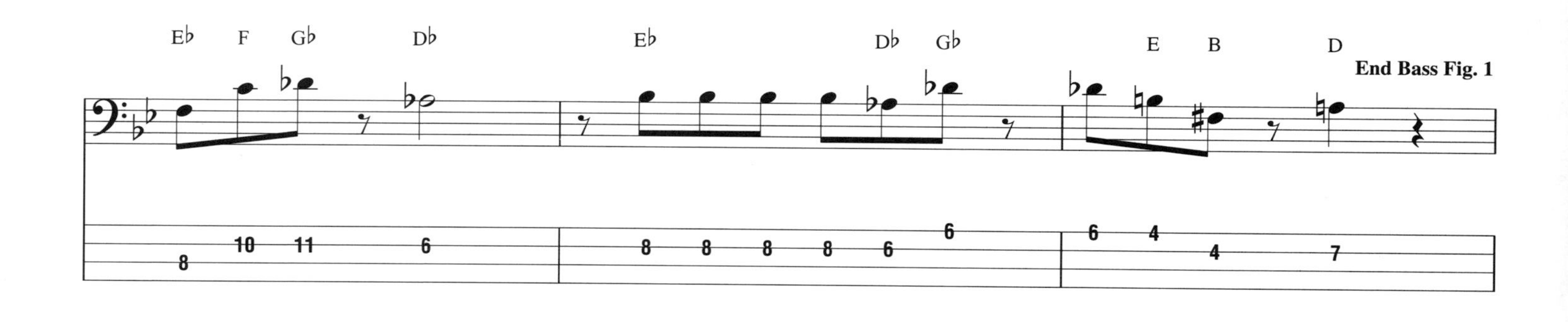

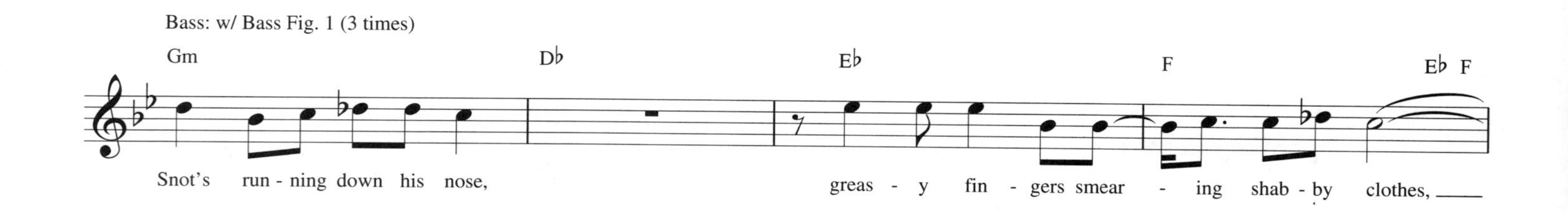

E♭ F G♭ D♭ E♭ D♭ G♭ E B D Gm
hey, Aq - ua - lung. Dry - ing in the cold sun,
D♭ E♭ F E♭ F E♭ F G♭ D♭
watch - ing as the fril - ly pant - ies run. Hey,

E♭ D♭ G♭ E B D Gm D♭ E♭
Aq - ua - lung. Feel-ing like a dead duck, spit-ting out pie-ces of his

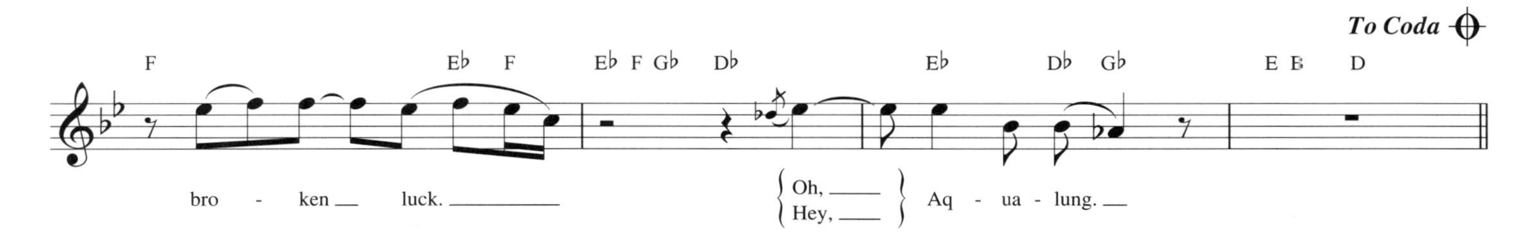
To Coda
F E♭ F E♭ F G♭ D♭ E♭ D♭ G♭ E B D
bro - ken luck. Oh, Hey, Aq - ua - lung.

Bridge
Bass tacet
Gm F C
Sun streak-ing cold, an old man wand'-ring lone - ly.

Cm Gm F
Tak-ing time the on - ly way he knows.

Gm F C
Leg hurt-ing bad, as he bends to pick a dog-end, he
mp

Cm
Gm
F
goes down to the bog ___ and ___ warms ___ his ___ feet.
Gm
F
Feel - ing a - lone, ___ the

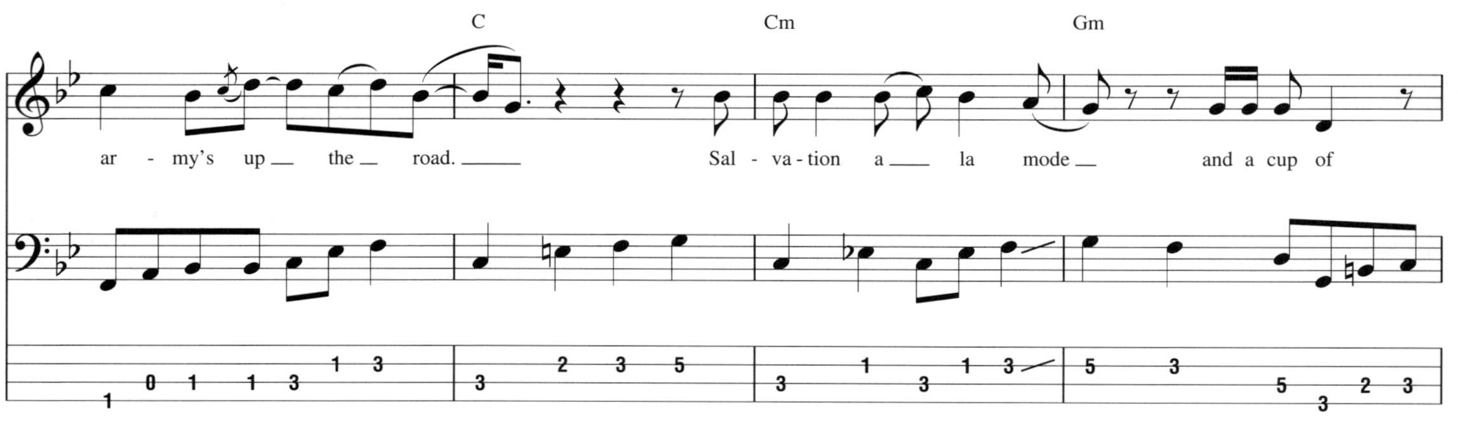
C
Cm
Gm
ar - my's up ___ the ___ road. ___ Sal - va - tion a ___ la mode ___ and a cup of

F
Gm
F
tea. Aq - ua - lung, my friend, ___ don't you

*Doubled, next 48 meas.

F
Gm
snatch your rat - tl - ing last breaths with deep sea div - er sounds and the
Cm
F
flow -ers bloom like mad - ness in the spring.
Gm
F
Sun streak-ing cold, an
Leg hurt - ing bad, as he
C
Cm
Gm
old man wand'- ring lone - ly, tak - ing time the on - ly way he
bends to pick a dog - end, he goes down to the park and warms his

F
knows.
feet.
Whoa, ho, ho, no.
Gm F C
Feel - ing a - lone, the ar - my's up the road. Sal -
Aq - ua - lung my friend, don't you start a - way un - eas - y. You
Cm Gm F
va - tion a la mode and a cup of tea.
poor old sod, you see it's on - ly me, me.
Interlude
Gm
Oh, ho, ho, ho, oh, ho.

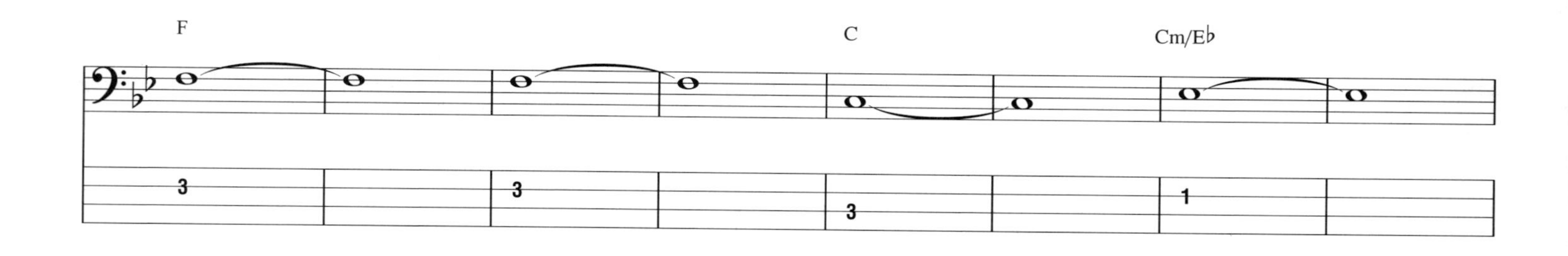

Guitar Solo

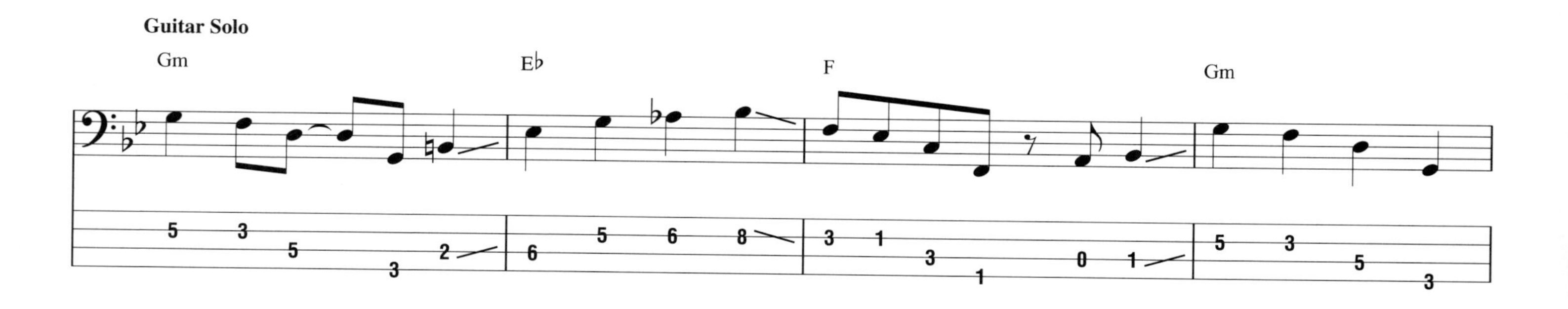

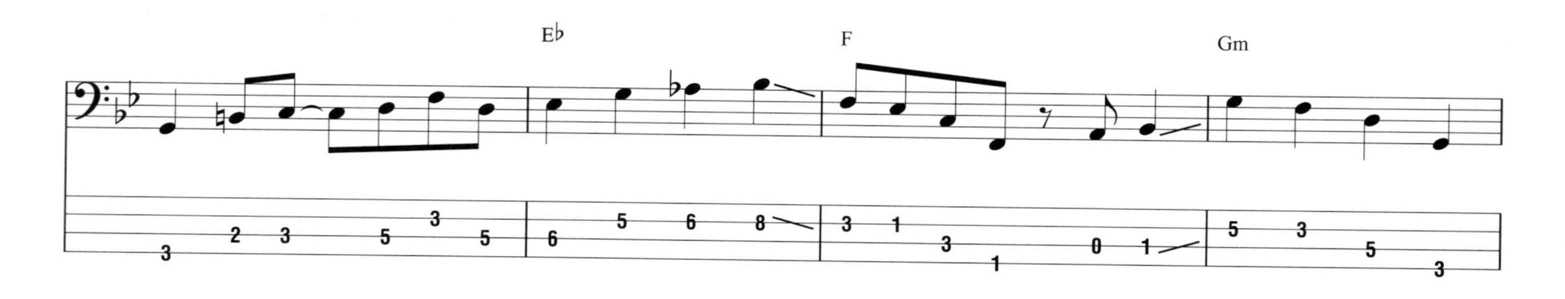

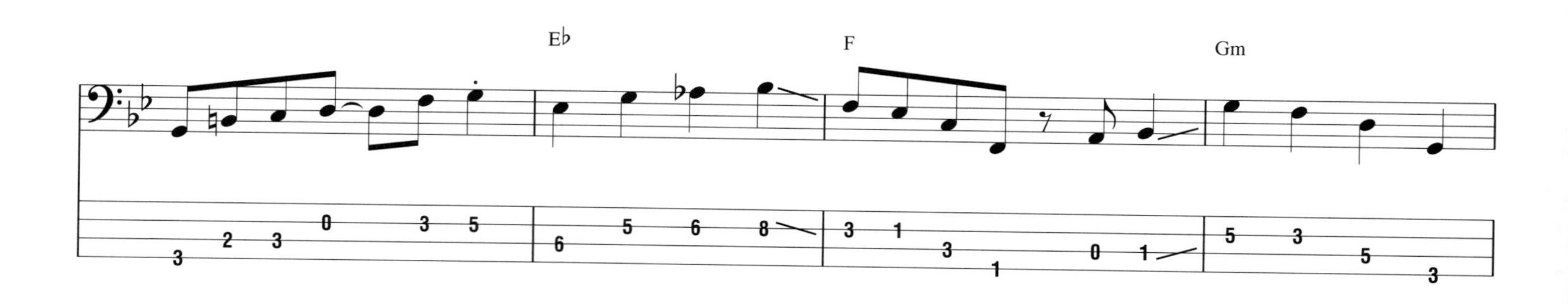

*Vocals doubled next 7 meas.

Cm
Gm
F
Gm
Dee, dee, dee, dee, dee, dee, dee, dee, dee, dee.
Aq - ua - lung, my

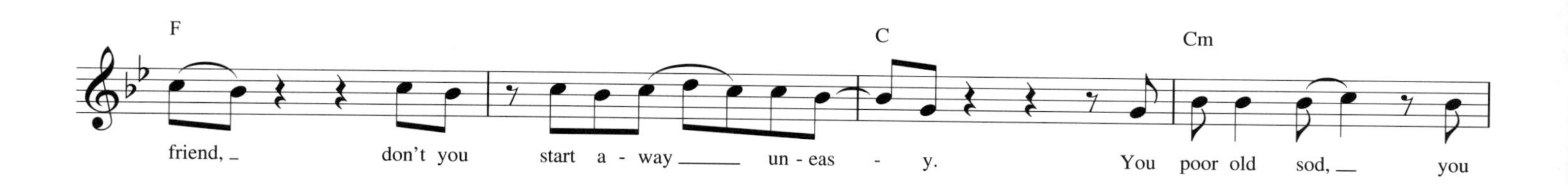
F
C
Cm
friend, don't you start a - way un - eas - y.
You poor old sod, you

Gm
F
D.C. al Coda
see it's on - ly me, yeah.
Hmm.

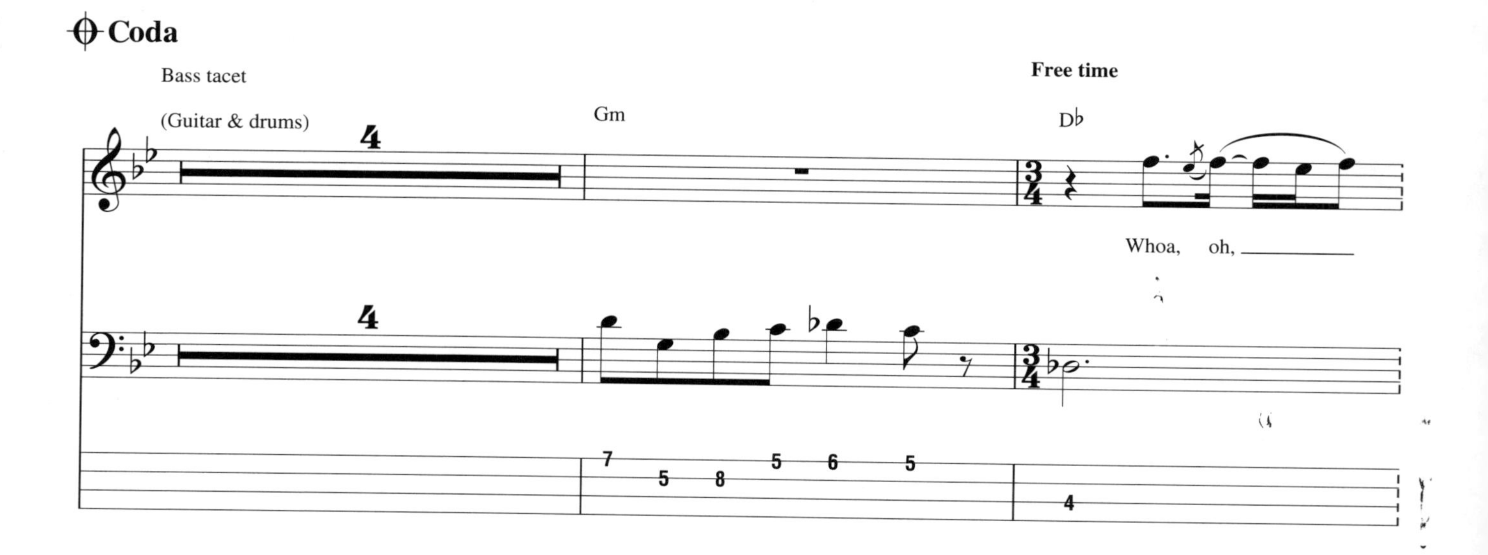
Coda
Bass tacet
(Guitar & drums)
Free time
Gm
D♭
Whoa, oh,

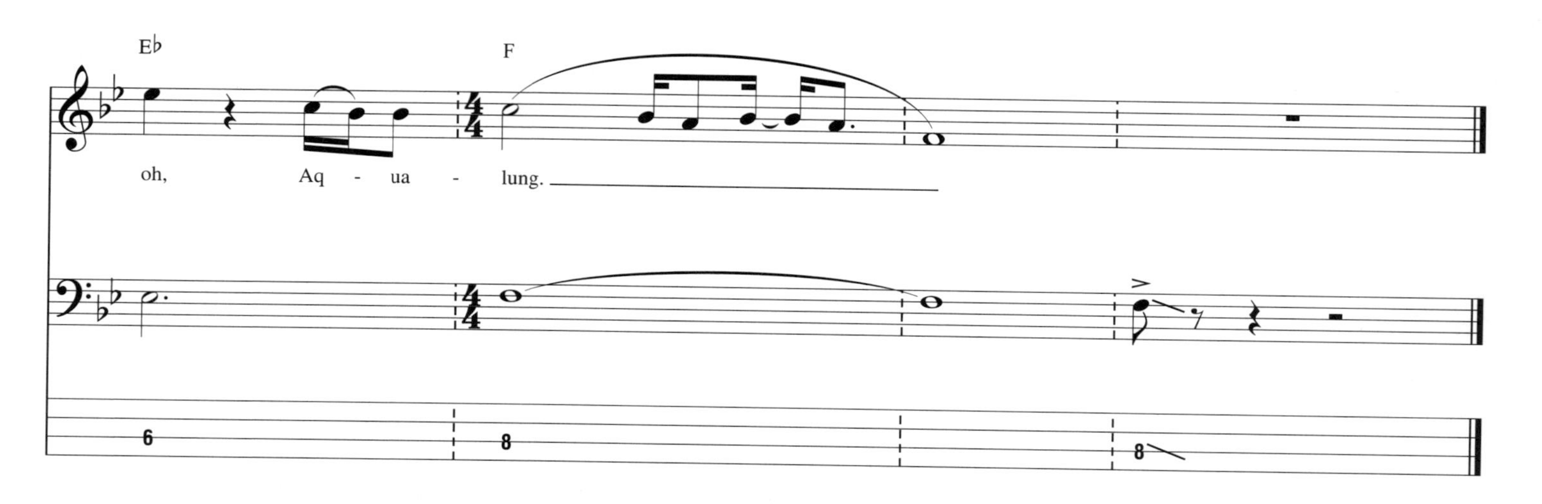
E♭
F
oh, Aq - ua - lung.

Barracuda

Words and Music by Nancy Wilson, Ann Wilson, Michael Derosier and Roger Fisher

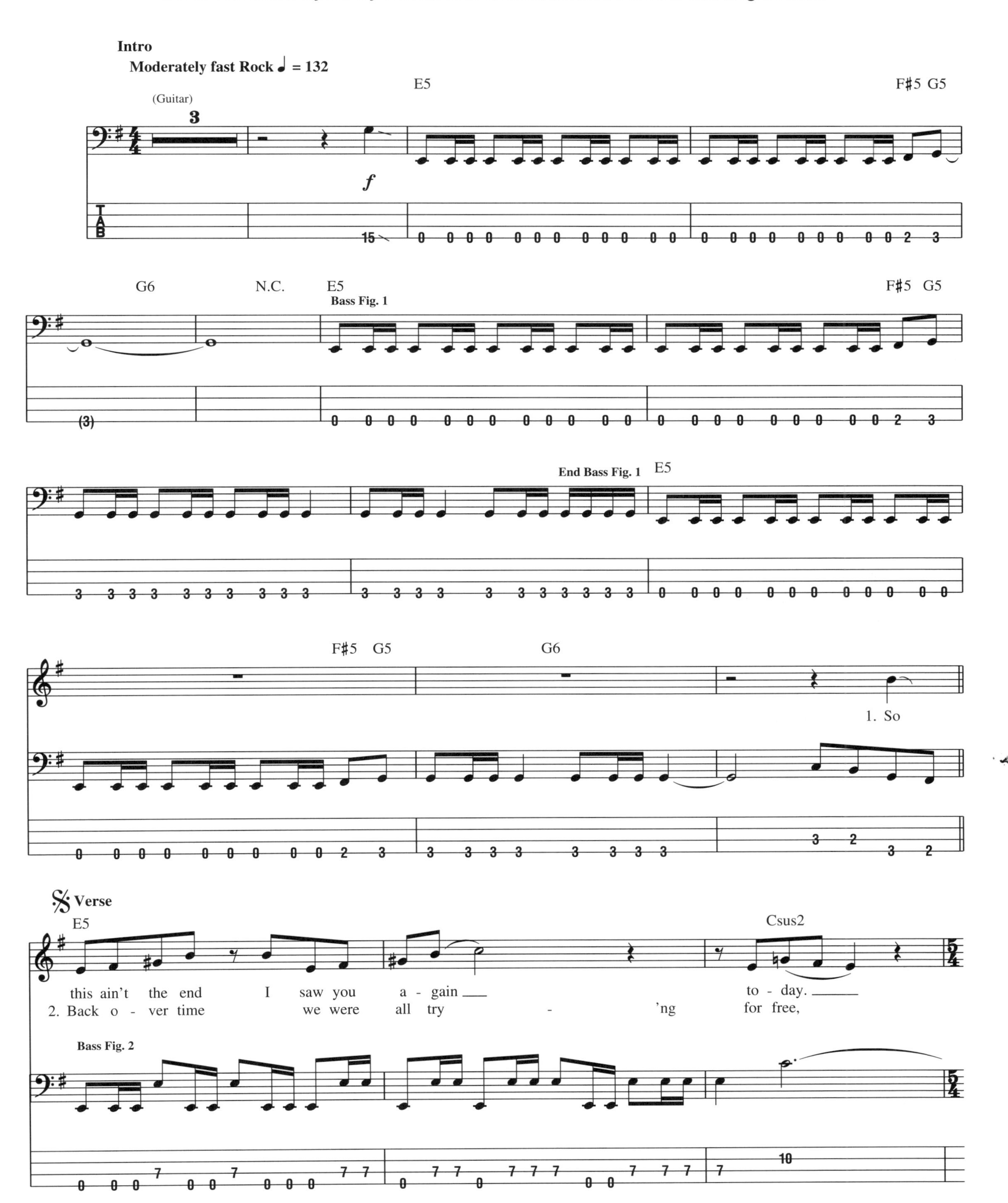

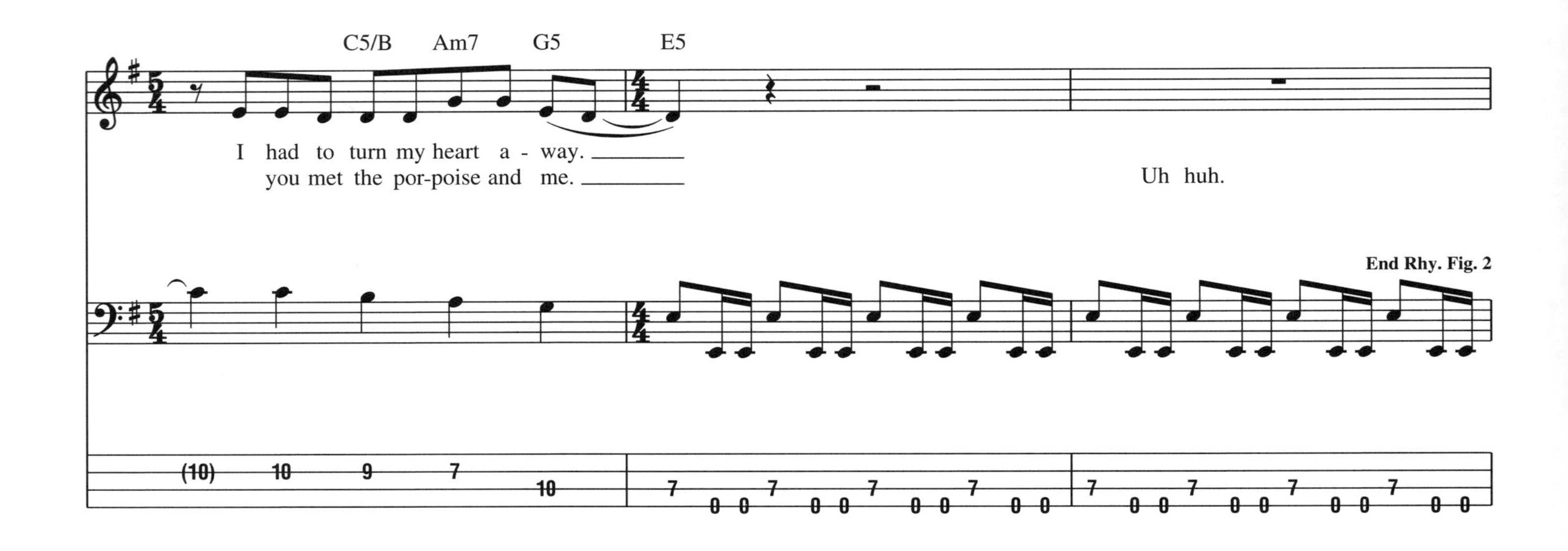
C5/B Am7 G5 E5
I had to turn my heart a - way.
you met the por-poise and me.
Uh huh.
End Rhy. Fig. 2

w/ Bass Fig. 2
E5
Csus2
Smile like the sun, kiss - es for ev - 'ry - one,
No right, no wrong; sell - ing a song, a name.

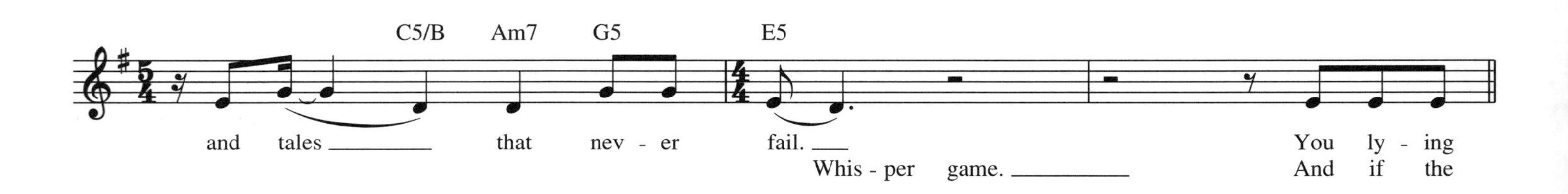
C5/B Am7 G5 E5
and tales that nev - er fail.
Whis - per game.
You ly - ing
And if the

Chorus
To Coda
2nd time, w/ Bass Fill 1
C5 C5/B N.C.(A5) E5 N.C.(C) (Am) E5
so low in - to the weeds. I bet you gon - na am - bush - me. You'd have me
real thing don't do the trick, you bet - ter make up some-thing - quick. You gon - na

Bass Fill 1

Dsus2
Asus2
down, down, down, down on my knees, now would-n't you, Bar - ra - cu -

w/ Bass Fig. 1
E5
F♯5 G5
da? Oh.

D.S. al Coda
E5
F♯5 G5
G6

Coda
Dsus2
Asus2
burn, burn, burn, burn, burn it to the wick.

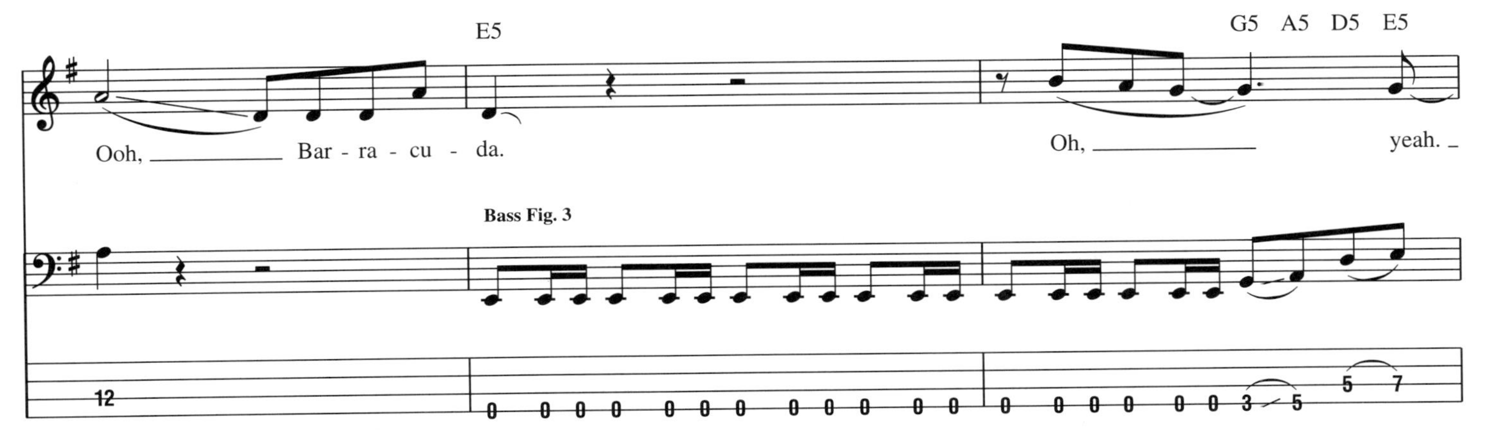
E5
G5 A5 D5 E5
Ooh, Bar - ra - cu - da. Oh, yeah.
Bass Fig. 3

Bridge
G5 A5 D5 E5
C
"Sell me, sell you," the por-poise said.
A
Dive down, deep down, save my head. You,
End Bass Fig. 3
Bass Fig. 4
End Bass Fig. 4
w/ Bass Fig. 3
E5
G5 A5 D5 E5
I think that you had the blues too.
G5 A5 D5 E5 C
w/ Bass Fig. 4
All that night and all the next,
A
swam with-out look-ing back,
made for the west-ern pools.
E5
F#5 G5 A5 E5
Sil-ly, sil-ly fools.
F#5 G5 A5

Guitar Solo
C
A

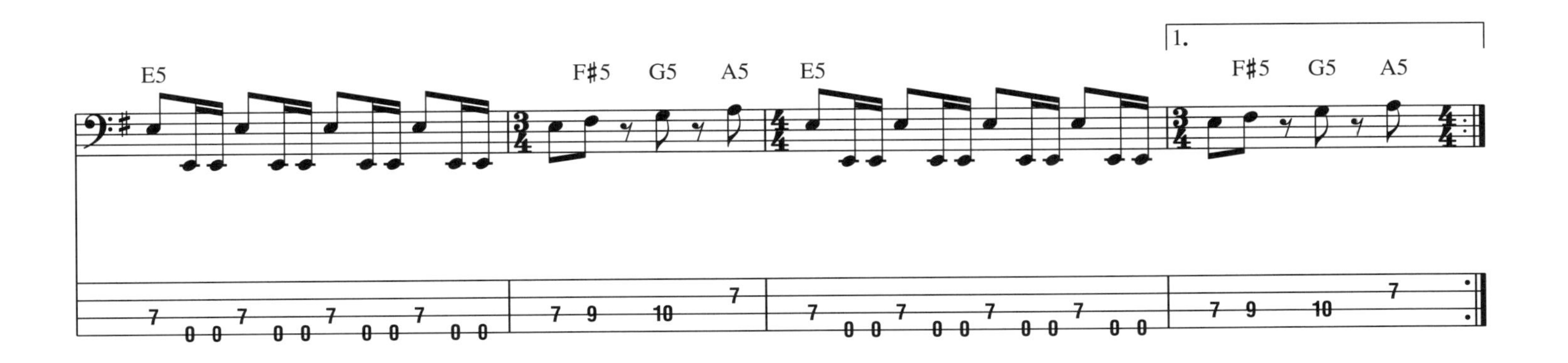
E5
F#5 G5 A5
E5
1.
F#5 G5 A5

2.
F#5 G5 A5
Chorus
C5 C5/B N.C.(A5) E5
The real thing don't do the trick, no, you bet - ter

N.C.(C) (Am) E5 Dsus2
make up some - thing quick. You gon - na burn, burn, burn,

Asus2
burn,
burn it to the wick.
(12)
14
12
11
14
12
11
14
12
12
E5
Oh,
Bar - ra - bar -
ra - cu - da.
Yeah.
Outro
N.C.(Em)
Play 3 times

1.
2.
E5
1.-4.
F#5
G5
A5
5.
F#5
G5
A5

Been Caught Stealing

Words and Music by Perry Farrell, Dave Navarro, Stephen Perkins and Eric Avery

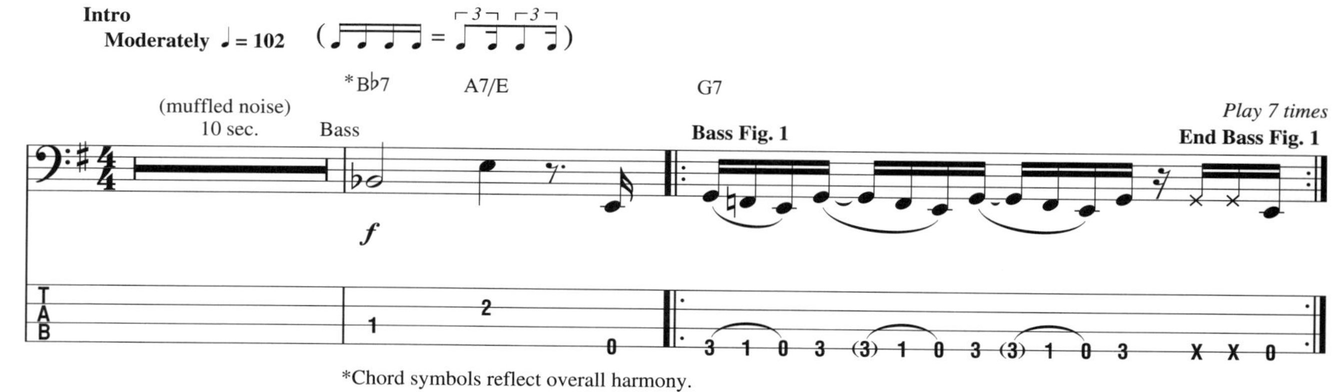

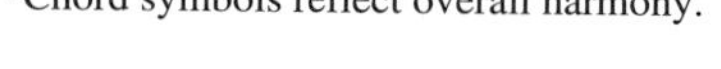

*Chord symbols reflect overall harmony.

Chorus

2nd time, Bass: w/ Bass Fill 1
3rd time, Bass: w/ Bass Fill 2

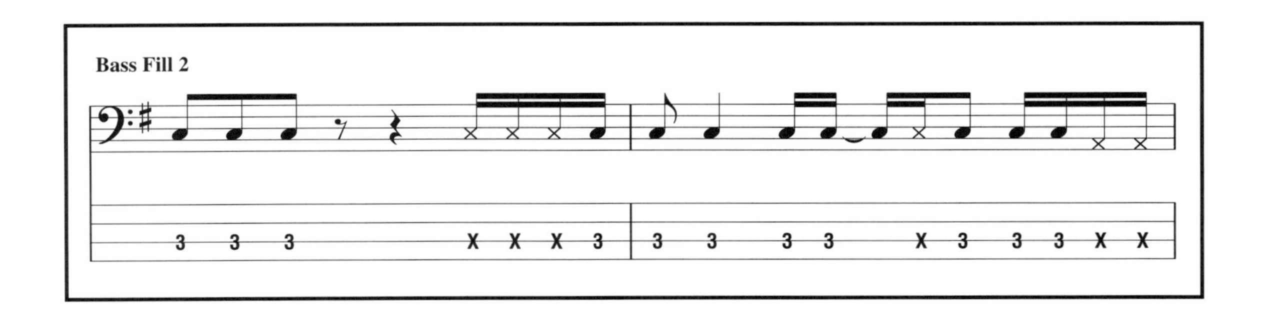

To Coda

G
Csus4
C
Csus4
C7
Hey, all right.
1.
B♭7
A7
If I get by
it's

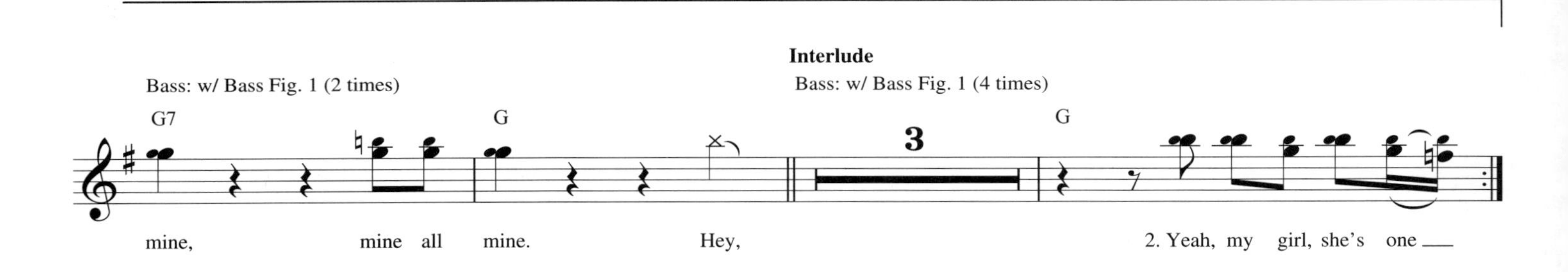
Interlude
Bass: w/ Bass Fig. 1 (2 times)
Bass: w/ Bass Fig. 1 (4 times)
G7
G
G
mine, mine all mine.
Hey,
2. Yeah, my girl, she's one

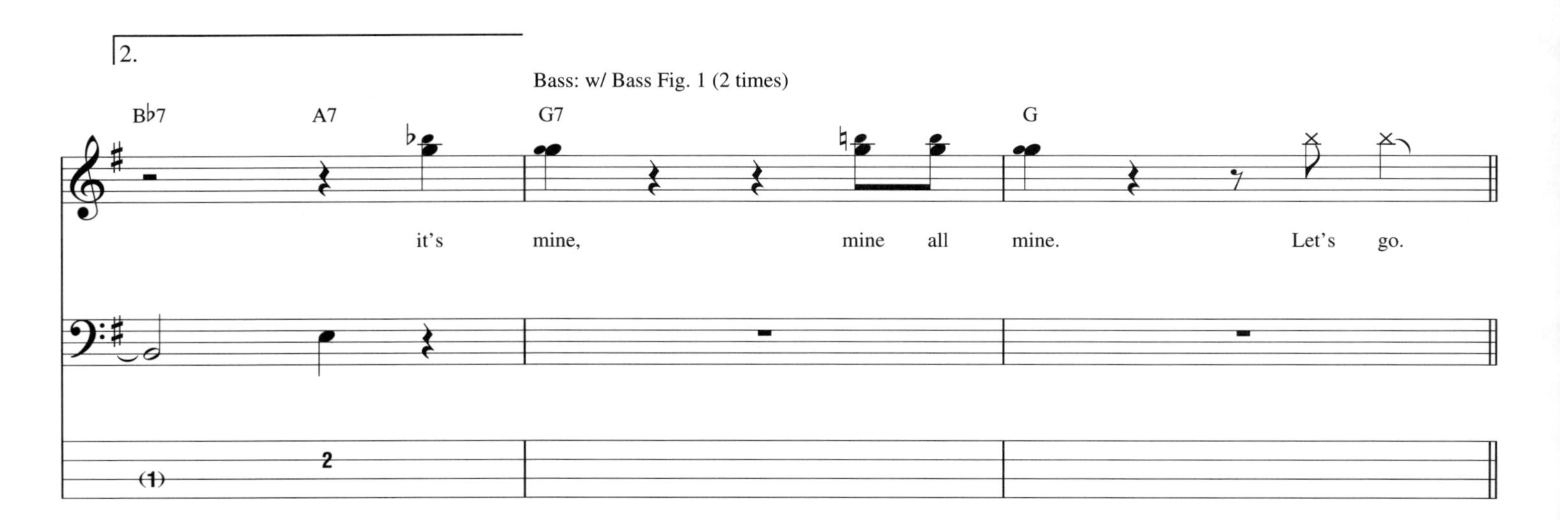
2.
Bass: w/ Bass Fig. 1 (2 times)
B♭7
A7
G7
G
it's mine, mine all mine.
Let's go.

D.S. al Coda

Bass: w/ Bass Fig. 1 (4 times)

N.C.(G)

3. Sat a - round the

Coda

B♭7
A7/E
If I get by
it's, a,

C
Csus4
C7
mine, all mine, all mine, all mine, all
mine, all mine, all mine, all mine, all mine.

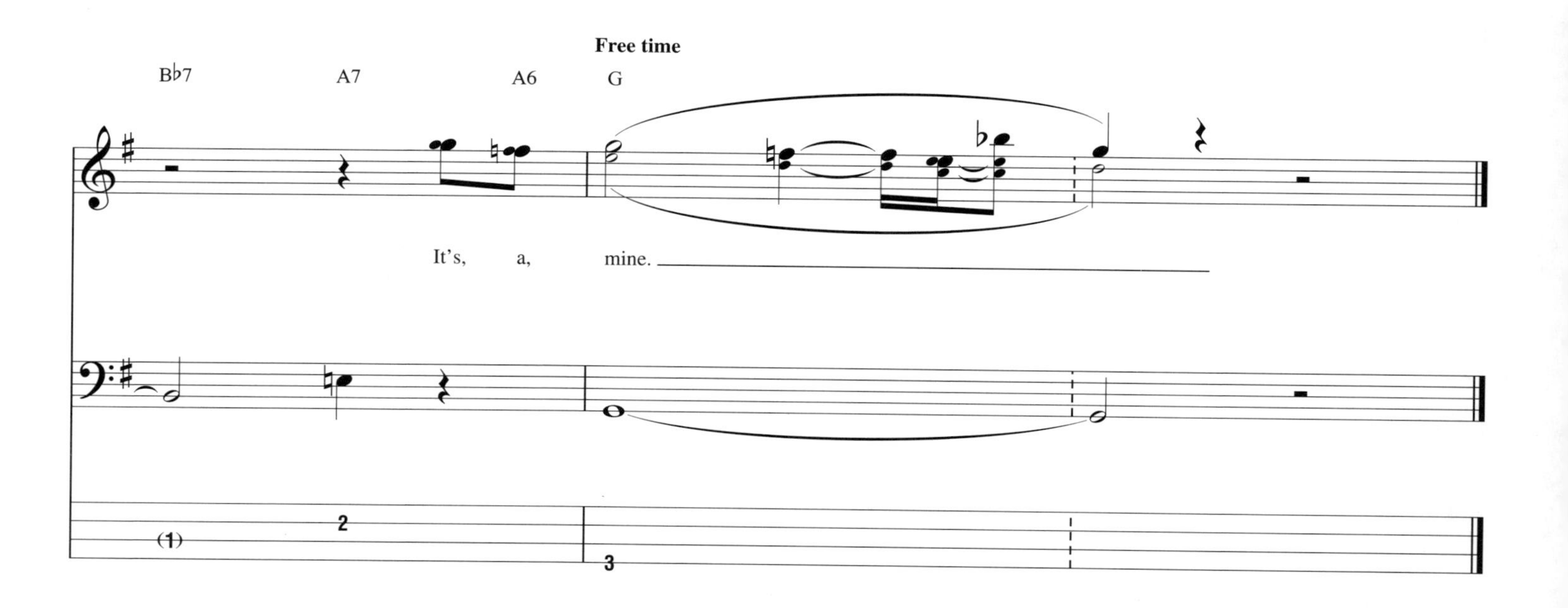
Free time
B♭7
A7
A6
G
It's, a, mine.

Bulls on Parade

Written and Arranged by Rage Against The Machine

Bass: w/ Bass Fig. 3, 3 times
sure shot, sure ta make tha bod-ies drop. Drop and don't cop-y. Yo, don't call this a co-opt.
walk tha cor-ner to tha rub-ble that used to be a li - brar-y. Line up to tha mind cem-e-tar-y now.

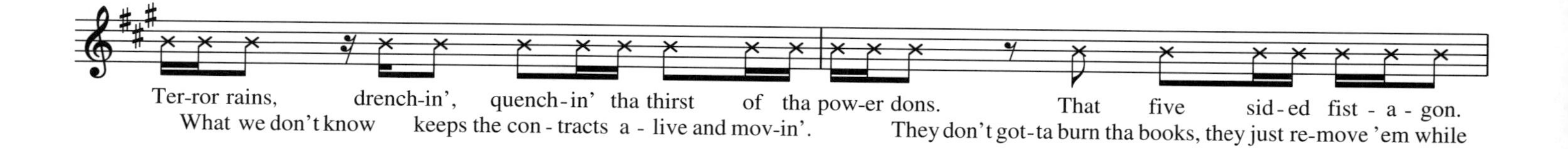
Ter-ror rains, drench-in', quench-in' tha thirst of tha pow-er dons. That five sid-ed fist - a - gon.
What we don't know keeps the con-tracts a - live and mov-in'. They don't got-ta burn tha books, they just re-move 'em while

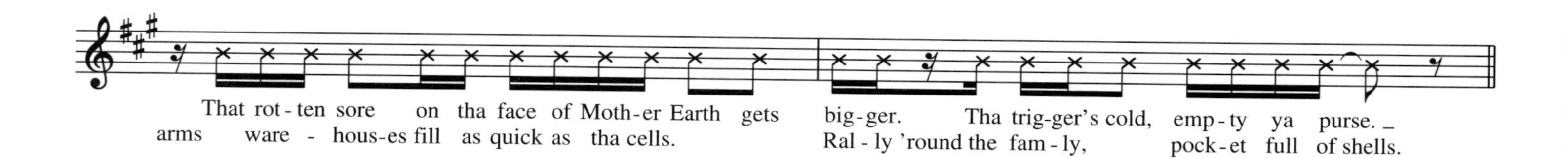
That rot-ten sore on tha face of Moth-er Earth gets big-ger. Tha trig-ger's cold, emp-ty ya purse.
arms ware - hous-es fill as quick as tha cells. Ral-ly 'round the fam-ly, pock-et full of shells.

Chorus
N.C.
Ral-ly 'round tha fam-'ly with a pock-et full of shells. They
Bass
Bass Fig. 4
End Bass Fig. 4

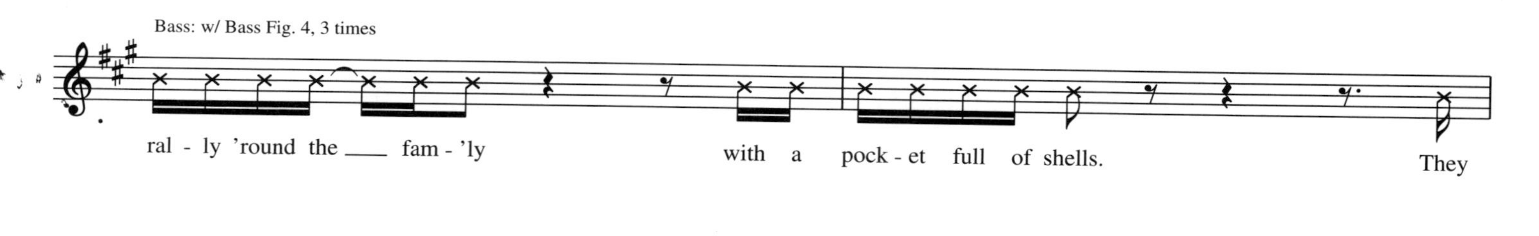
Bass: w/ Bass Fig. 4, 3 times
ral-ly 'round the fam-'ly with a pock-et full of shells. They

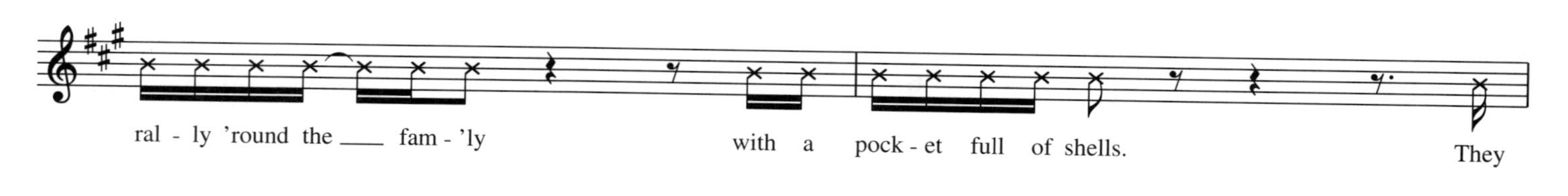
ral-ly 'round the fam-'ly with a pock-et full of shells. They

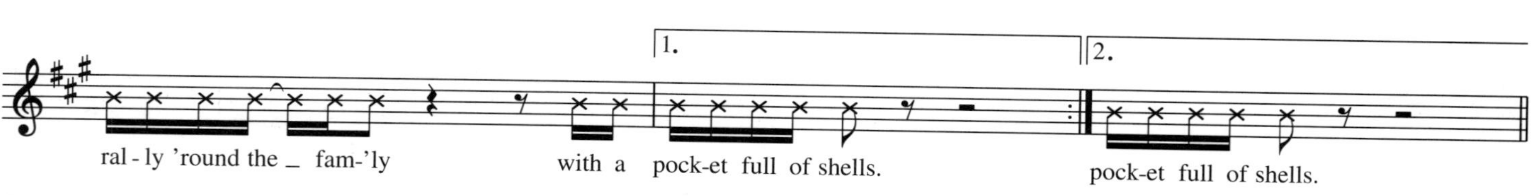
1.
2.
ral-ly 'round the fam-'ly with a pock-et full of shells. pock-et full of shells.

Interlude
Bass
B5
6

Bulls on pa - rade!

Guitar Solo
N.C.
play 4 times
Uh.
*Sing 1st time only.

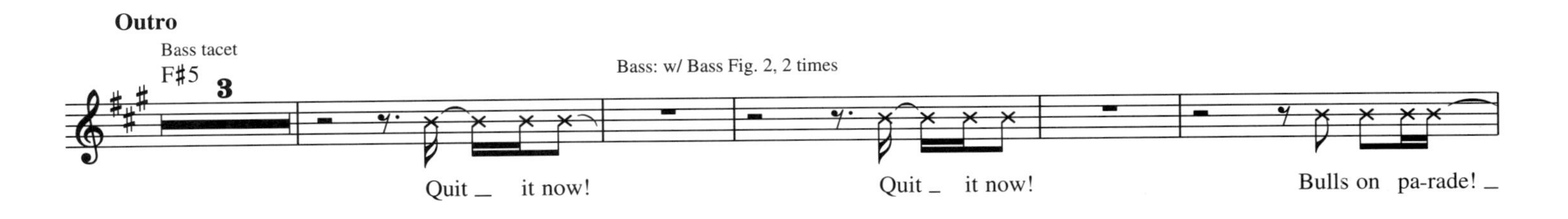
Outro
Bass tacet
F#5
Bass: w/ Bass Fig. 2, 2 times
Quit it now!
Quit it now!
Bulls on pa-rade!

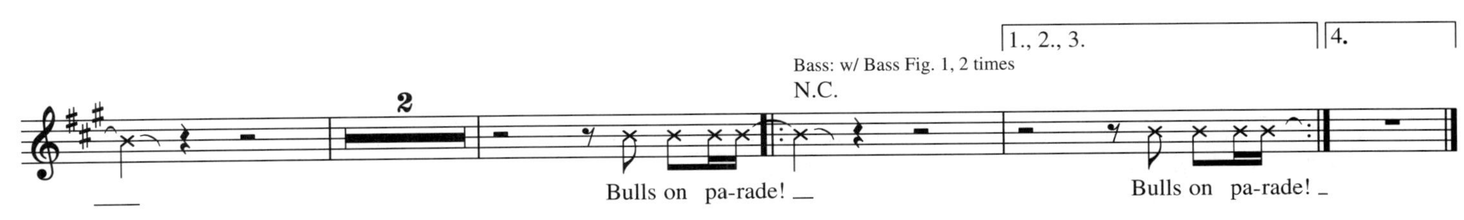
1., 2., 3.
4.
Bass: w/ Bass Fig. 1, 2 times
N.C.
Bulls on pa-rade!
Bulls on pa-rade!

Calling Dr. Love

Words and Music by Gene Simmons

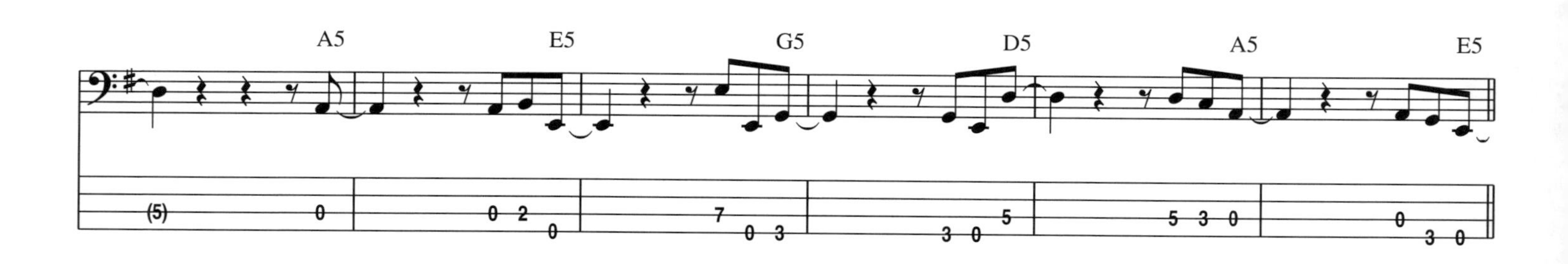

Chorus
D
N.C.
They call me,
they call me Doc - tor Love.
(Doc - tor Love.
Call-ing Doc - tor Love.
Bass Fig. 1
I've got the cure you're think-in' of.
Call-ing Doc - tor Love.)
End Bass Fig. 1
E5
G5
Verse
D5
A5
E5
G5
2. And e - ven though I'm
full of sin,
in the end you'll let me in.
You'll let me through, there's noth-in'
you can do.
You need my lov-in', don't you know it's true.
So an-swer please. Get

D A7 E5 G5
on your knees. There are no bills, there are no fees. Ba-by I know what the
N.C. G D C D
prob-lem is. The first step of the cure is a kiss. So
Chorus
Bass: w/ Bass Fig. 1, 1st 5 meas.
N.C.
Bkgd. Voc. Fig. 1
call me, they call me Doc - tor Love.
1. I am your doc - tor of
2. I've got the cure you're think-in'
(Doc - tor Love. Call-ing Doc - tor Love.
1.
E5
End Bkgd. Voc. Fig. 1
love.
of.
Call-ing Doc - tor Love.)
Ha! They
2.
Guitar Solo
E5 G5 D5 A5
(sing 1st time only)

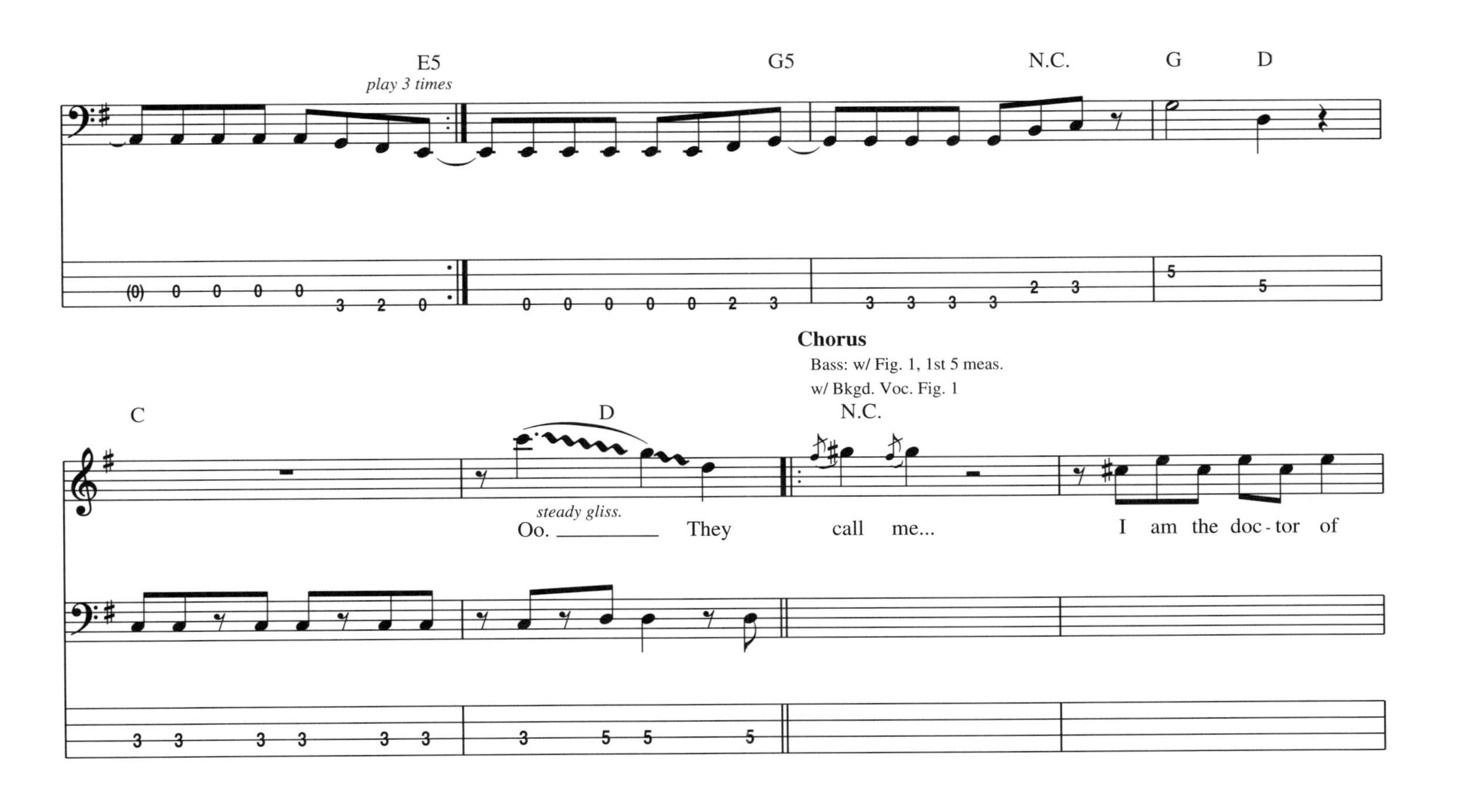
E5
play 3 times
G5
N.C.
G
D
(0) 0 0 0 0 3 2 0
0 0 0 0 0 2 3
3 3 3 3 2 3
5 5
Chorus
Bass: w/ Fig. 1, 1st 5 meas.
w/ Bkgd. Voc. Fig. 1
C
D
N.C.
steady gliss.
Oo. They call me... I am the doc-tor of
3 3 3 3 3 3
3 5 5 5

Bass: w/ Fill 1
E5
love. I've got the cure you're think-in' of.

1.
2.
Bass: w/ Bass Fig. 1
w/ Bkgd. Voc. Fig. 1
N.C.
Oo. They Yeah. They call me... They call me Doc - tor Love.

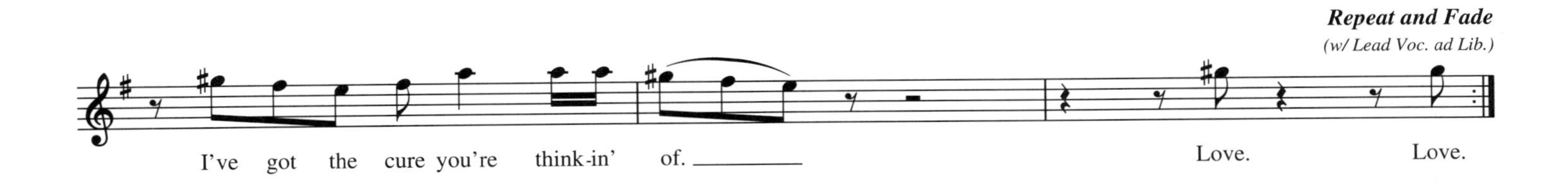
Repeat and Fade
(w/ Lead Voc. ad Lib.)
I've got the cure you're think-in' of. Love. Love.

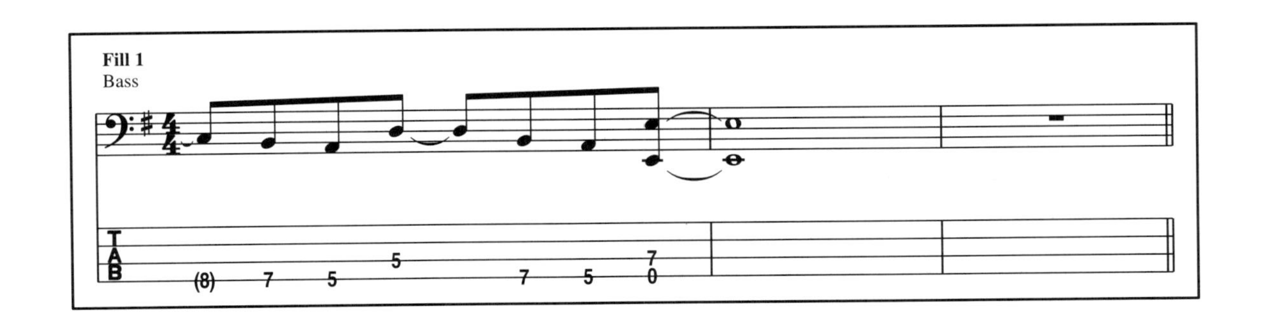
Fill 1
Bass
(8) 7 5 5 7 5 7 0

Crazy Train

Words and Music by Ozzy Osbourne, Randy Rhoads and Bob Daisley

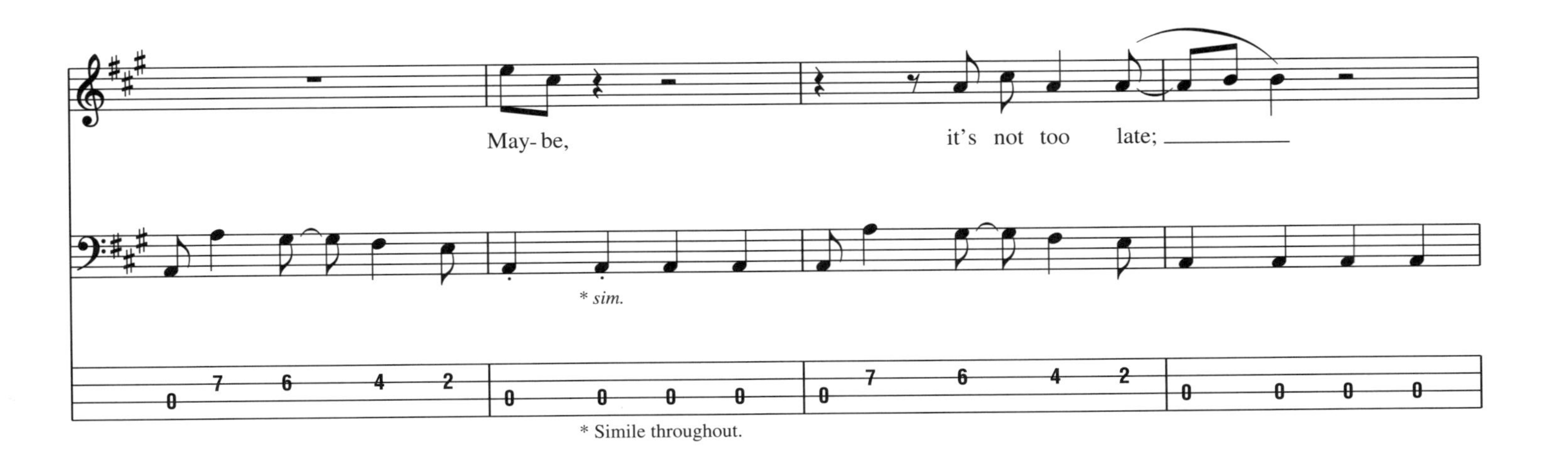
May- be,
it's not too late;
* sim.
* Simile throughout.

To learn how to love,
and for - get how to hate.

Chorus
F♯m E F♯m
D
Men - tal wounds not heal -

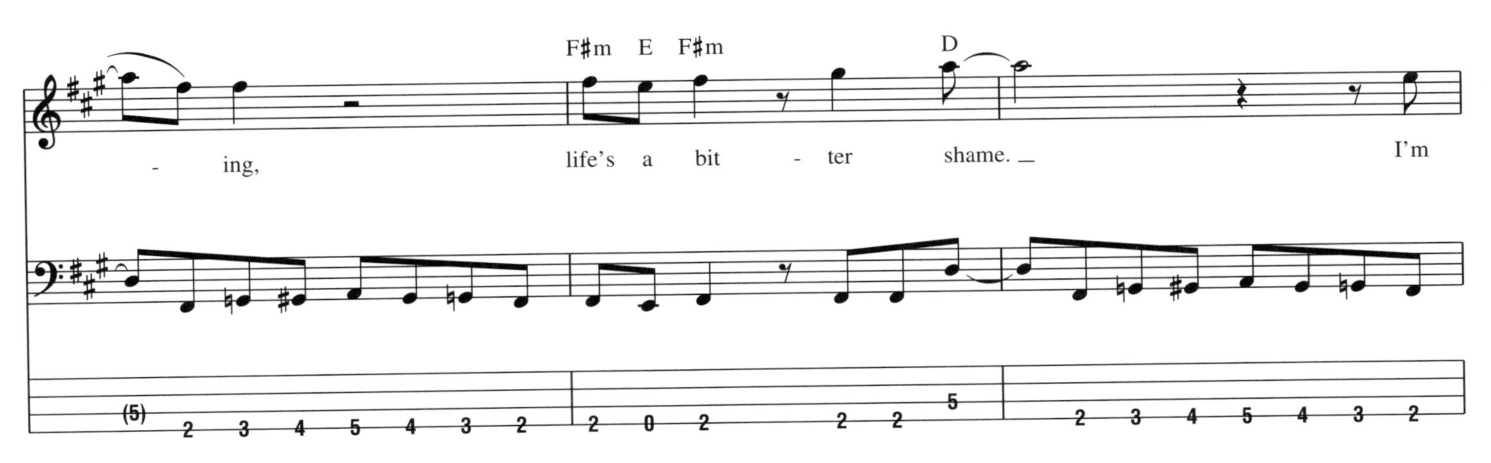
F♯m E F♯m
D
- ing,
life's a bit - ter shame.
I'm

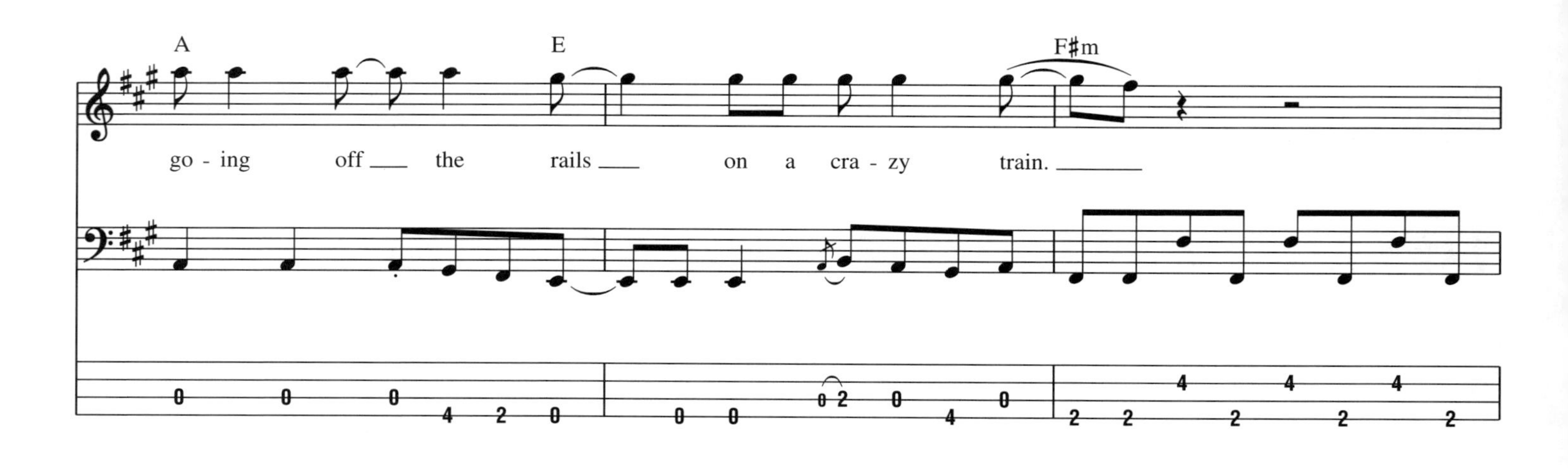

A E F♯m
go - ing off the rails on a cra - zy train.
0 0 0 4 2 0 0 0 0 2 0 4 0 2 2 4 2 4 2 2 4 2

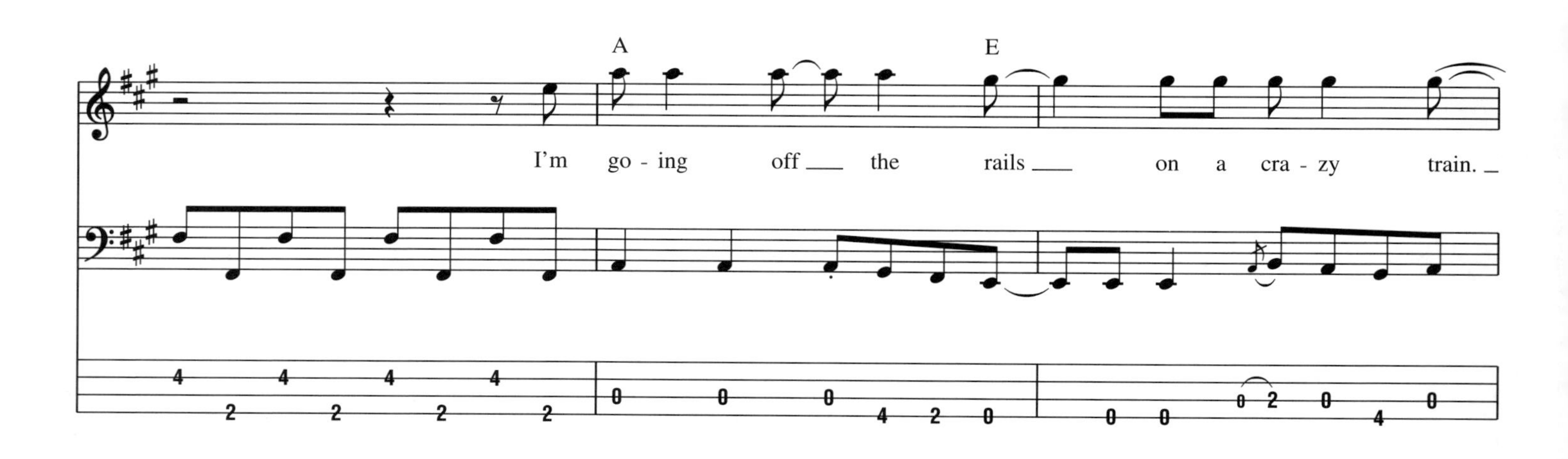

A E
I'm go - ing off the rails on a cra - zy train.
4 2 4 2 4 2 4 2 0 0 0 4 2 0 0 0 0 2 0 4 0

F♯m E F♯m A E F♯m E F♯m D E
Let's go...
2 0 2 2 4 0 4 2 0 2 4 2 0 2 2 2 5 0 2 4

Interlude
A
2. I've
0 0 0 0 0 7 6 4 2 0 0 0 0 0 7 6 4 2

Verse
A
lis-tened to preach-ers, I've lis-tened to fools. I've
3. Heirs of the cold war that's what we've be-come. In-

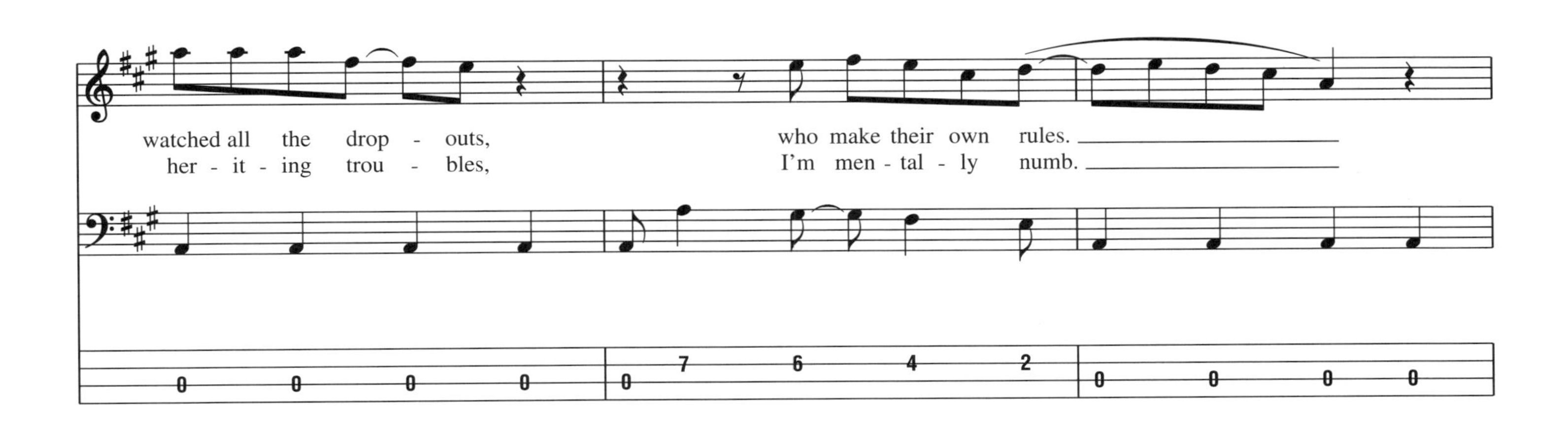
watched all the drop-outs, who make their own rules.
her-it-ing trou-bles, I'm men-tal-ly numb.

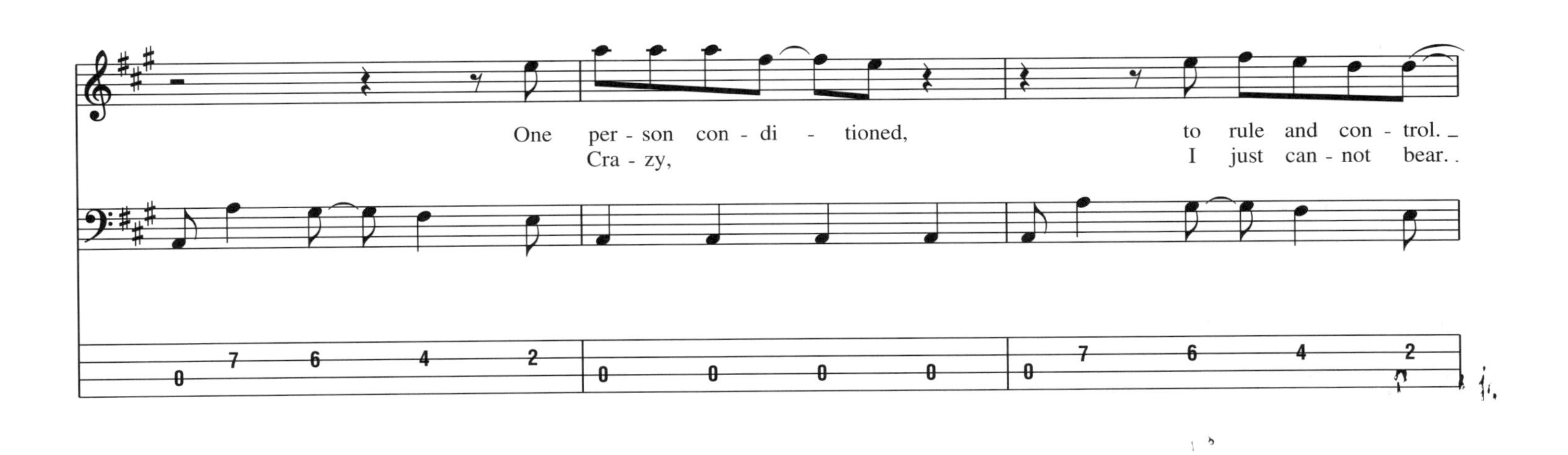
One per-son con-di-tioned, to rule and con-trol.
Cra-zy, I just can-not bear.

The me-di-a sells it and you live the role.
I'm liv-ing with some-thing that just is-n't fair.

Chorus
F#m E F#m D
Men-tal wounds still scream - ing,
Men-tal wounds not heal - ing,
F#m E F#m D
driv - ing me in - sane.
who and what's to blame?
A E
I'm go - ing off the rails
on a cra - zy train.
F#m
I'm
A E F#m E F#m A
go - ing off the rails on a cra - zy train.

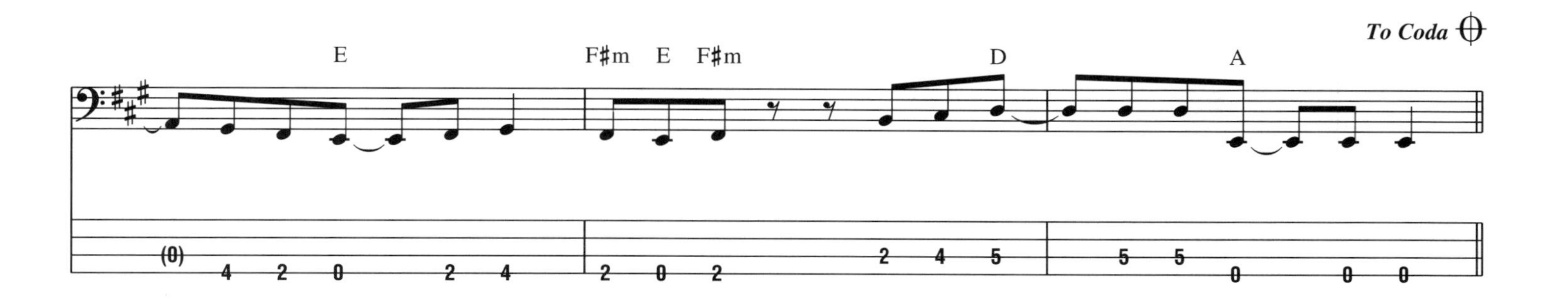
To Coda
E
F♯m E F♯m
D
A

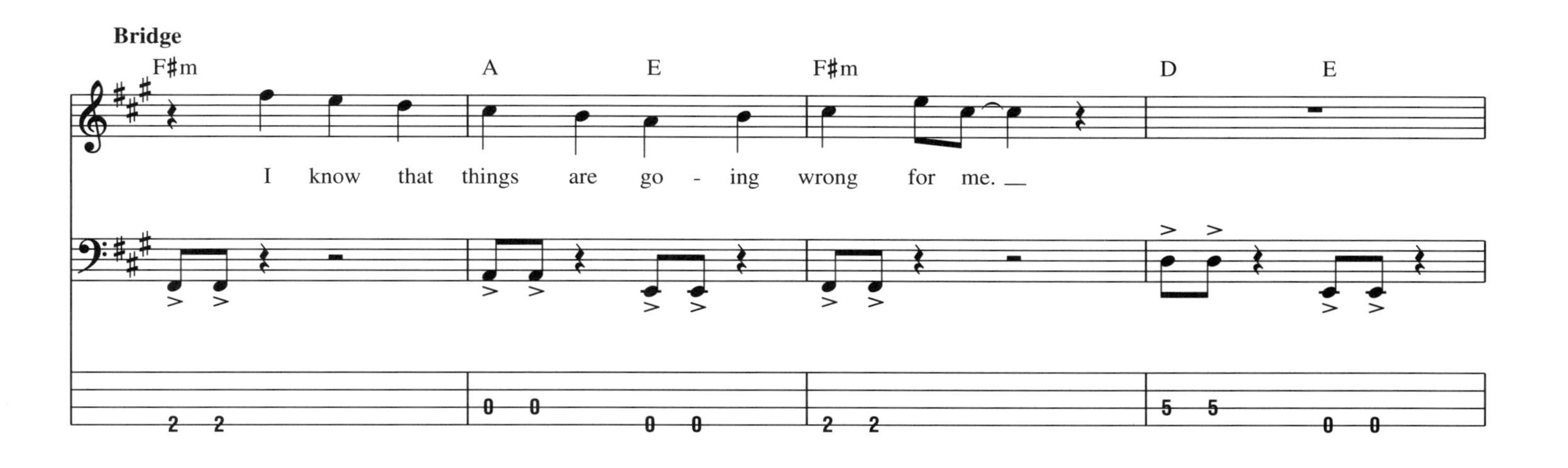
Bridge
F♯m
A
E
F♯m
D
E
I know that things are go - ing wrong for me.

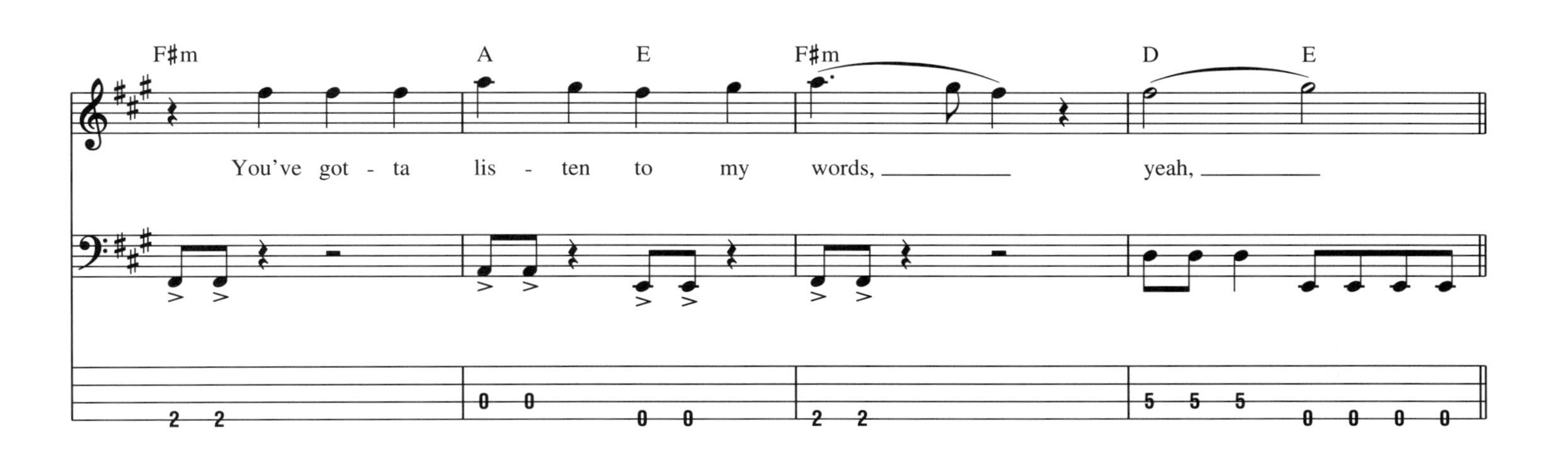
F♯m
A
E
F♯m
D
E
You've got - ta lis - ten to my words,
yeah,

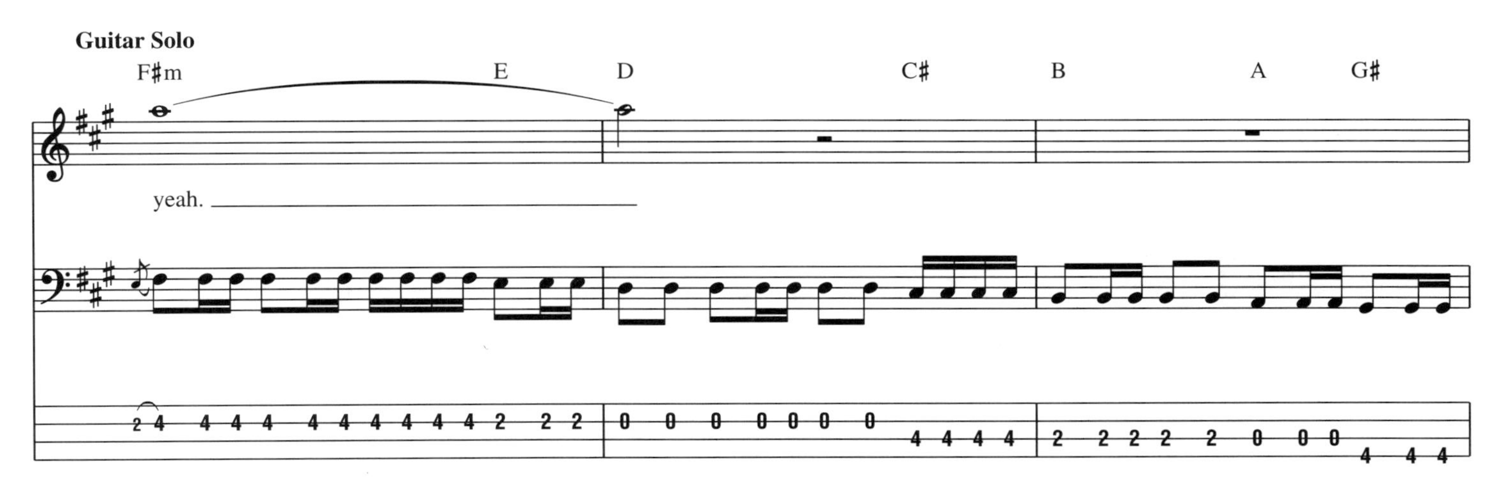
Guitar Solo
F♯m
E
D
C♯
B
A
G♯
yeah.

F♯m
F♯m
E

D
C♯
B
A
G♯

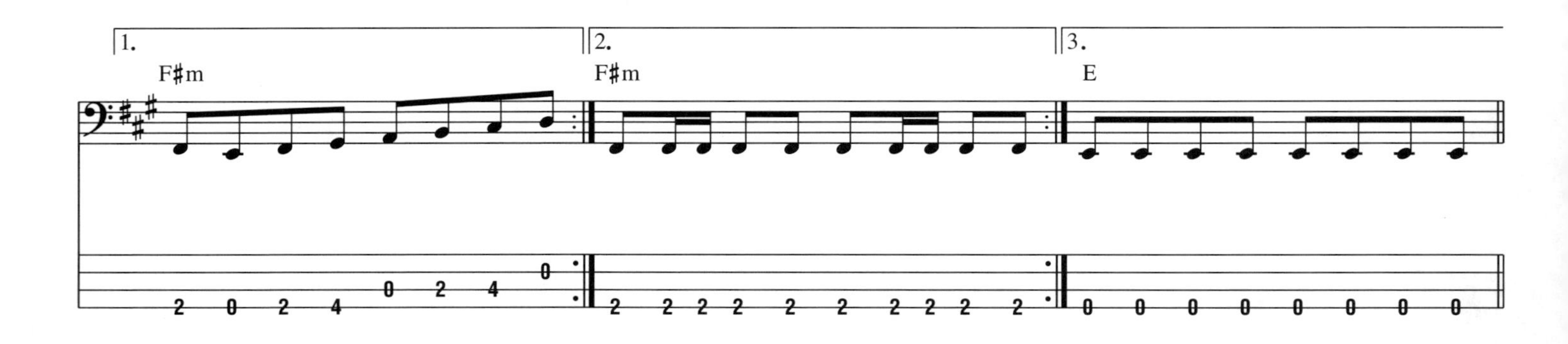
1.
2.
3.
F♯m
F♯m
E

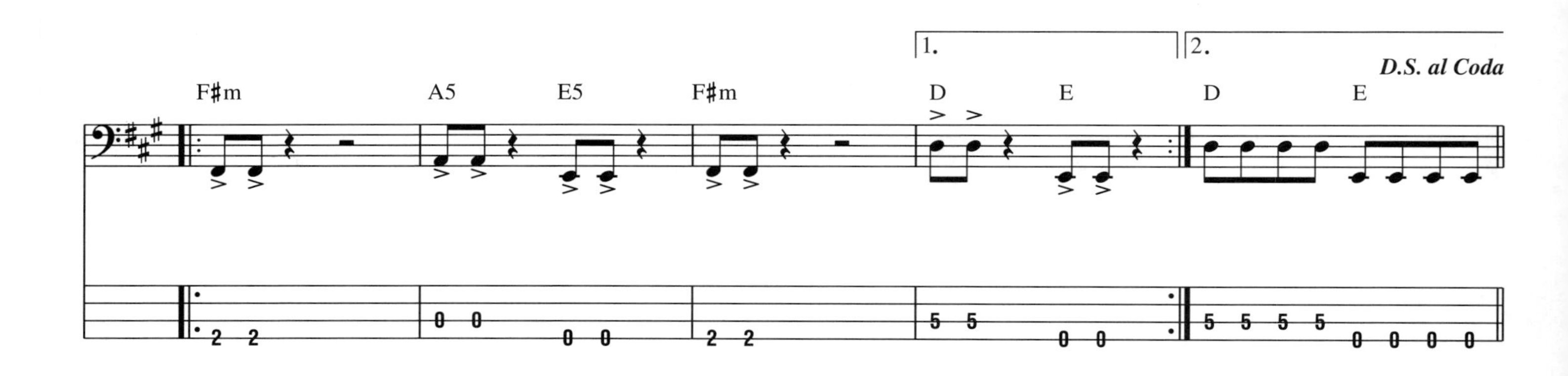
1.
2.
D.S. al Coda
F♯m
A5
E5
F♯m
D
E
D
E

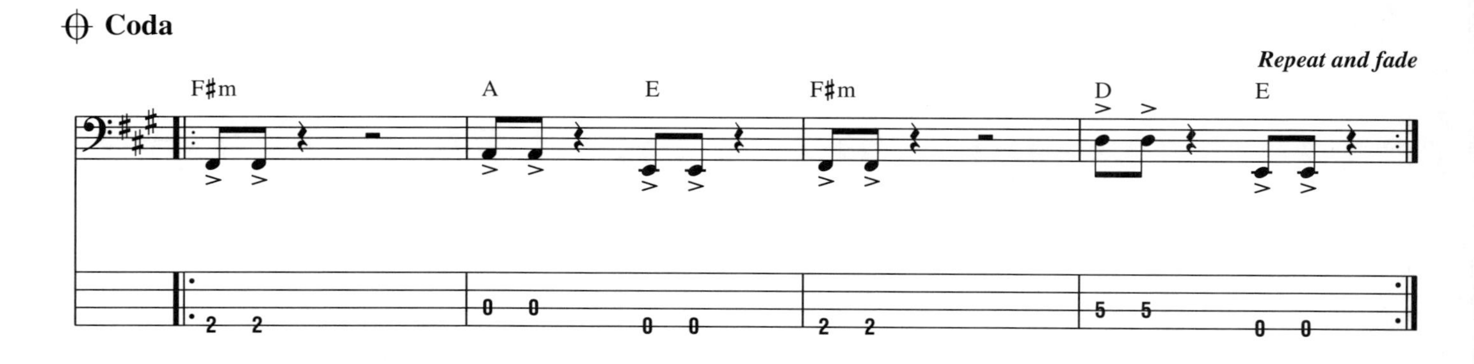
Coda
Repeat and fade
F♯m
A
E
F♯m
D
E

Cult of Personality

Words and Music by William Calhoun, Corey Glover, Muzz Skillings and Vernon Reid

(Spoken:) "And during the few moments that we have left, we want to talk right down to earth in a language that everybody here can easily understand."

Intro

Moderate Rock ♩ = 92

N.C.

(Guitar) Bass

f

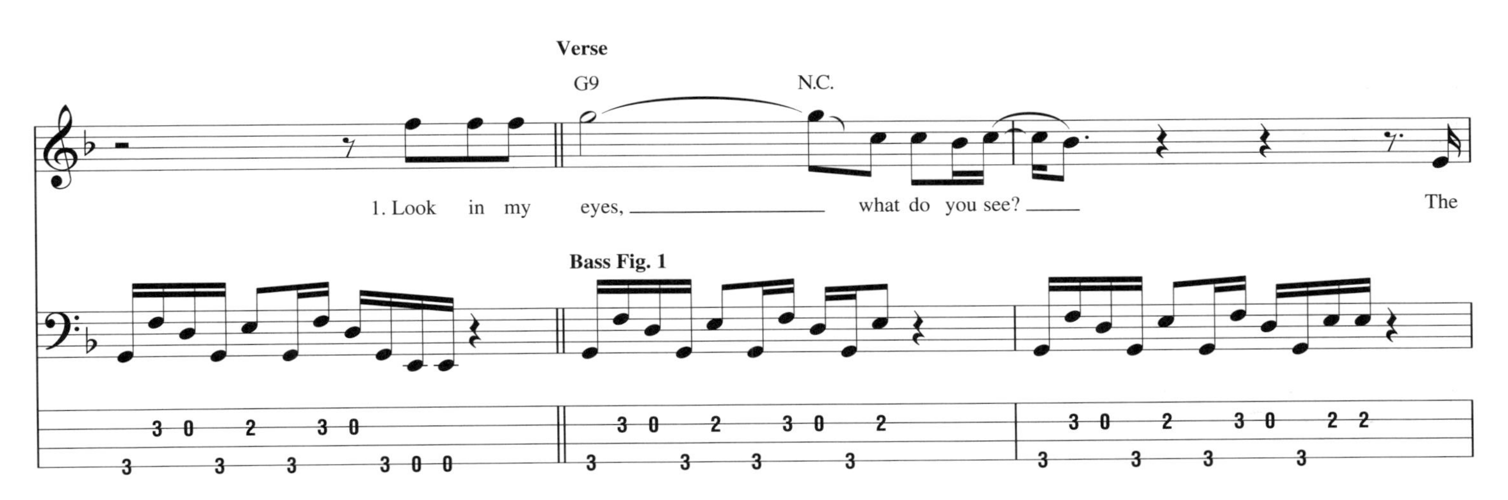

I've been ev-'ry-thing you wan - na be. Oh, I'm the
3 0 2 3 0 2
3 3 3 3
3 0 2 3 0 2 2
3 3 3 3
3 0 2 3 0 2
3 3 3 3
Bb5
C5
N.C.
cult of per-son - al - i - ty. Like Mus-sol-i - ni an' Ken-ne-dy,
1
3
3 0 2 3 0 2
3 3 3 3
3 0 2 3 0 2 2
3 3 3 3
Bb5
F5
N.C.
I'm the cult of per-son - al - i - ty, the cult of per-son - al - i - ty, the
3 0 2 3 0 2
3 3 3 3
1
1
3 0 2 3 0 2
3 3 3 3
Bb5
C5
N.C.
cult of per-son - al - i - ty.
1
3
3 0 5 3 0 2 3 0 3 2
3 3
3 0 2 3 0 5 4 0 3 0
3 3

Chorus
*B♭
F
Ne - on lights,
End Bass Fig. 1
*Chord symbols reflect implied harmony.
C
G
D
A/D
F
C
No - bel Prize, when a mir - ror speaks the re - flec - tion lies.
B♭5
F
C
G
D
A/D
You won't have to fol - low me, on - ly you can
F
C
Interlude
N.C.
set me free.

2. I sell the things

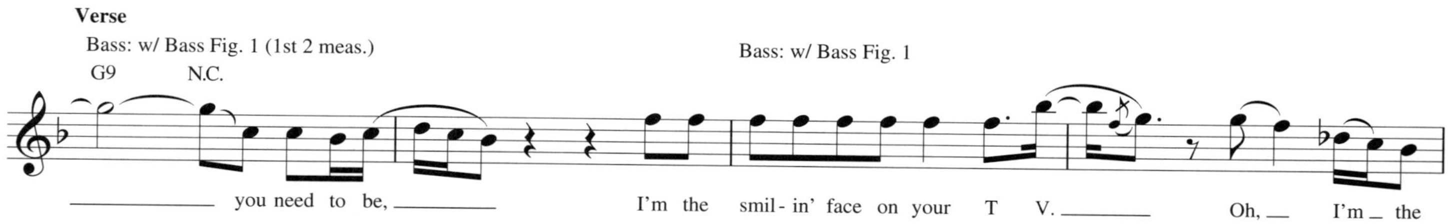
Verse
Bass: w/ Bass Fig. 1 (1st 2 meas.)
Bass: w/ Bass Fig. 1
G9
N.C.
you need to be, I'm the smil- in' face on your T V. Oh, I'm the

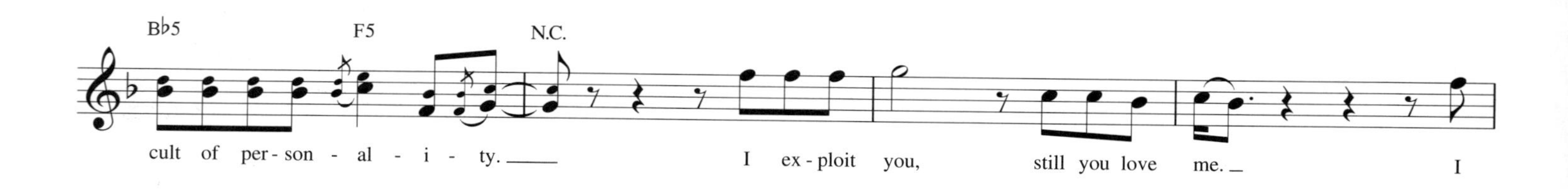
B♭5
F5
N.C.
cult of per- son - al - i - ty. I ex- ploit you, still you love me. I

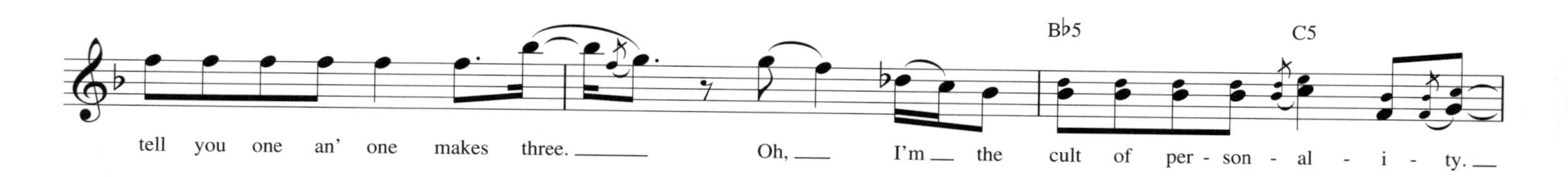
B♭5
C5
tell you one an' one makes three. Oh, I'm the cult of per- son - al - i - ty.

N.C.
Like Jo - seph Stal - in and Ghand - i, oh, I'm the

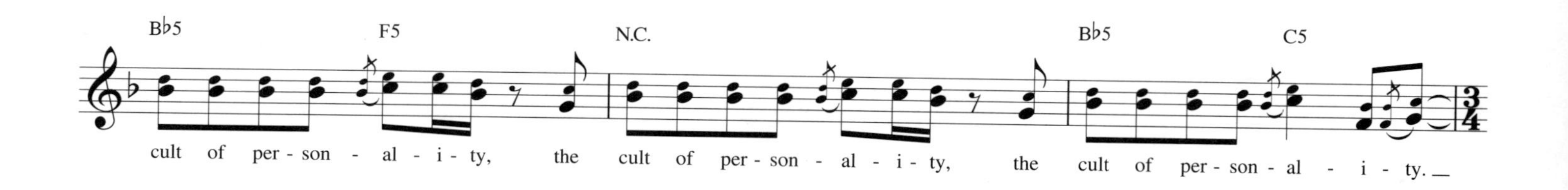
B♭5
F5
N.C.
B♭5
C5
cult of per- son - al - i - ty, the cult of per- son - al - i - ty, the cult of per- son - al - i - ty.

N.C.

Chorus
B♭ F C G D A/D
Ne - on lights, No - bel Prize, when a lead - er speaks, that
F C B♭ F C G
lead - er dies. You won't have to fol - low me,
D A/D F C
on - ly you can set you free.
let ring
let ring
Guitar Solo
N.C.

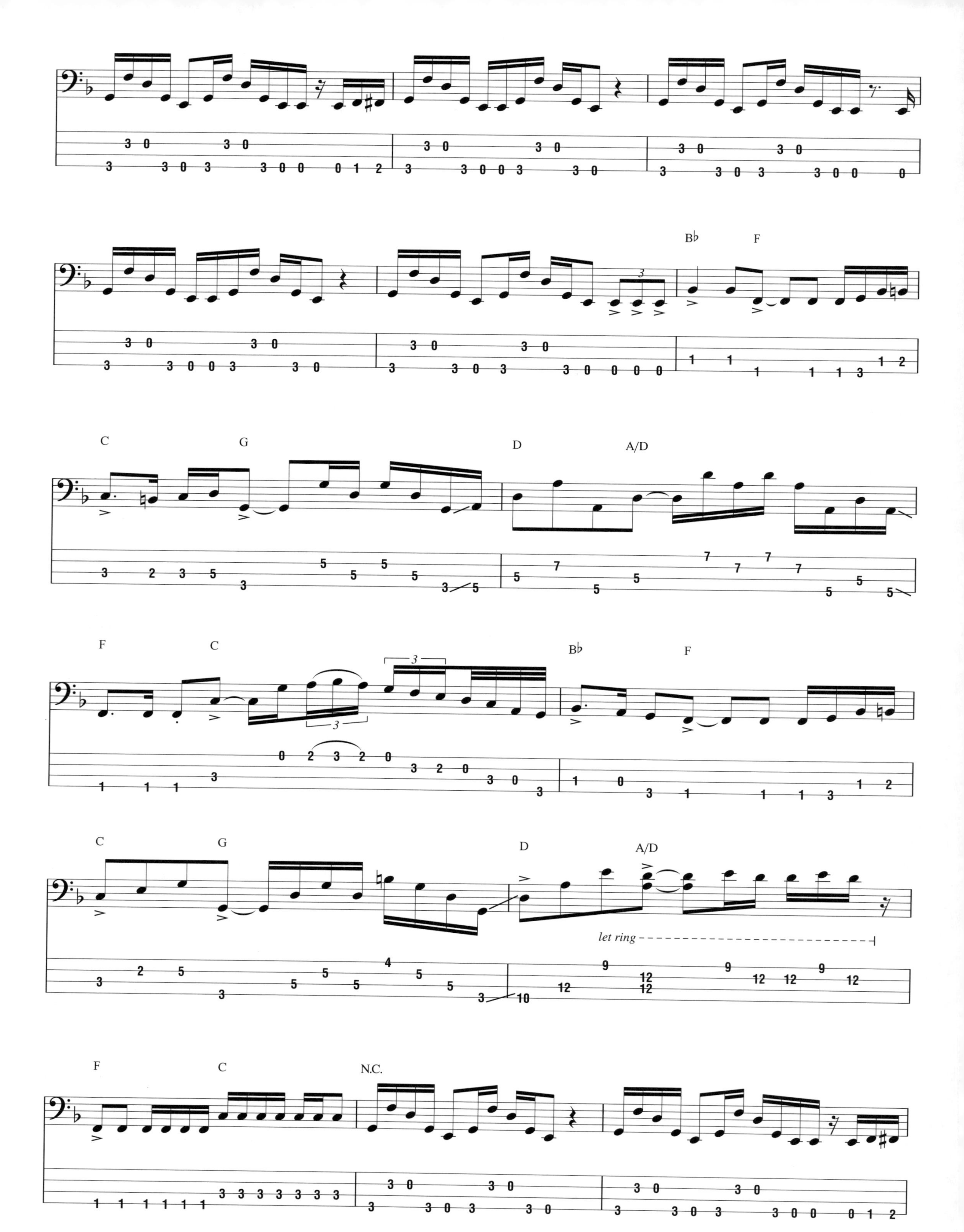
B♭
F
C
G
D
A/D
F
C
B♭
F
C
G
D
A/D
let ring
F
C
N.C.

3. You gave me for -
Verse
Bass: w/ Bass Fig. 1 (1st 2 meas., 3 times)
G9
N.C.
- tune, you gave me fame.
You gave me pow - er in your God's
name. I'm ev - 'ry per - son you need to be.
Oh,
B♭5
F5
N.C.
B♭5
C
Voc. Fig. 1
I'm the cult of per - son -
(I'm the cult of, I'm the
N.C.
Bkgd. Voc.: w/ Voc. Fig. 1
B♭5
F5
N.C.
End Voc. Fig. 1
- al - i - ty.
I am the cult of, I am the cult of, I am the cult of, I am the cult of
cult of.)

B♭5
C
N.C.
I am the cult of, I am the cult of I am the cult of, I am the cult of
per - son - al - i - ty.
(Spoken:) "Ask not what your coun - try can do for you..."
Outro
N.C.
(Spoken:) "The only thing we have to fear, it fear itself."

Empire

Words and Music by Geoff Tate and Michael Wilton

(Spoken:) *Next message, saved, Saturday at 9:24 P.M. "Sorry, I'm just... it's starting to hit me like a, um, um, two ton heavy thing."*

Intro
Moderately slow Rock ♩ = 80

A5
G
F5
In - no - cent, their on - ly crime was be - ing the wrong place at the wrong time.
A5
G5
C5
Too bad, peo - ple say, what's wrong with the kids to - day?
A5
G5
F5
A5
I tell you right now they've got noth - in' to lose. They're build - ing em - pire.
Verse
G5
C5
2. John - ny used to work af - ter school at the cin - e - ma show.

A5
G
F5
Got - ta hus - tle if he wants an ed - u - ca - tion, yeah, he's got - ta long way to go.
A5
G5
C5
Now he's out on the streets all day sell - ing crack to the peo - ple who pay. Got an
A5
G5
F5
A - K - for - ty - sev - en for his best friend, busi - ness the A - mer - i - can way.
Pre-Chorus
F5/D
D5
G5/D
D5
F5/D
D5
E5
C5
East - side meets West - side down - town.

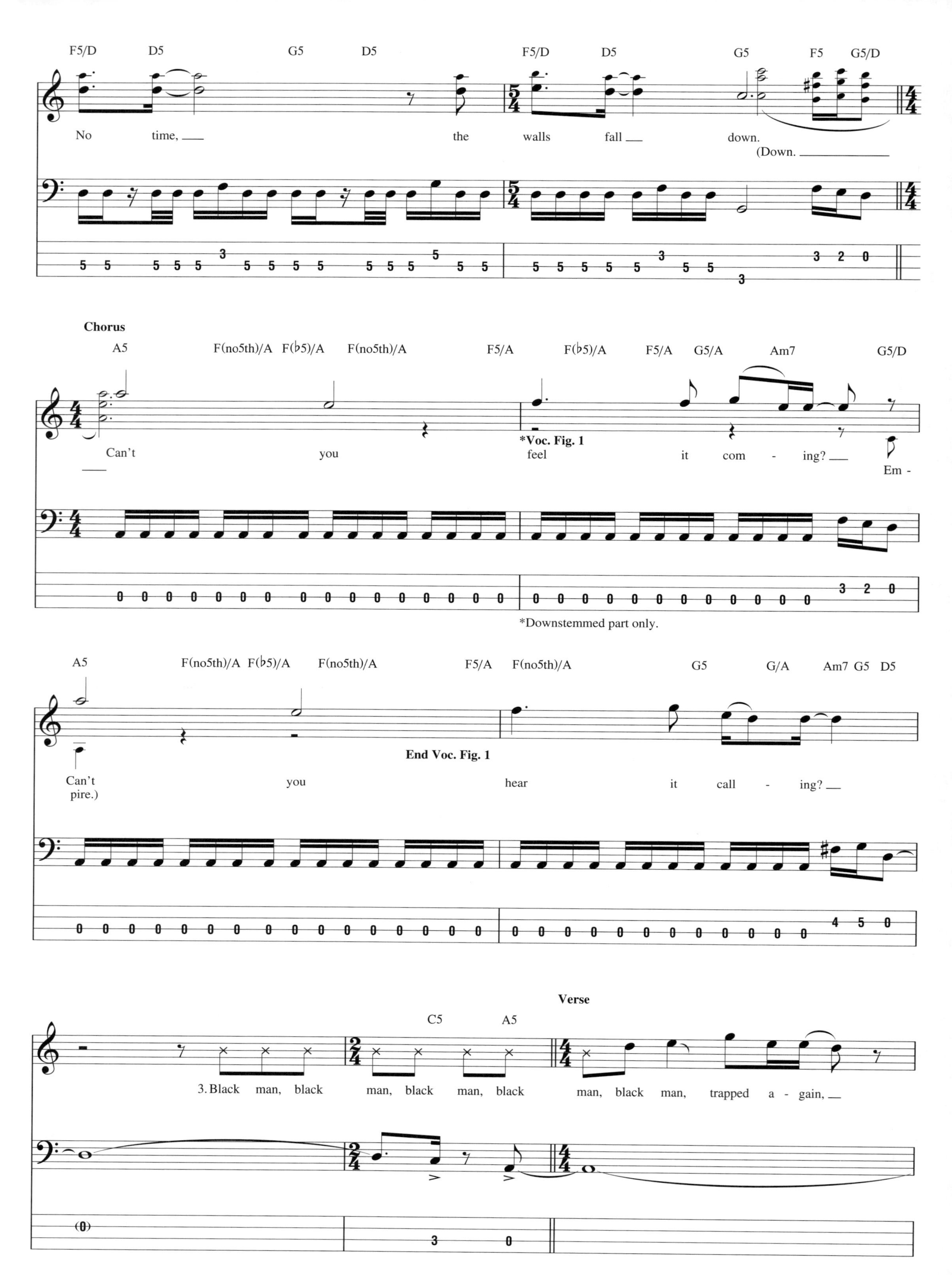
F5/D
D5
G5
D5
F5/D
D5
G5
F5
G5/D
No time, the walls fall down.
(Down.
Chorus
A5
F(no5th)/A
F(♭5)/A
F(no5th)/A
F5/A
F(♭5)/A
F5/A
G5/A
Am7
G5/D
Can't you feel it com - ing? Em -
*Voc. Fig. 1
*Downstemmed part only.
A5
F(no5th)/A
F(♭5)/A
F(no5th)/A
F5/A
F(no5th)/A
G5
G/A
Am7 G5 D5
Can't you hear it call - ing?
pire.)
End Voc. Fig. 1
Verse
C5
A5
3. Black man, black man, black man, black man, black man, trapped a - gain,

G5
C5
A5
holds his chains in his hand.
Broth - er kill - ing broth - er for the prof - it of an - oth - er,
G
F5
A5
game point, no - bod - y wins.
De - clines right on time.
G5
C5
A5
What hap-pened to the dream sub - lime?
Tear it all down we'll build it up a - gain.
G5
F5
Pre-Chorus
F5/D
D5
G5/D
D5
An - oth - er em - pire?
East - side
meets

F5/D
D5
E5
C5
F5/D
D5
G5/D
D5
West - side
down - town.
No time,
(No time.)
the
F5/D
D5
G5
F5
G5/D
Chorus
A5
F(no5th)/A
F(♭5)/A
F(no5th)/A
F5/A
walls fall,
down.
(Down.)
Can't
you
Bass Fig. 1
Bkgd. Voc.: w/ Voc. Fig. 1 (2 times)
F(♭5)/A
F5/A
G5/A
Am7
G5/D
A5
F(no5th)/A
F(♭5)/A
F(no5th)/A
F5/A
feel
it com - ing?
Can't
you
F(♭5)/A
F5/A
G5/A
Am7
G5/D
A5
F(no5th)/A
F(♭5)/A
F(no5th)/A
F5/A
hear
it com - ing?
Can't
some - one
End Bass Fig. 1

F(♭5)/A
F5/A
G5/A
Am7
G5/A
F5/A
C/E G5/D
C5
G5
C5
G5
C5
here
stop
it?
Interlude
Dsus2
B♭/D
D5
C/D Dm7 C/D D5
G5/D
C
Csus4
dim.
Dsus2
B♭/D
D5
C/D
Dm7
C/D
D5
G5/D
C
Csus4
Spoken: In the fiscal year 1986 to '87 the local, state, and federal governments spent a combined total of 60.6 million dollars on law enforcement.
Bass Fig. 2
End Bass Fig. 2
mf
Bass: w/ Bass Fig. 2 (2 times)
Dsus2
B♭/D
D5
C/D
Dm7
C/D D5
G5/D
C
Csus4
Federal law enforcement expenditures ranked last in absolute dollars and accounted for only 6 percent of all federal spending.
Dsus2
B♭/D
D5
C/D
Dm7
C/D
By way of comparison, the federal government spent 24 million more on space exploration,
D5
G5/D
C
Csus4
and 43 times more on national defense and international relations than on law enforcement.

Guitar Solo

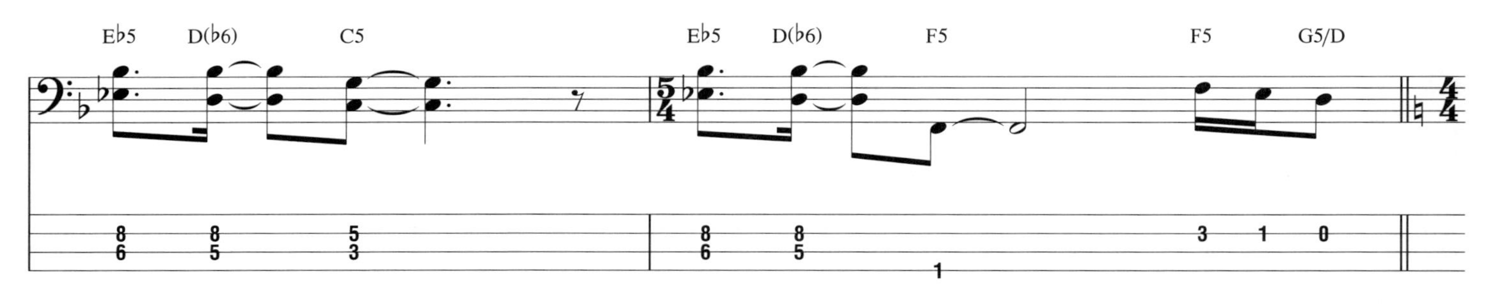

Chorus

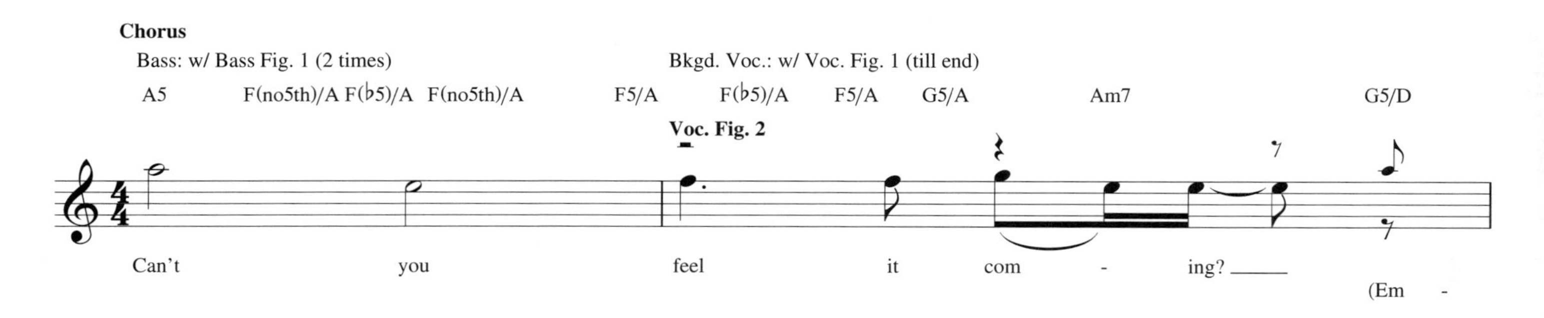

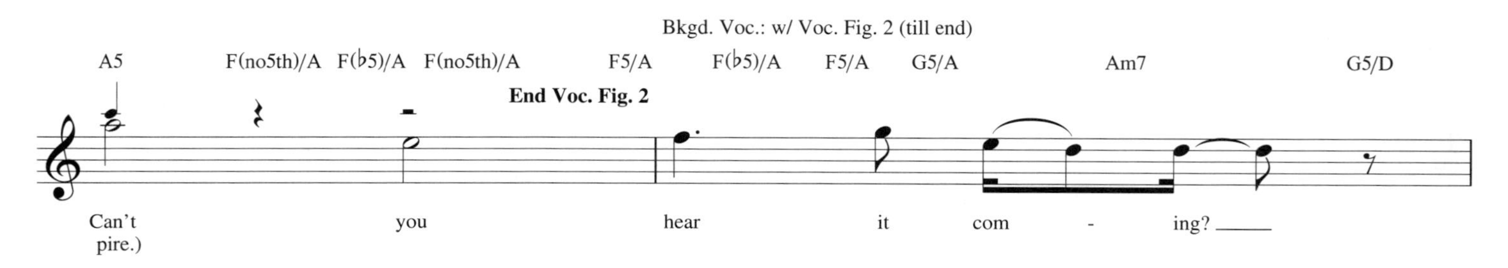

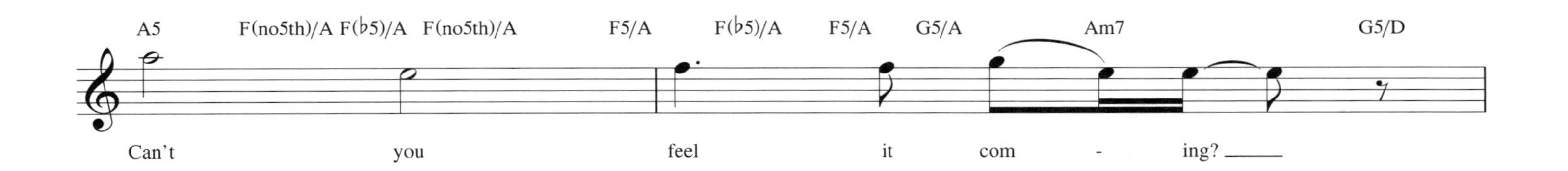
A5 F(no5th)/A F(♭5)/A F(no5th)/A F5/A F(♭5)/A F5/A G5/A Am7 G5/D
Can't you feel it com - ing?

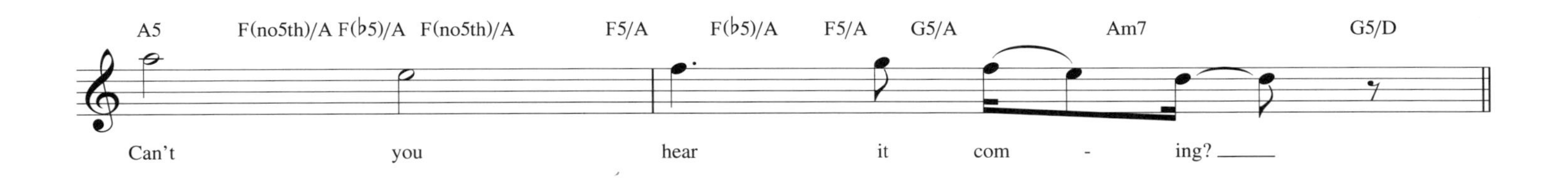
A5 F(no5th)/A F(♭5)/A F(no5th)/A F5/A F(♭5)/A F5/A G5/A Am7 G5/D
Can't you hear it com - ing?

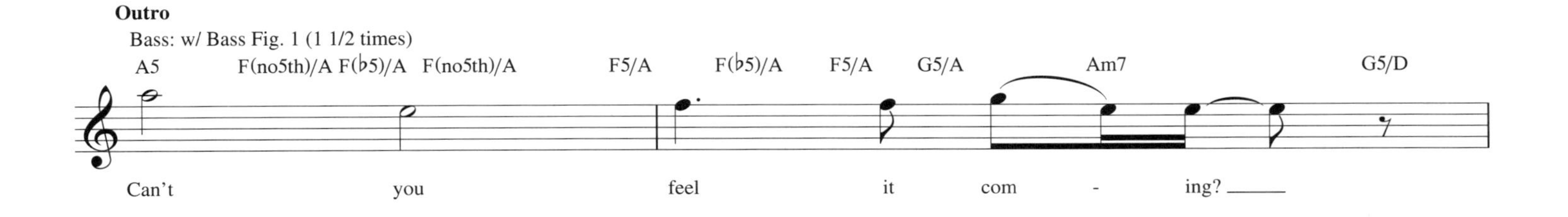
Outro
Bass: w/ Bass Fig. 1 (1 1/2 times)
A5 F(no5th)/A F(♭5)/A F(no5th)/A F5/A F(♭5)/A F5/A G5/A Am7 G5/D
Can't you feel it com - ing?

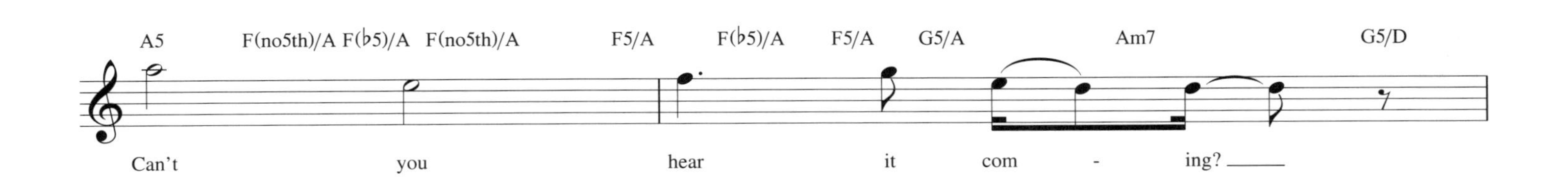
A5 F(no5th)/A F(♭5)/A F(no5th)/A F5/A F(♭5)/A F5/A G5/A Am7 G5/D
Can't you hear it com - ing?

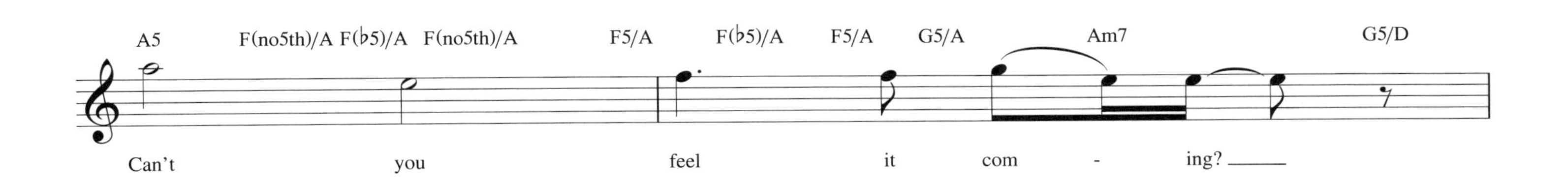
A5 F(no5th)/A F(♭5)/A F(no5th)/A F5/A F(♭5)/A F5/A G5/A Am7 G5/D
Can't you feel it com - ing?

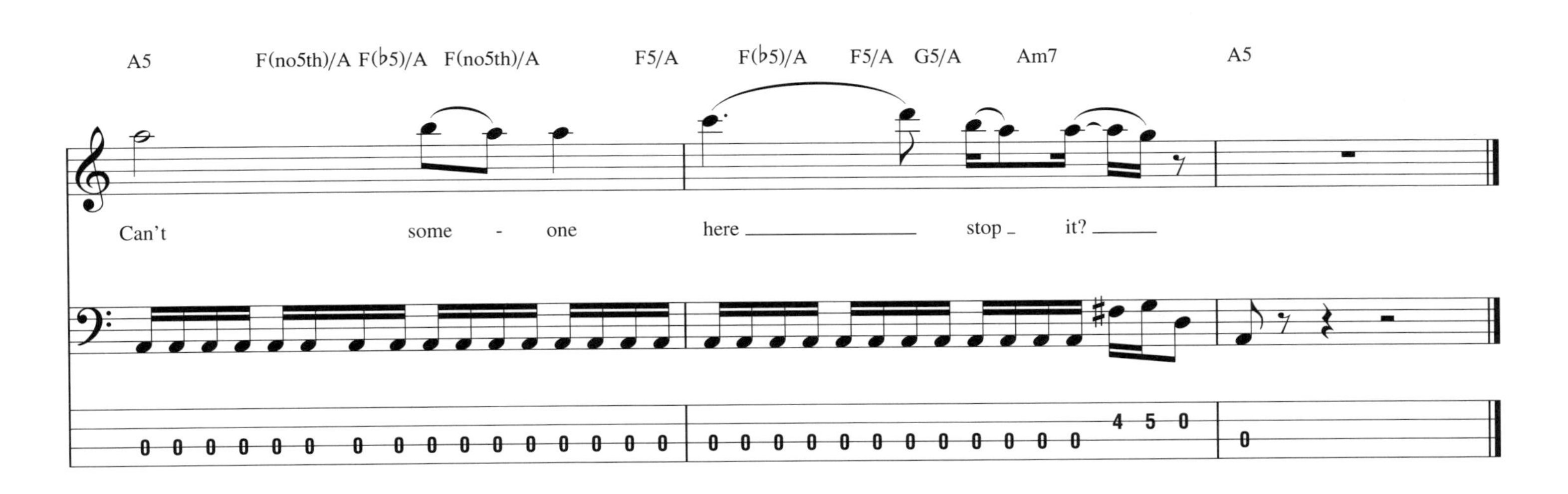
A5 F(no5th)/A F(♭5)/A F(no5th)/A F5/A F(♭5)/A F5/A G5/A Am7 A5
Can't some - one here stop it?

Fool for Your Loving

Words and Music by Bernie Marsden, Mick Moody and David Coverdale

G5
A5
C5
D5
C5
G5
I'm a lone - ly man who knows just what it means to lose con -
A5 C5 D5 C5
G5
A5 C5 D5 C5
trol.
But I took all my heart - ache
Bass Fig. 1
D5 G5 A5 C5 D5 C5
G5
and turned it to shame.
Now I'm
A5 C5 D5 C5
D5 G5 A5 C5 D5 C5
mov - in', mov - in' on
and I ain't tak - ing the blame.

Pre-Chorus
G5
Dm
Em7
Don't come run - ning to me, I know I've done all I
End Bass Fig. 1

Am
Dm
Em7
can.
A hard lov - ing wom - an like you

2nd time, Bass: w/ Bass Fill 1
Am
just makes a hard lov - ing man.
So I can say it to you, babe, I'll be a

Bass Fill 1

Chorus
F
G
Am7
Voc. Fig. 1
fool for your lov - ing no more.
(Fool for your lov - ing no more.
A fool for your lov - ing no more.
A fool for your lov - ing no more.
I'm so tired of try - ing, I al - ways end up cry - ing.
Em7
3

2nd time, Bass: w/ Bass Fill 2
To Coda
Dm
E5
N.C.
End Voc. Fig. 1
Fool for your lov - ing no more.
Fool for your lov - ing no more.)
I'll be a fool for you lov - ing no more.

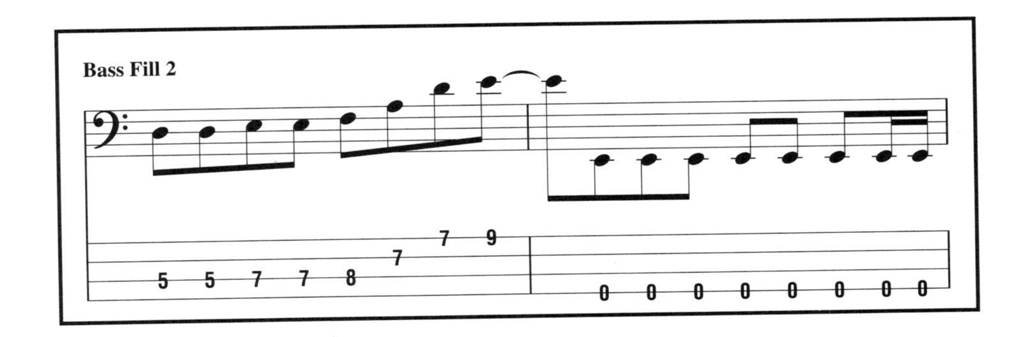
Bass Fill 2

Interlude
A5 E5 D5 C5 B5 G5 A5 E5 D5 C5 B5 G5
I'm tired of hid - ing my feel -
Verse
Bass: w/ Bass Fig. 1
A5 C5 D5 C5 D5 G5 A5 C5 D5 C5 G5
- ings, you left me lone - ly too long. I
A5 C5 D5 C5 D5 G5 A5 C5 D5 C5 G5
D.S. al Coda
gave my heart and you tore it a - part. Ooh, ba - by, you done me wrong.
Coda
Interlude
A5 E5 D5 C5 B5 G5 A5 E5 D5
I'll be a
Bass Fig. 2
C5 B5 G5 A5 E5 D5 C5 B5 G5
fool for your lov - ing no more, no more, no more.
End Bass Fig. 2

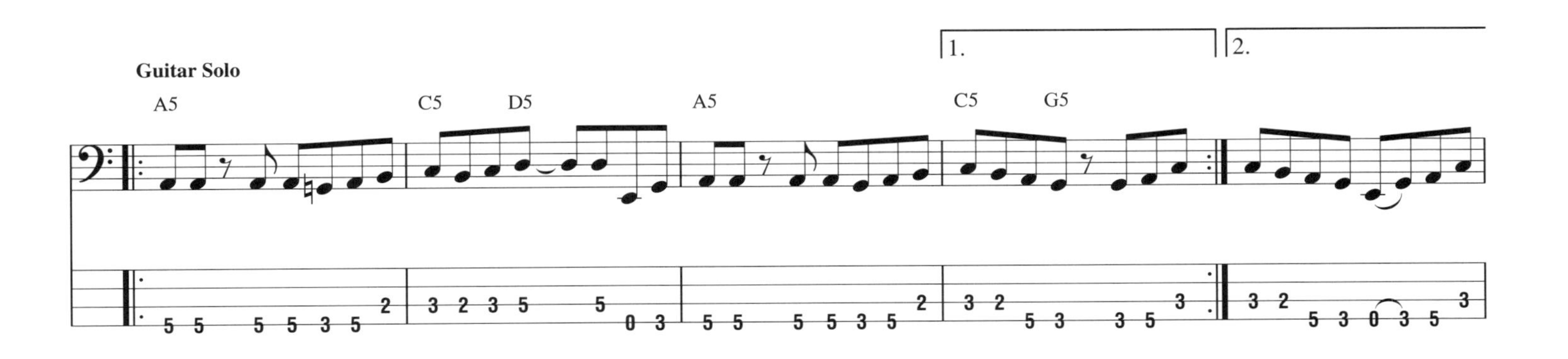
Guitar Solo
1.
2.
A5
C5
D5
A5
C5
G5

Dm
Em7
Am

Dm
Em7
Am
So I can say it to you, babe, _ I'll be a

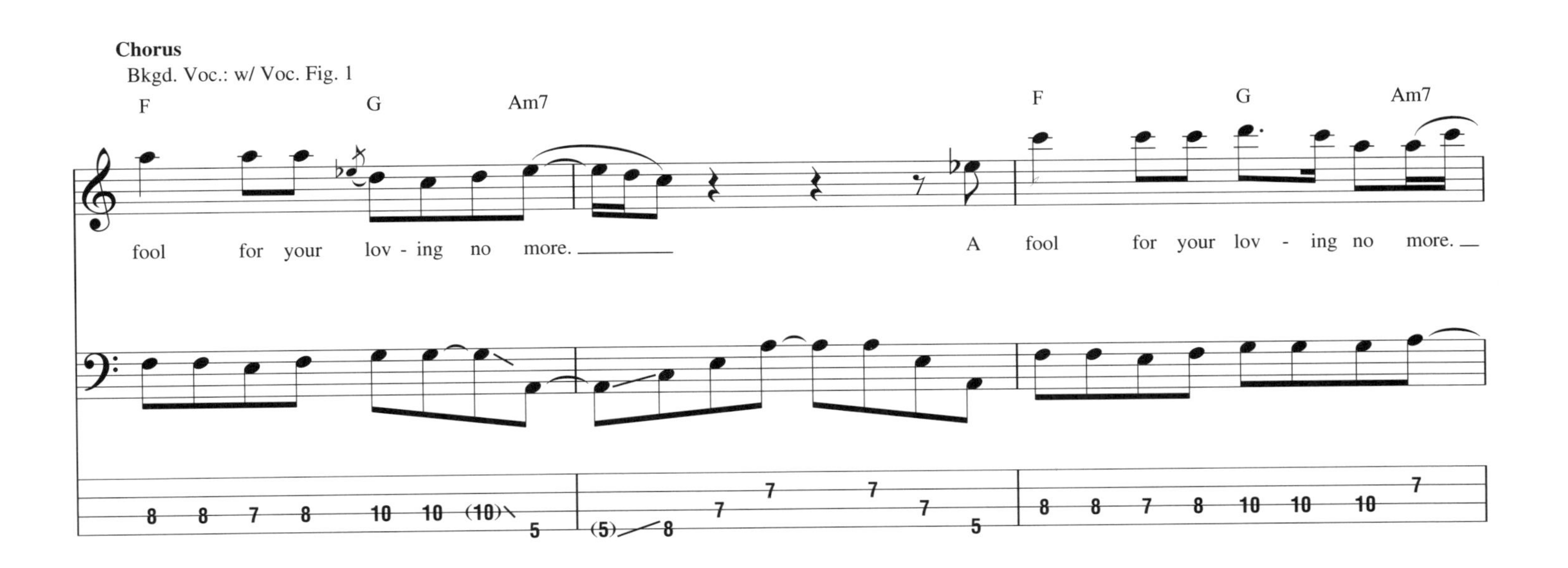
Chorus
Bkgd. Voc.: w/ Voc. Fig. 1
F
G
Am7
F
G
Am7
fool for your lov - ing no more. _
A fool for your lov - ing no more. _

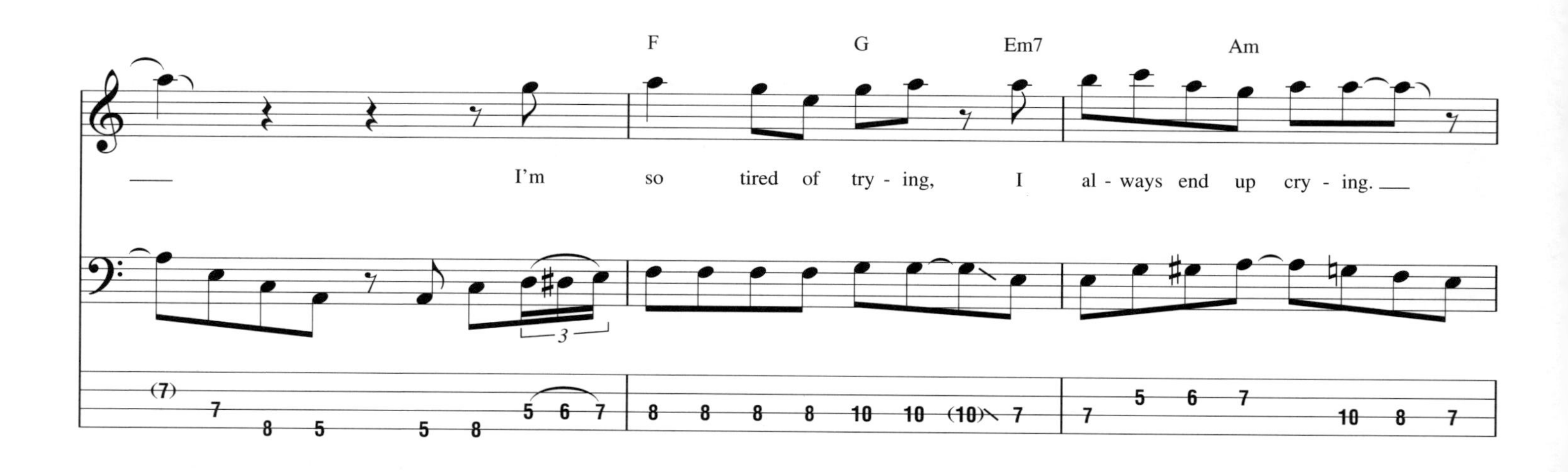
F
G
Em7
Am
I'm so tired of try - ing, I al - ways end up cry - ing.

Dm
E5
Fool for your lov - ing no more.
A fool for your lov - ing no

Outro

A5
E5 D5
C5 B5
G5 A5
Bass: w/ Bass Fig. 2 (6 1/2 times)
E5 D5
more.
No more.

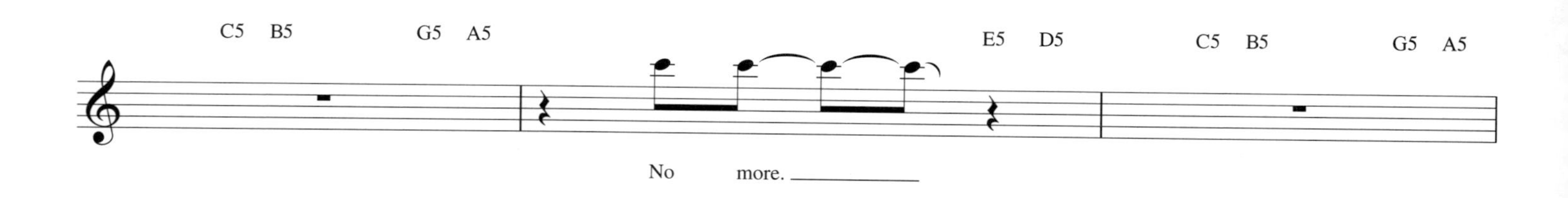
C5 B5
G5 A5
E5 D5
C5 B5
G5 A5
No more.

E5 D5 C5 B5 G5 A5 E5 D5
Fool for your lov - ing no more. Fool
(Fool for your lov - ing no more. Fool
C5 B5 G5 A5 E5 D5 C5 B5 G5 A5
for your lov - ing no more. Fool for your lov - ing no more.
for your lov - ing no more. Fool for your lov - ing no more.
E5 D5 C5 B5 G5 A5 E5 D5
Fool for your lov - ing no more. Fool
Fool for your lov - ing no more. Fool
C5 B5 G5 A5 E5 D5 C5 B5 A5
for your lov - ing no more.
for your lov - ing no more.)
N.C. G5 A5
rit.
A fool for your lov - ing no more.
rit.

Get the Funk Out

Words and Music by Nuno Bettencourt and Gary Cherone

Tune down 1/2 step:
(low to high) E♭-A♭-D♭-G♭

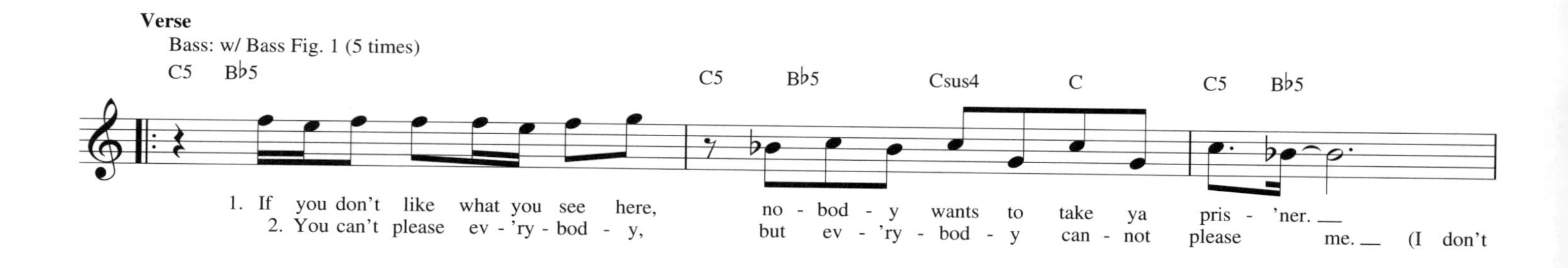

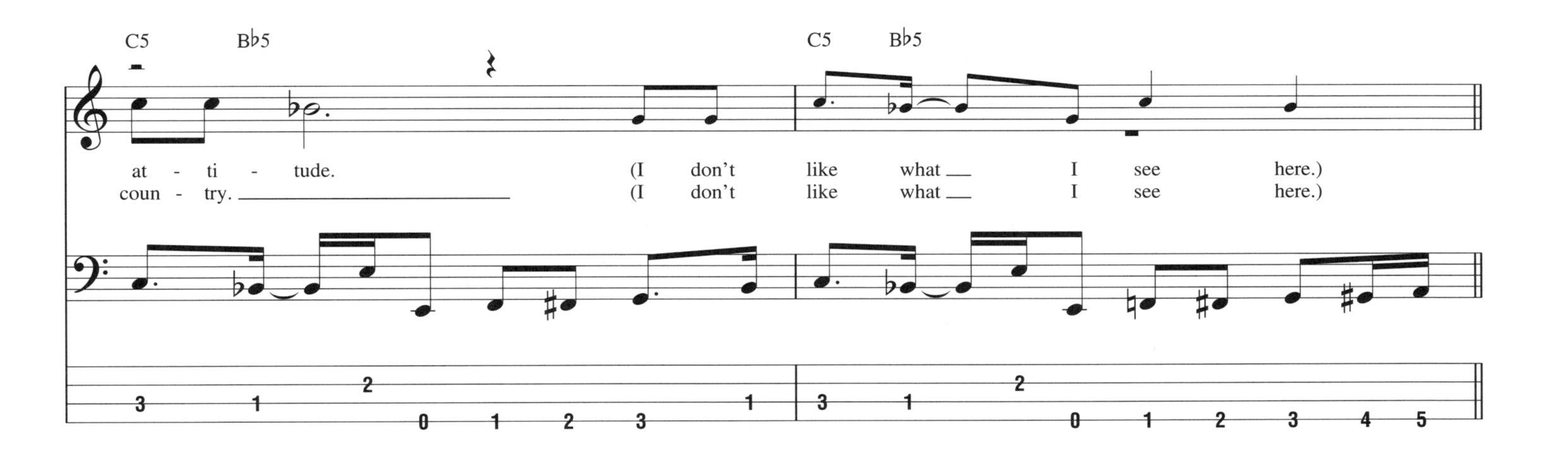
C5
B♭5
C5
B♭5
at - ti - tude. (I don't like what I see here.)
coun - try. (I don't like what I see here.)

Pre-Chorus

2nd time, w/ additional vocal ad lib.
B♭5
C5
You're all in - vit - ed to the par - ty, You know you did - n't have to come.

2nd time, Bass: w/ Bass Fill 1
E♭9
F9
N.C.
No rot - ten ap - ple's gon - na spoil all the funk. If you

Bass Fill 1

Chorus
2nd & 3rd times, w/ additional vocal ad lib.
N.C.(G5)
don't like what you see here, get the
Bass Fig. 3

(C)
(F)
funk out! We won't
End Bass Fig. 3

Bass: w/ Bass Fig. 3
(G5)
try to force feed you, get the
(C)
1.
(F)
funk out. Hey, Pat - rick!
Bass: w/ Bass Fig. 2
C5 B♭5
C5 B♭5
Not bad for a ba - si - c'ly white boy.
2.
(F)
If you

(G5)
don't like what you see here, get the
Bass Fig. 4
(C)
(F)
funk out! We won't
End Bass Fig. 4
G7
N.C.
try to force feed you. Get the
Bass Fig. 5
To Coda
Interlude
N.C.(C)
funk out!
End Bass Fig. 5
*1st time only

(G)
Guitar Solo
B♭
C
E♭
1.
2.
F
F
Bass: w/ Bass Fig. 4
(2 times)
(F)
Chorus
w/ additional vocal ad lib.
Bass: w/ Bass Fig. 3
N.C.(G5)
(C)
If you don't like what you see here, get the funk out!
(F)
Bass: w/ Bass Fig. 5
(G5)
We won't try to force feed you. Get the...
N.C.
D.S. al Coda
(take 2nd ending)
If you
Coda
(C)
G5

Highway Star

Words and Music by Ritchie Blackmore, Ian Gillan, Roger Glover, Jon Lord and Ian Paice

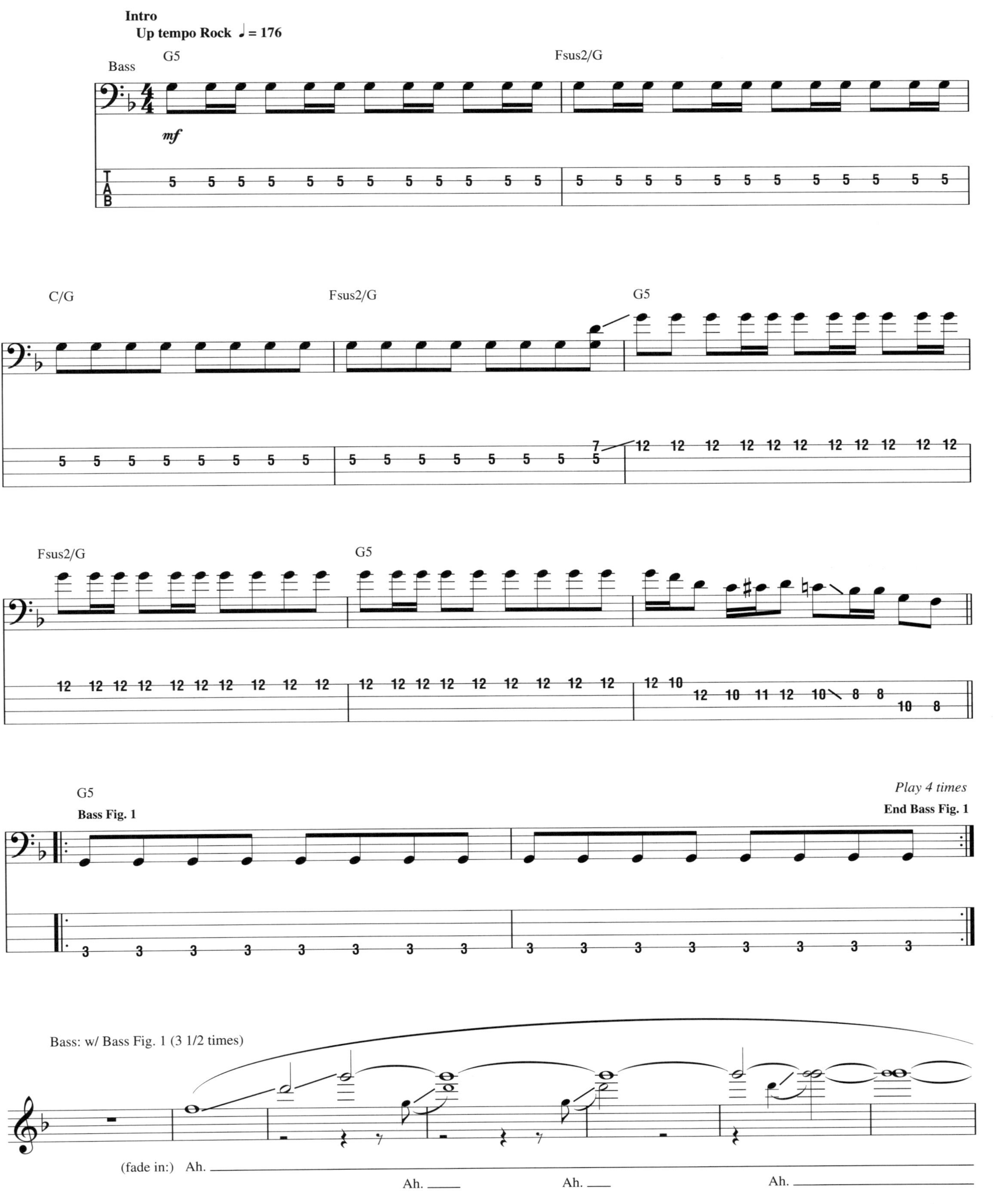

Verse
2nd & 3rd times, Bass: w/ Bass Fill 1
4th time, Bass: w/ Bass Fill 4
C
B♭
F5 G5
1., 4. No - bod - y gon - na take my car, I'm gon - na
2. No - bod - y gon - na take my girl, I'm gon na
3. No - bod - y gon - na take my head, I got
race it to the ground.
keep her to the end.
speed in - side my brain.
A no - bod - y gon - na
2nd time, Bass: w/ Bass Fill 1
4th time, Bass: w/ Bass Fill 5
beat my car, it's gon - na break the speed of sound.
have my girl, she stays a close on ev - 'ry bend.
steal my head, now that I'm on the road a - gain.

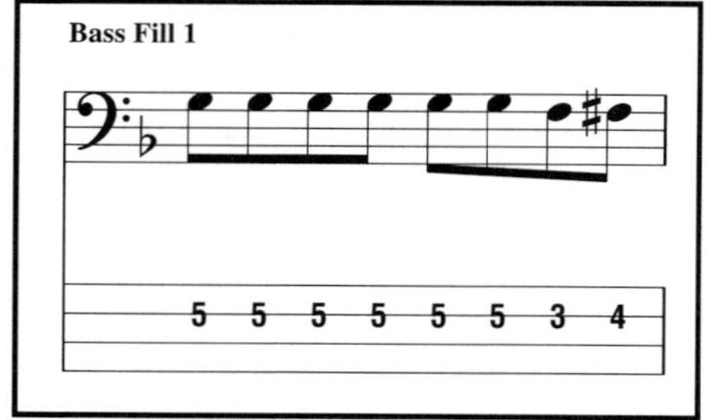
Bass Fill 1

Bass Fill 4

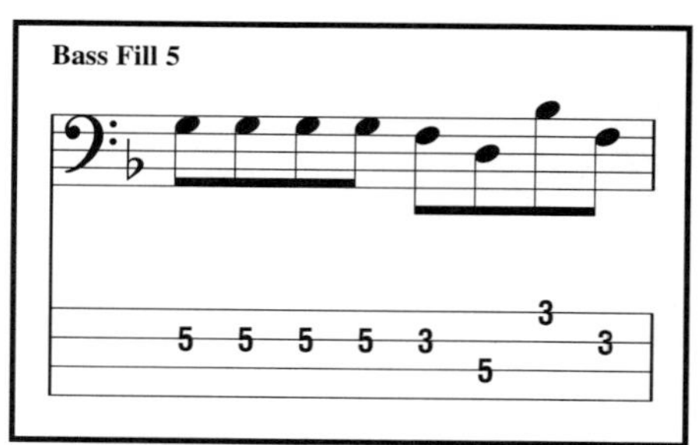
Bass Fill 5

F5
Ooh, it's a kill - in' ma - chine,
Ooh, she's a kill - in' ma - chine,
Ooh, I'm in heav - en a - gain,

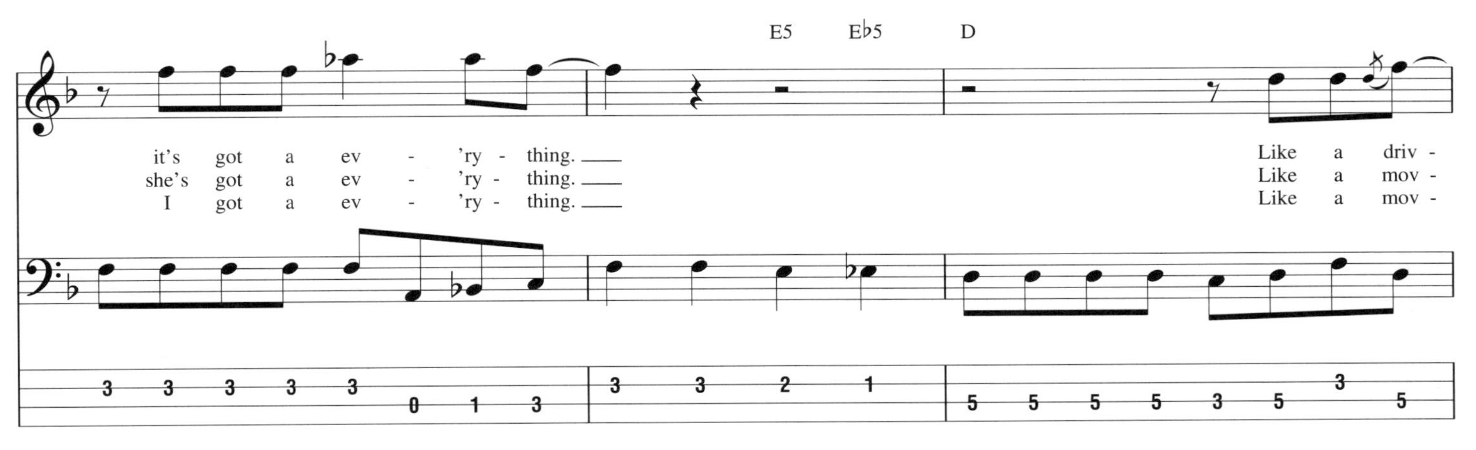
E5 E♭5 D
it's got a ev - 'ry - thing.
she's got a ev - 'ry - thing.
I got a ev - 'ry - thing.
Like a driv -
Like a mov -
Like a mov -

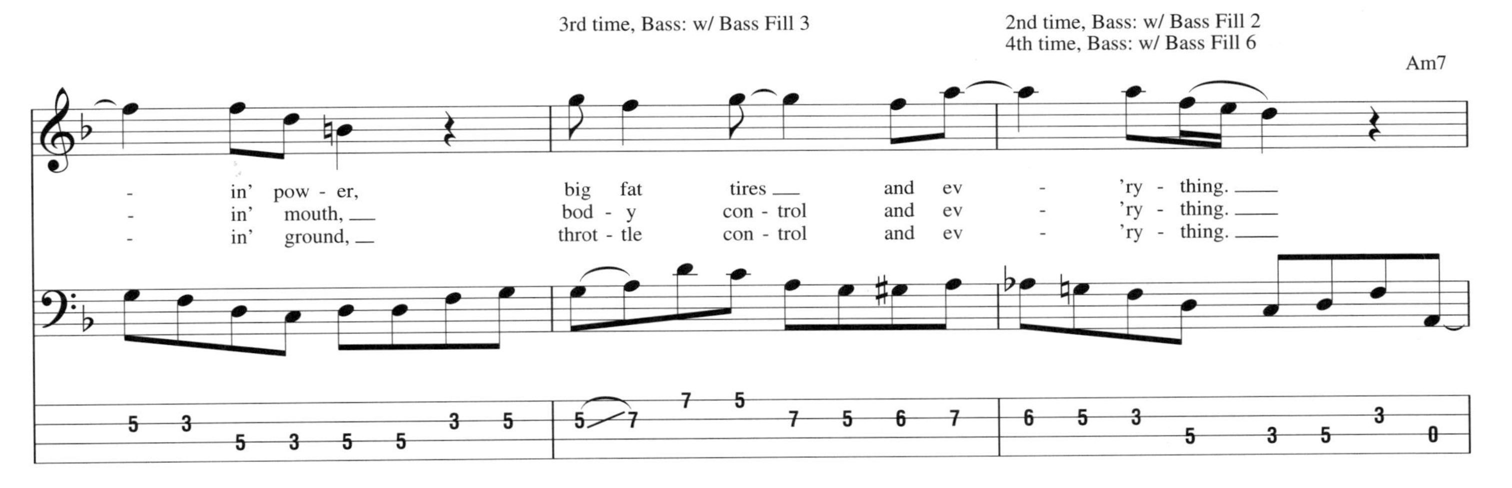
3rd time, Bass: w/ Bass Fill 3
2nd time, Bass: w/ Bass Fill 2
4th time, Bass: w/ Bass Fill 6
Am7
- in' pow - er, big fat tires and ev - 'ry - thing.
- in' mouth, bod - y con - trol and ev - 'ry - thing.
- in' ground, throt - tle con - trol and ev - 'ry - thing.

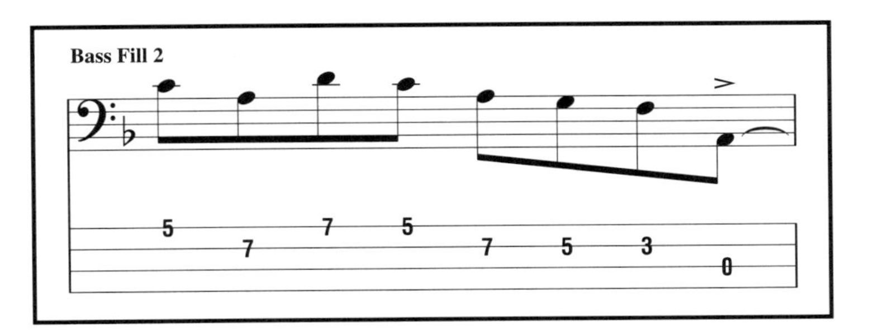
Bass Fill 2

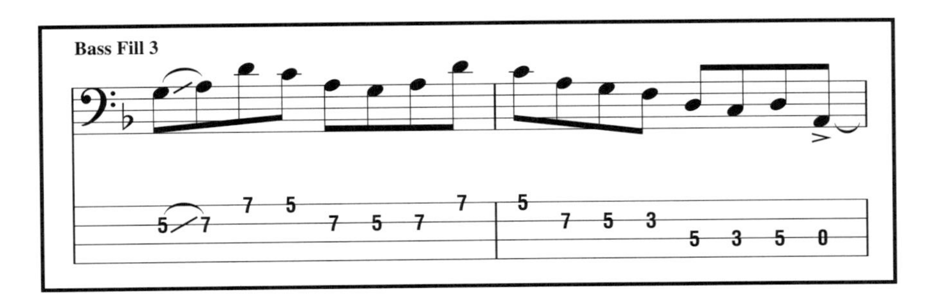
Bass Fill 3

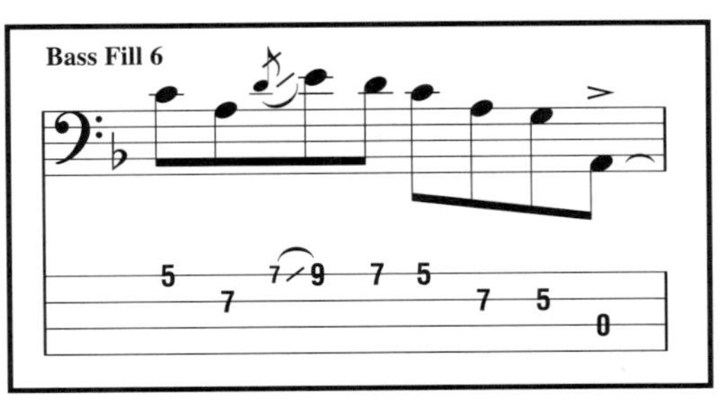
Bass Fill 6

I love it! And I need it! I bleed it!
I love her! And I need her! I seed her!
I love it! And I need it! I seed it!

C
Yeah, it's a wild hurricane!
Yeah, she turns me on
Eight cylinders, all mine!
All

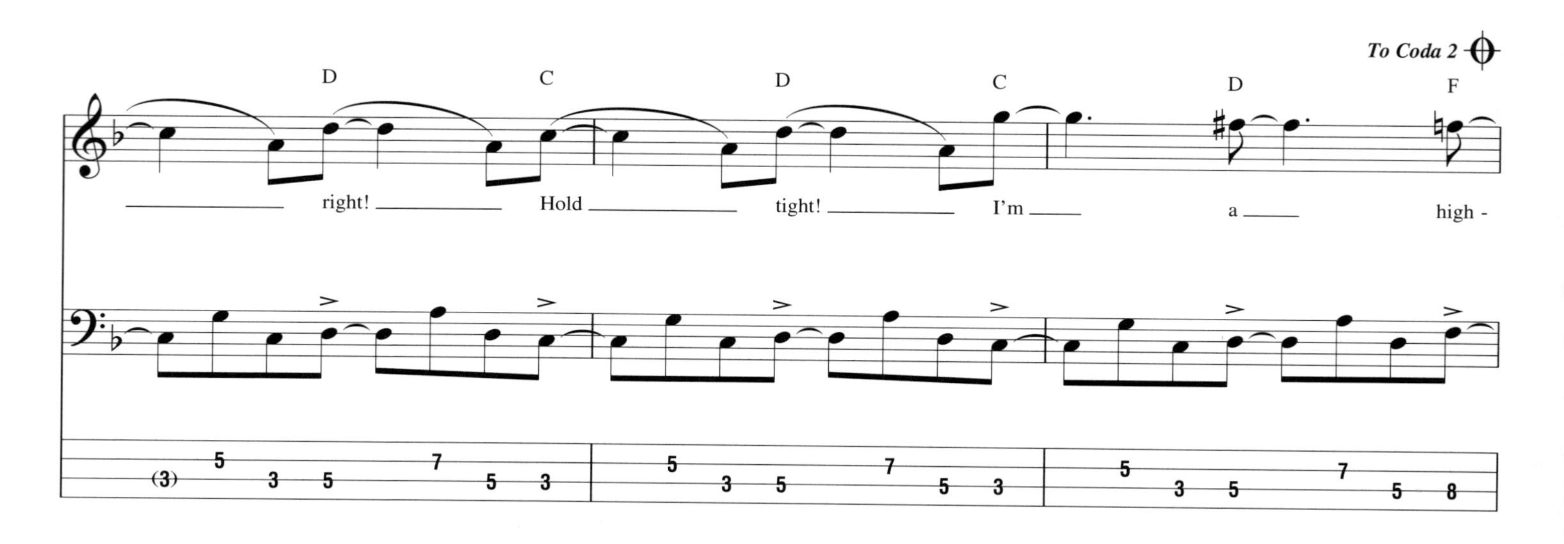
To Coda 2
D C D C D F
right! Hold tight! I'm a high-

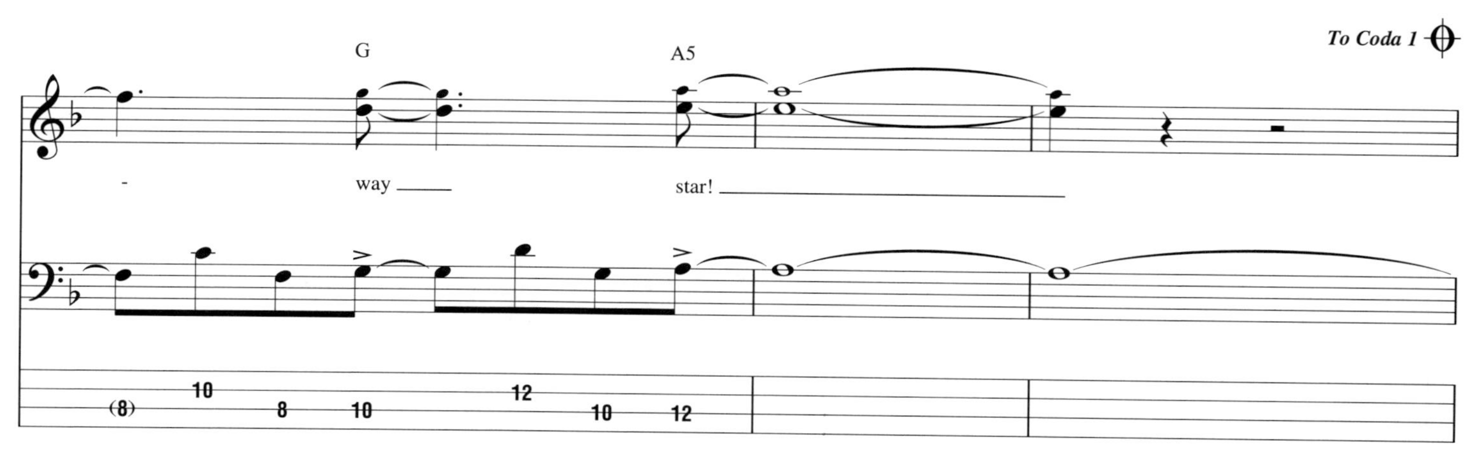
To Coda 1
G A5
-way star!

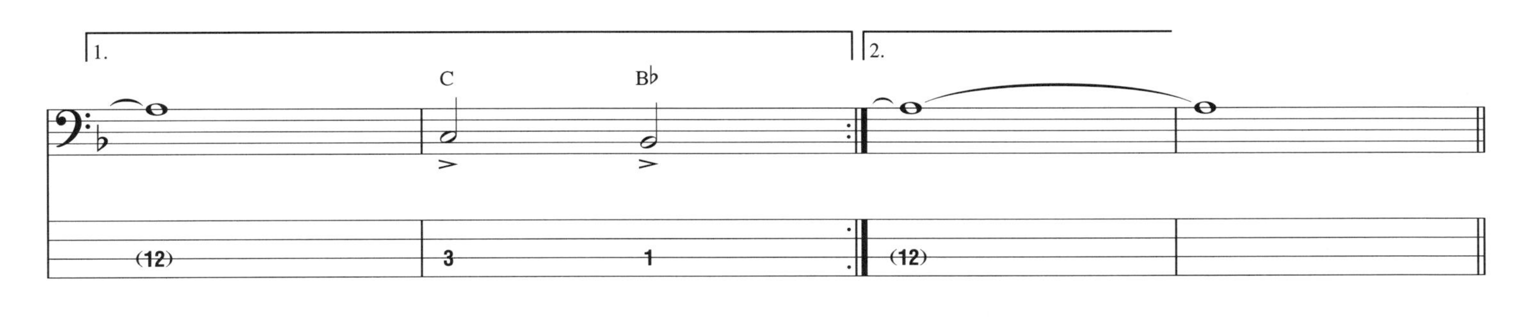
1.
C
B♭
2.

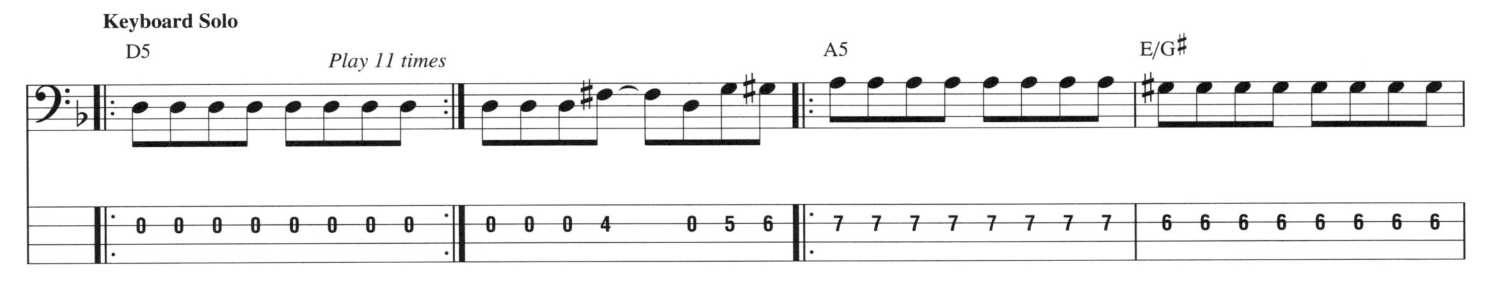
Keyboard Solo
D5
Play 11 times
A5
E/G♯

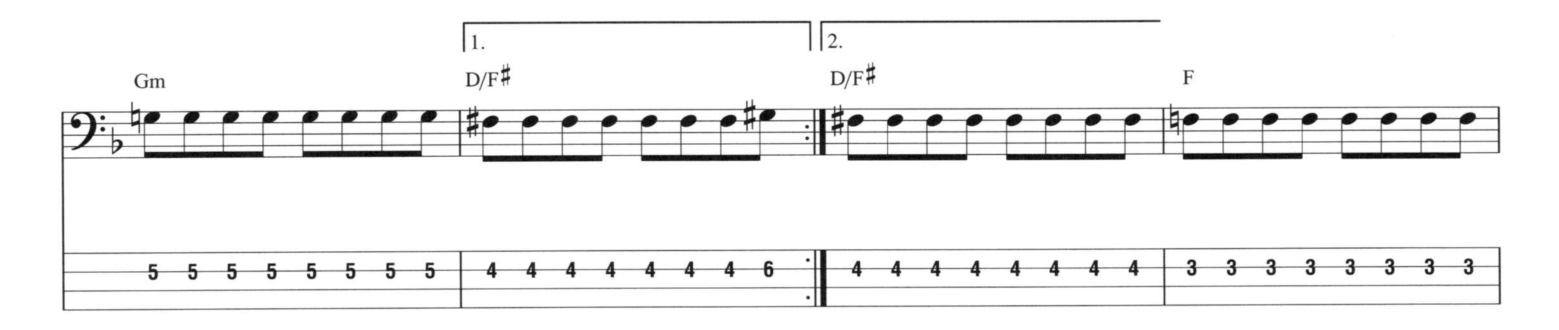
Gm
1.
D/F♯
2.
D/F♯
F

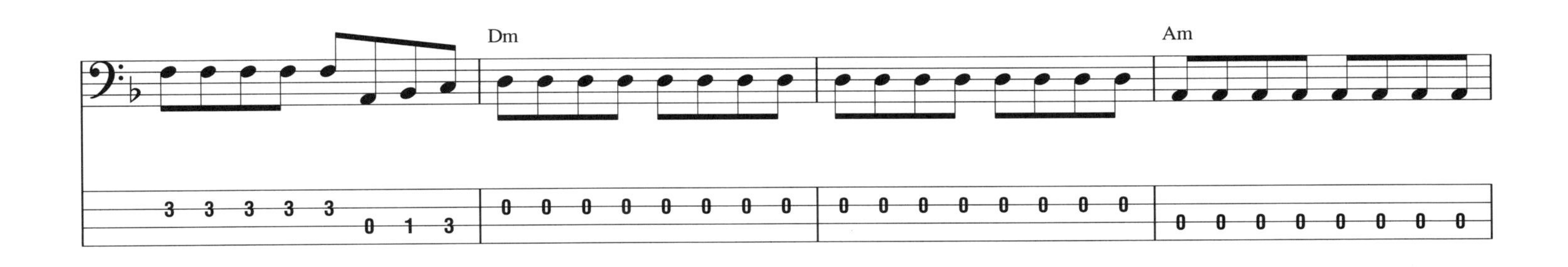
Dm
Am

D5
F5
G5
F5
Play 4 times

N.C.

D.S. al Coda 1
C5
B♭5

Coda 1
Guitar Solo
D5
Play 7 times

A5

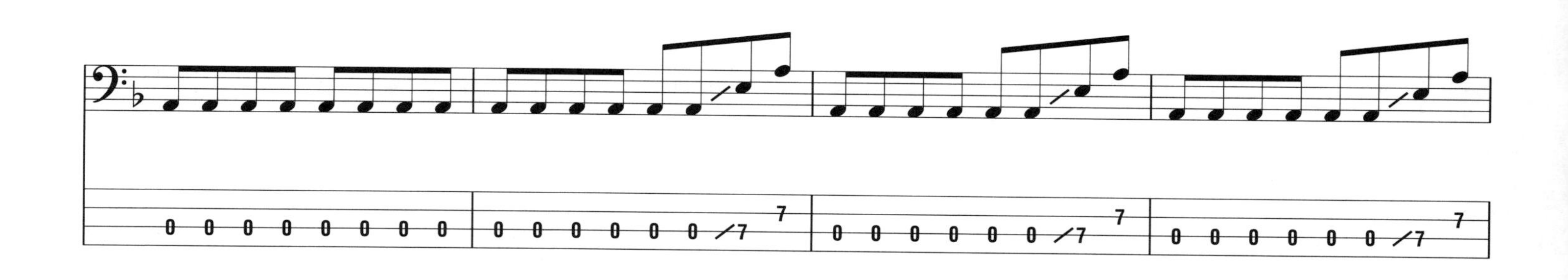

D5
G5

C5
A5

D5
G5

C5
A5

D5
G5

C5
3
A5

D5
G5

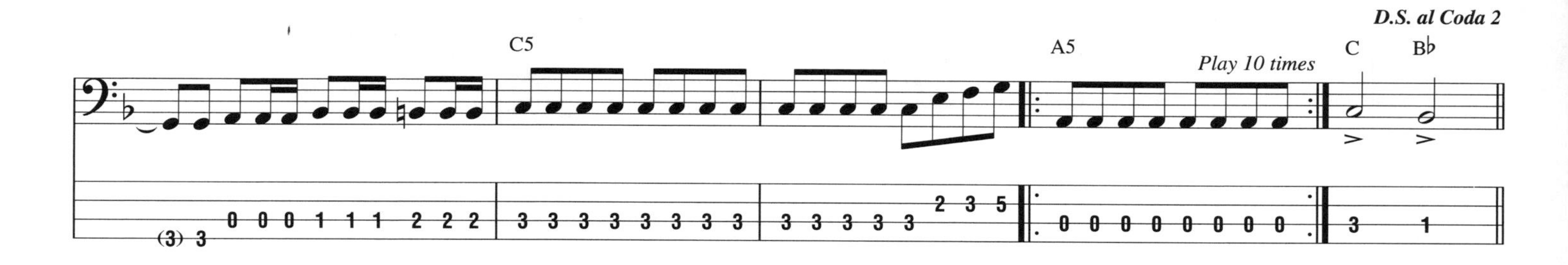
D.S. al Coda 2
C5
A5
Play 10 times
C
B♭

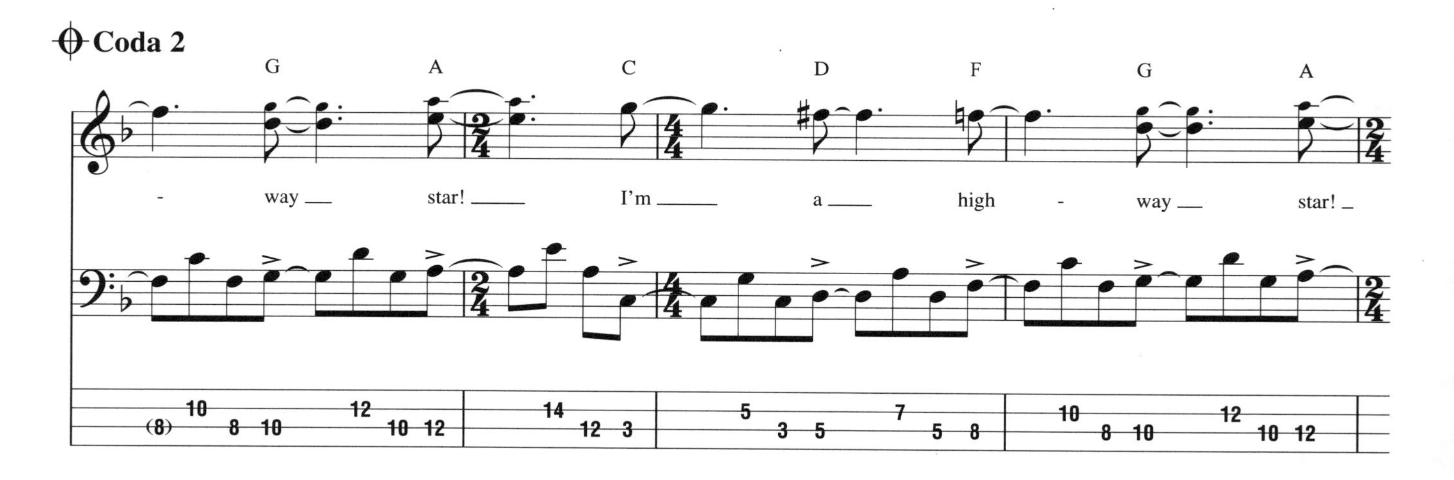
Coda 2
G
A
C
D
F
G
A
- way star! I'm a high - way star!

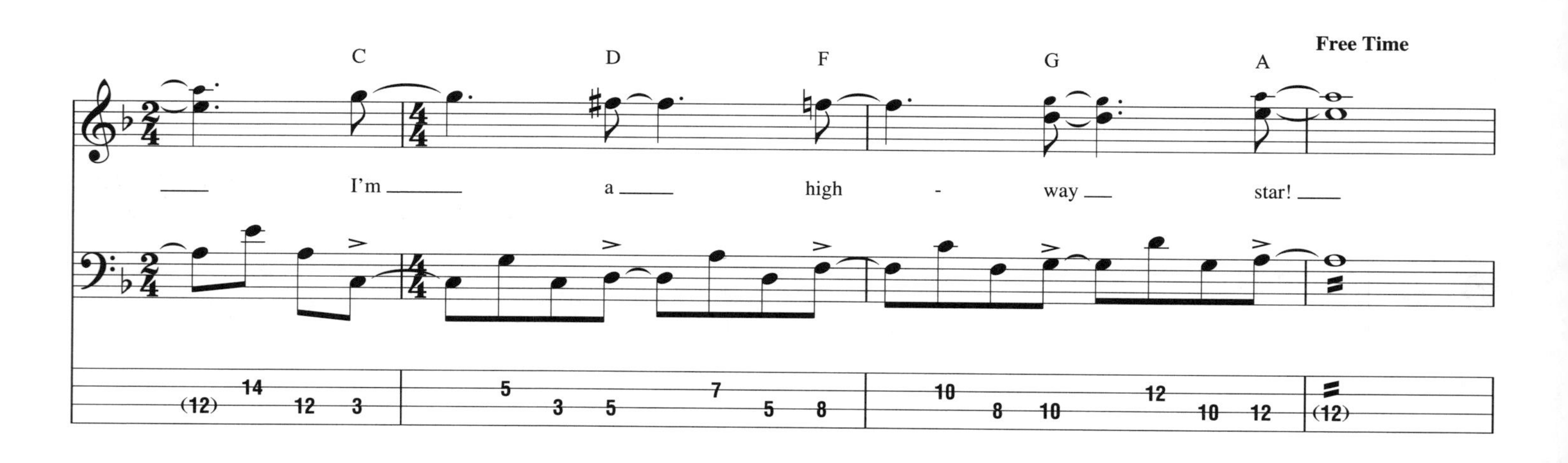
Free Time
C
D
F
G
A
I'm a high - way star!

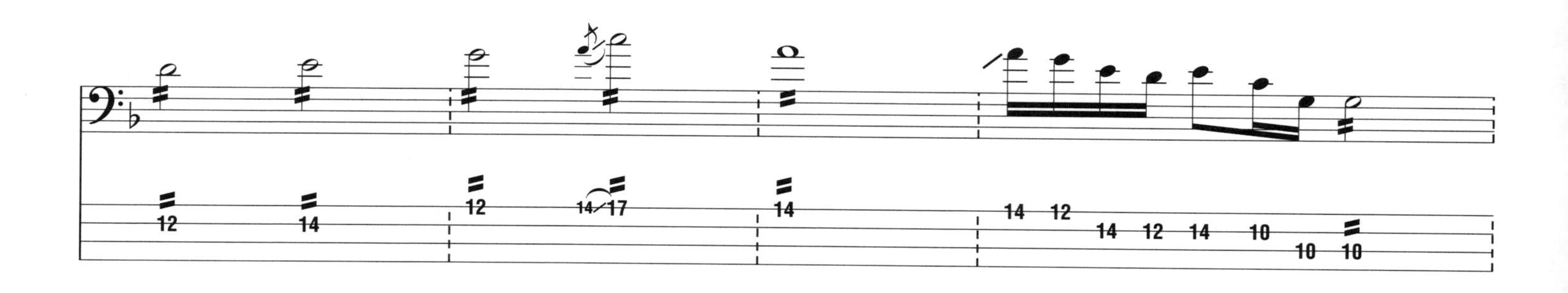

I'll See the Light Tonight

Words and Music by Yngwie Malmsteen and Jeff Scott Soto

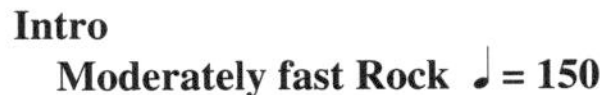

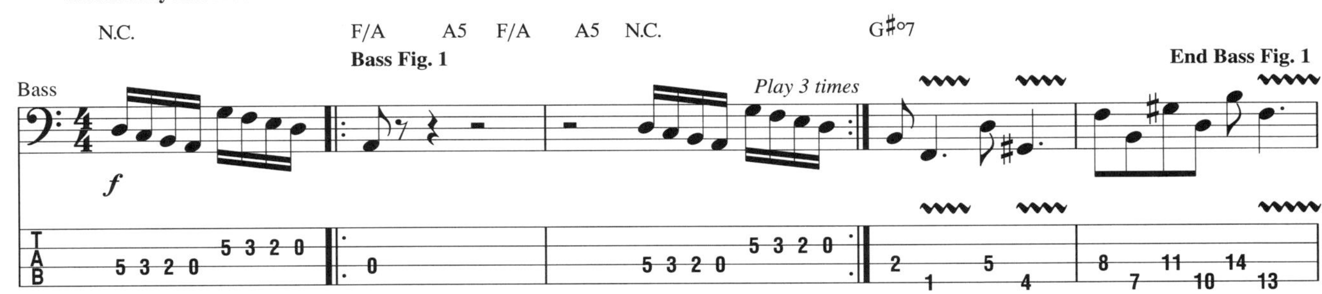

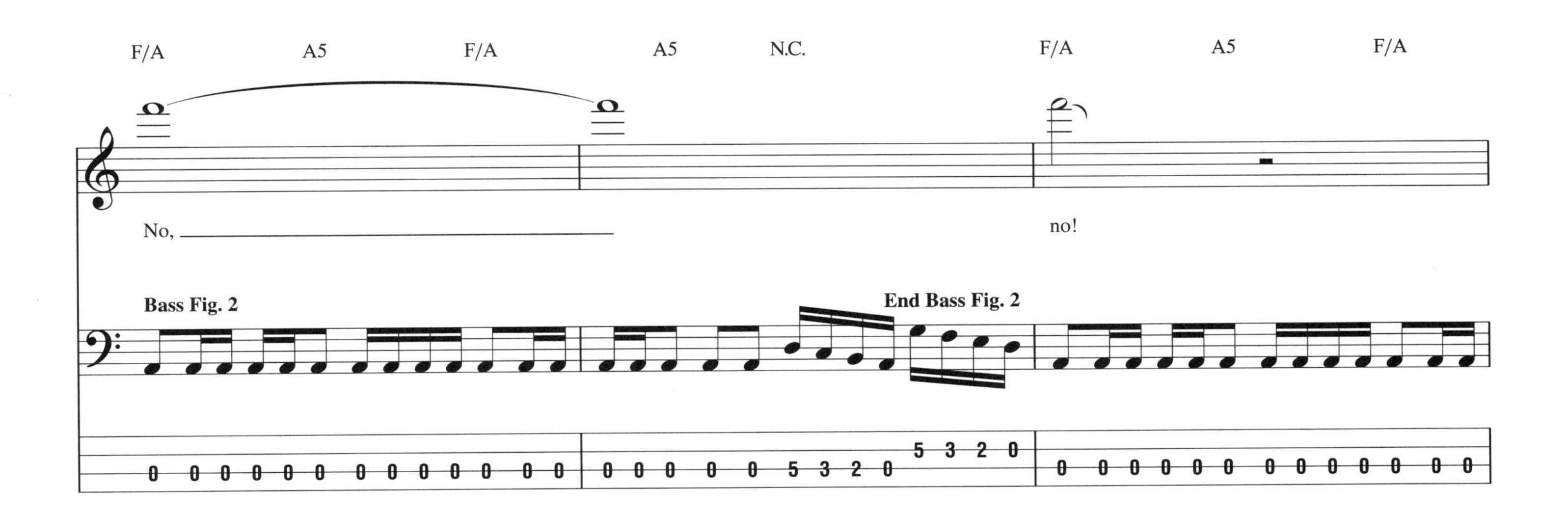

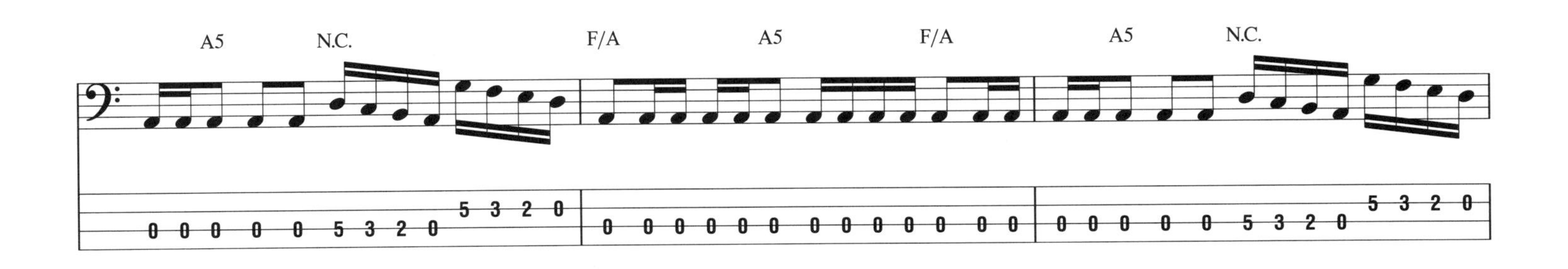

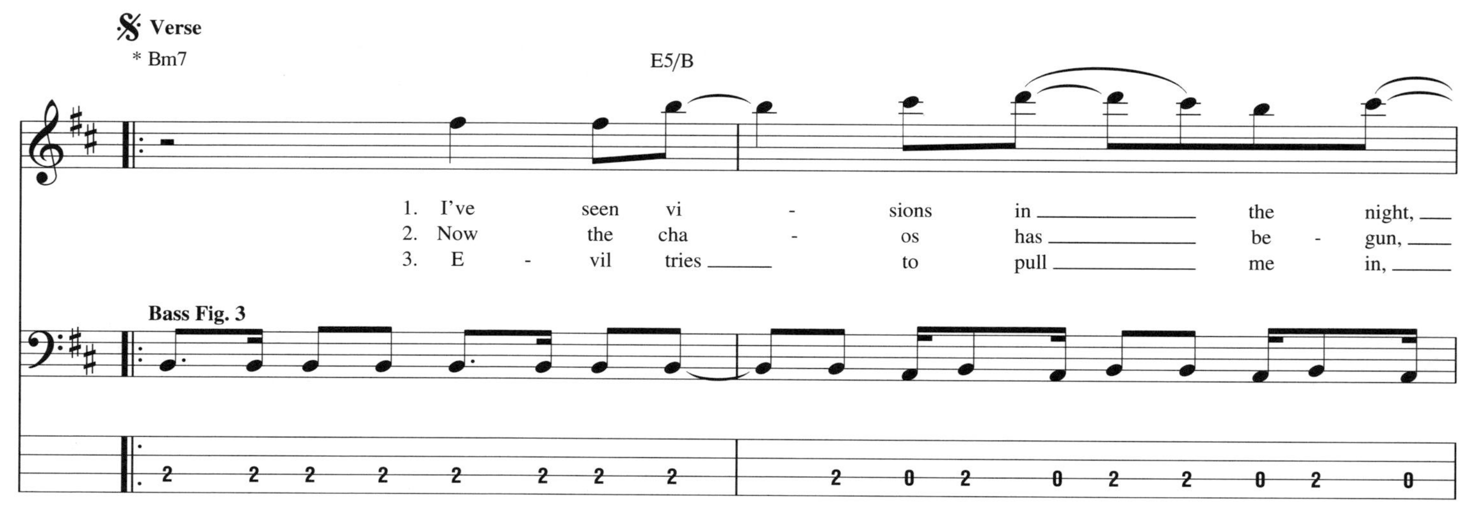

*Chord symbols reflect overall tonality.

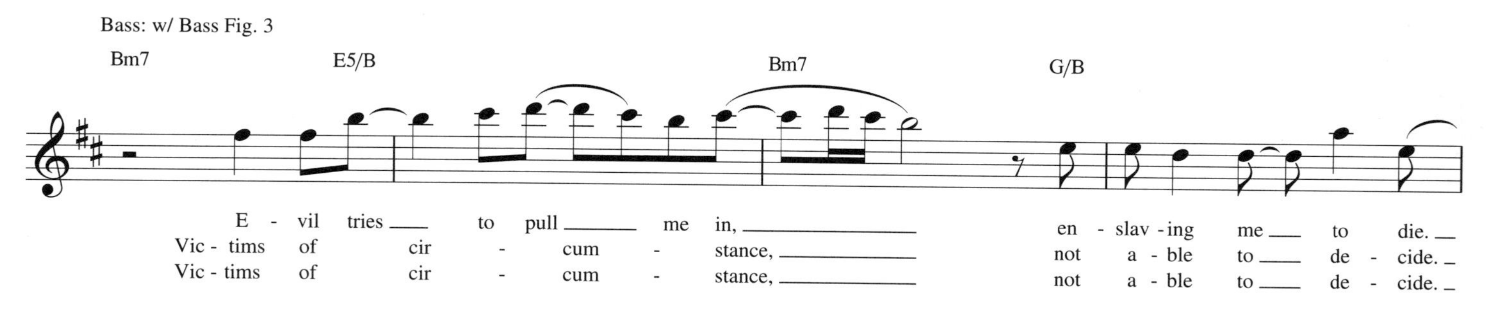

Bm7 E5/B A/B E5
Who's to lose and who's to win?
No, we nev - er had a chance.
No, we nev - er had a chance.
Chorus
Bass: w/ Bass Fig. 2 (3 times)
To Coda
F/A A5 F/A A5 N.C. F/A A5 F/A A5 N.C. F/A A5 F/A A5 N.C.
I'll see the light to - night flash - ing through the sky. Take my life to -
1.
G#°7 A5
night.
Bass Fig. 4
End Bass Fig. 4
2.
G#°7 A5
night.
Guitar Solo
Dm C E7/G# Am Dm C E7/G# Am G#° Am

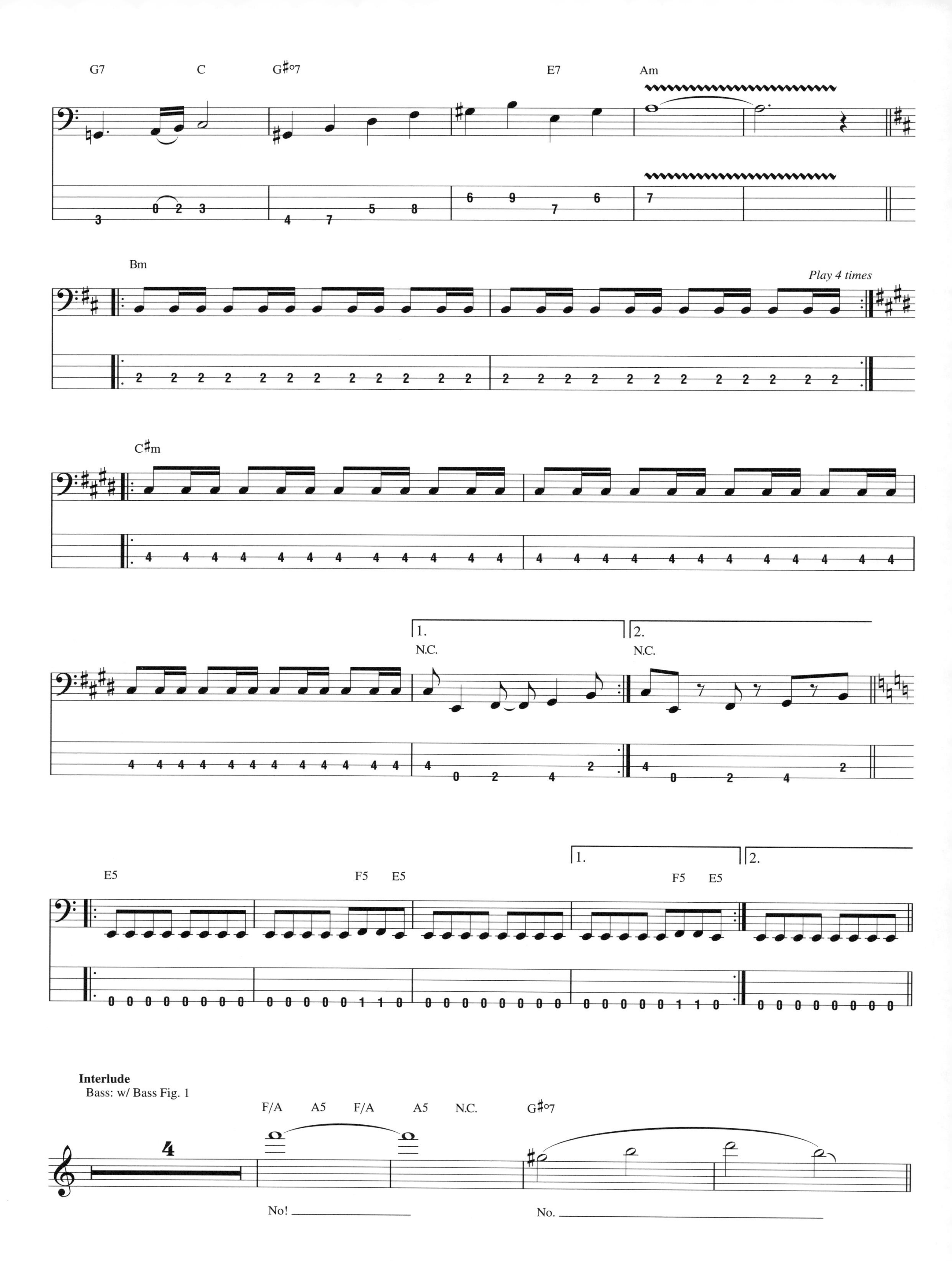
G7
C
G♯°7
E7
Am
Bm
Play 4 times
C♯m
1.
2.
N.C.
N.C.
E5
F5
E5
1.
2.
F5
E5
Interlude
Bass: w/ Bass Fig. 1
F/A
A5
F/A
A5
N.C.
G♯°7
No!
No.

Chorus
Bass: w/ Bass Fig. 2 (3 times)
F/A A5 F/A A5 N.C. F/A A5 F/A A5 N.C.
I'll see the light to - night flash - ing through the
D.S. al Coda
Bass: w/ Bass Fig. 4
F/A A5 F/A A5 N.C. G#o7 A5 N.C.
sky. Take my life to - night.
Coda
Bass: w/ Bass Fig. 4 (1st 2 meas.)
Bass: w/ Bass Fig. 2 (3 times)
G#o7 F/A A5 F/A A5 N.C. F/A A5 F/A
night. I'll see the light to - night
Bass: w/ Bass Fig. 4 (1st 2 meas.)
A5 N.C. F/A A5 F/A A5 N.C. G#o7
flash - ing through the sky. Take my life to - night.
Outro
Free time
A5 F/A G/B N.C.
No!
A tempo
G#o7 A5

The Lemon Song

Words and Music by Chester Burnett, John Bonham, Jimmy Page, Robert Plant and John Paul Jones

E
E7♯9
I would-n't
B7♯9
be here, my chil - dren,
A7
down on this kill - in' floor.
E
2. I should have
Verse
E
lis - tened, ba - by,
E7♯9
to my sec - ond mind.

E
E7♯9
A
Oh.
I should have lis - tened, ba - by,
A5
E
E7♯9
to my sec - ond mind.
B7♯9
A7
Ev - 'ry time I go a - way and leave you, dar - lin',
you send me the blues way
E
Faster ♩ = 150
down the line.
No.

Guitar Solo
Double-time feel

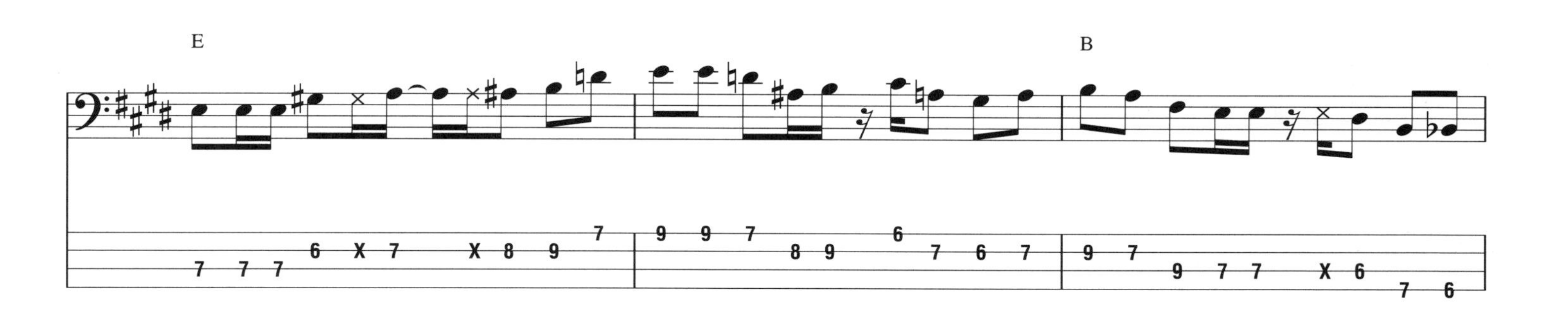

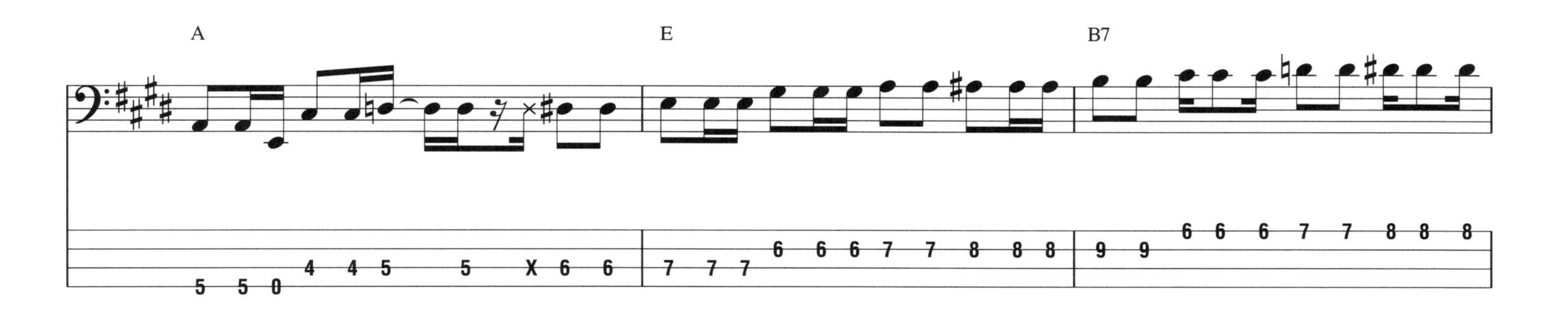

A

E
B

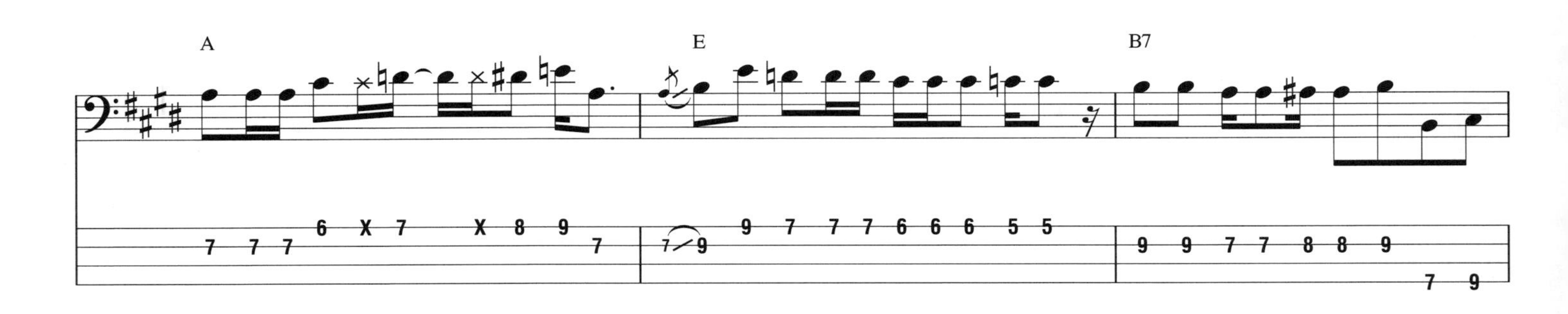
A
E
B7

E

A

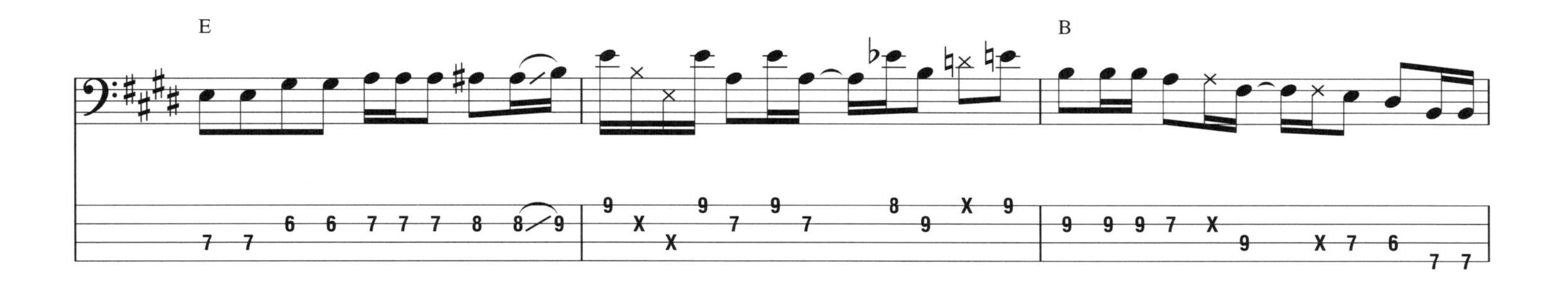
E
B

End double-time feel
A
E
rit.

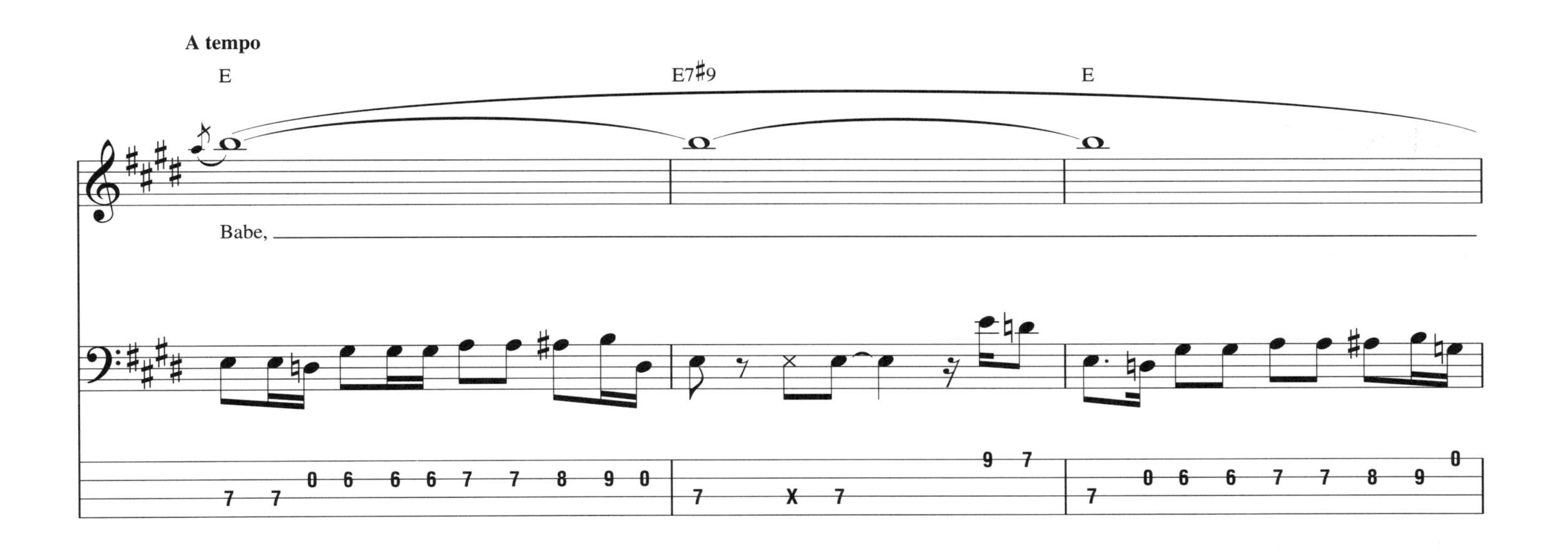
A tempo
E
E7♯9
E
Babe,

E7♯9
A
A5
yeah.
Treat me right, ba - by.

E
E7#9
B7#9
Oh, oh, oh.
A7
E
My, my, my, my.
Spoken: Alright, take it down a little bit.
Verse
E
3. Peo-ple tell me, ba - by, can't be sat - is - fied.
Try to wor-ry me, ba - by, but I nev - er get you in my eyes, and...

A
People worry, ba - by,
can't keep you sat - is -
E
fied.
Huh, let me tell ya,
B
babe,
oh, you ain't noth - in' but a, mm,
A
two - bit, no good
E
jive.

Verse
E
4. I went to sleep last night. _
I worked as hard as I can. _
I bring home my mon - ey, you take _ my mon - ey, give it to an - oth - er man. _
I
A
should-'ve quit you, ba - by,
oh, _ such a long time
E
a - go, _
oh.

B
A
I would-n't be here with all my trou-bles,
down on this kill-in'
E
floor.
Verse
E
5. Squeeze me, babe,
till the juice runs
down my leg.
Ooh.

A
Squeeze, squeeze me ba - by, till the juice runs down my
E
leg.
B
The way you squeeze my lem - on, I,
A
I'm gon - na fall right out of bed,
E
bed, bed, bed.

Guitar Solo

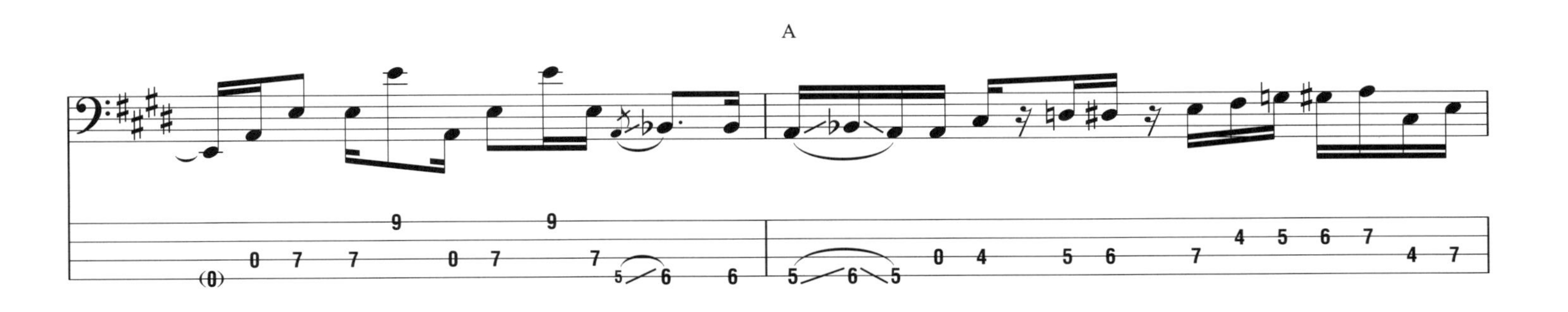

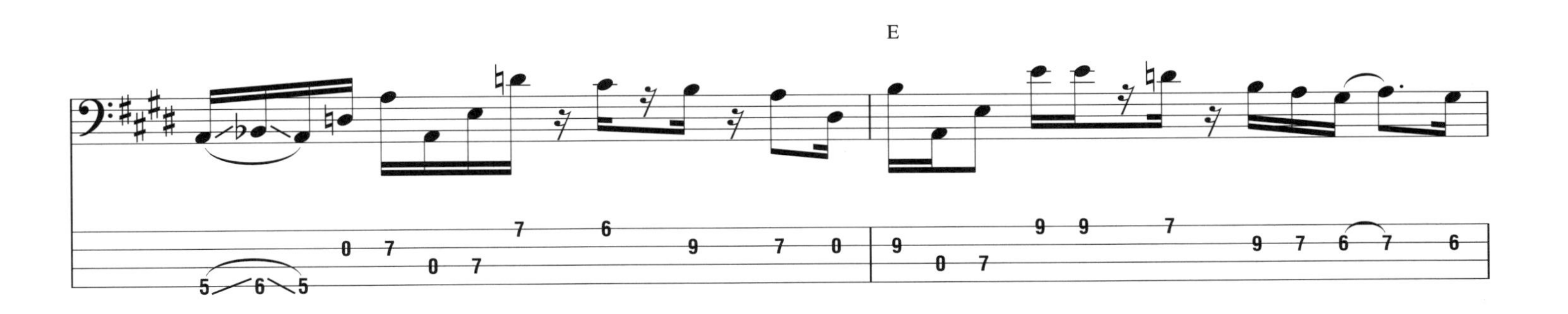

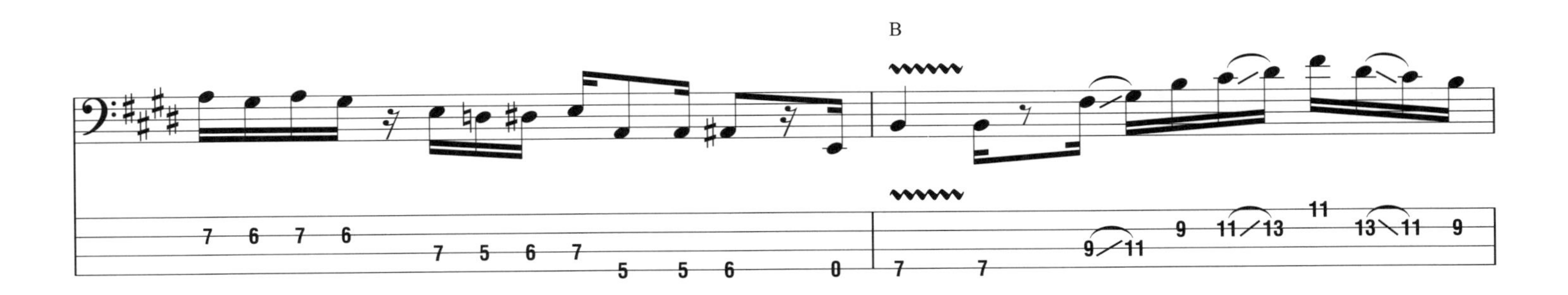

Hey.
Hey.
Hey,
hey.
Hey,
hey,
hey,
hey,
A
do.
Ba - by, ba - by, ba -
E
by, ba - by, ba - by, ba - by, ba - by, ba - by, ba - by, ba - by, ba - by, ba - by.
B
Hey,
hey.
Oh,
hey,

A
E
Faster ♩ = 150
hey.
Uh,
oh.

Guitar Solo
Double-time feel
E

A

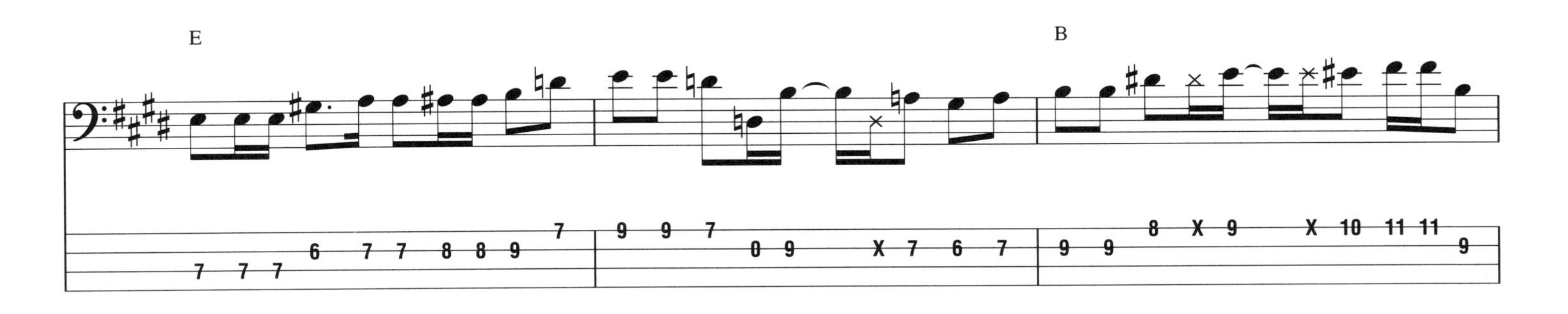
E
B

A
E
B7

E

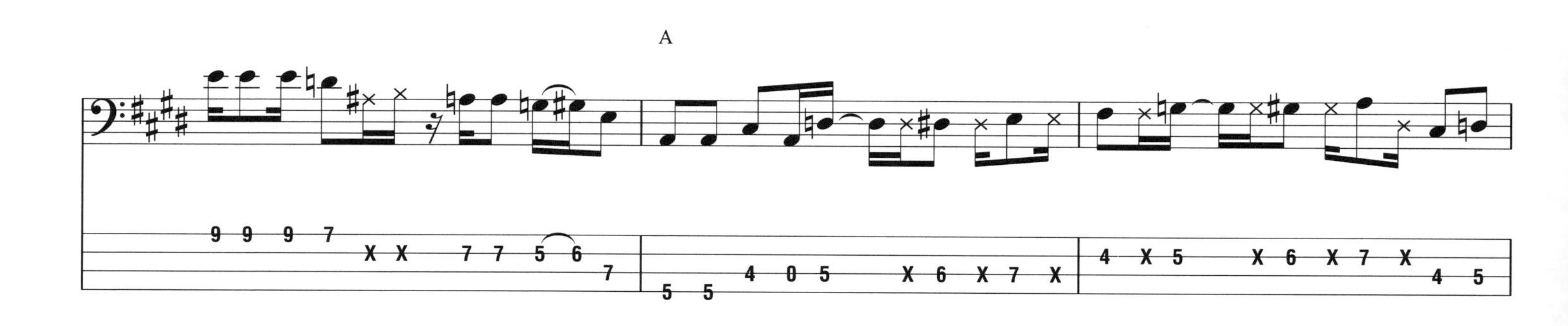
A

E
I'm gon - na

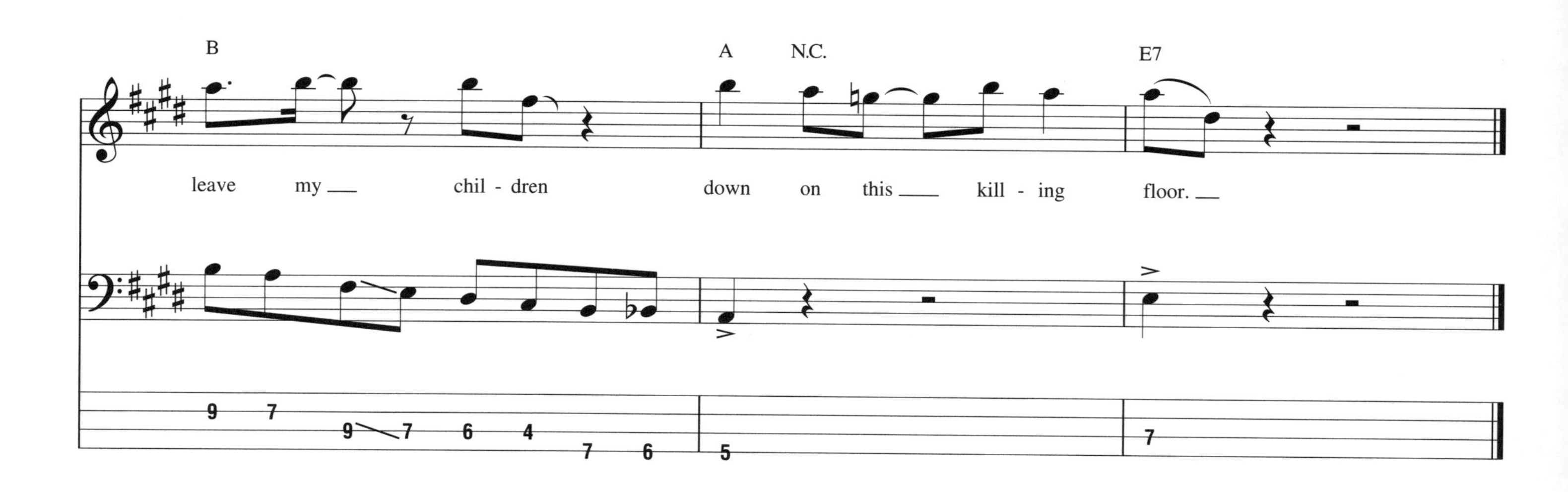
B
A N.C.
E7
leave my chil - dren down on this kill - ing floor.

Livin' on a Prayer

Words and Music by Jon Bon Jovi, Richie Sambora and Desmond Child

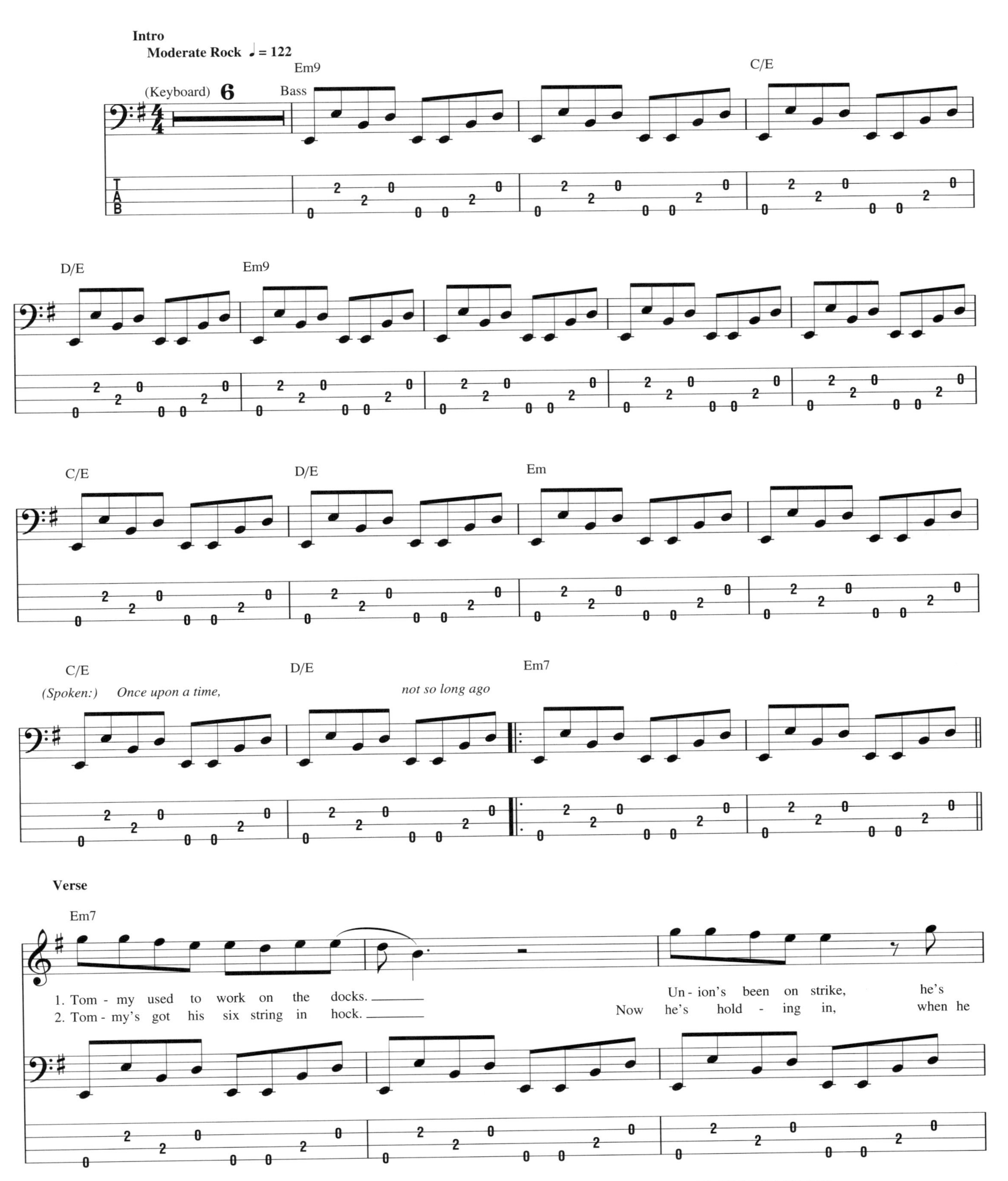

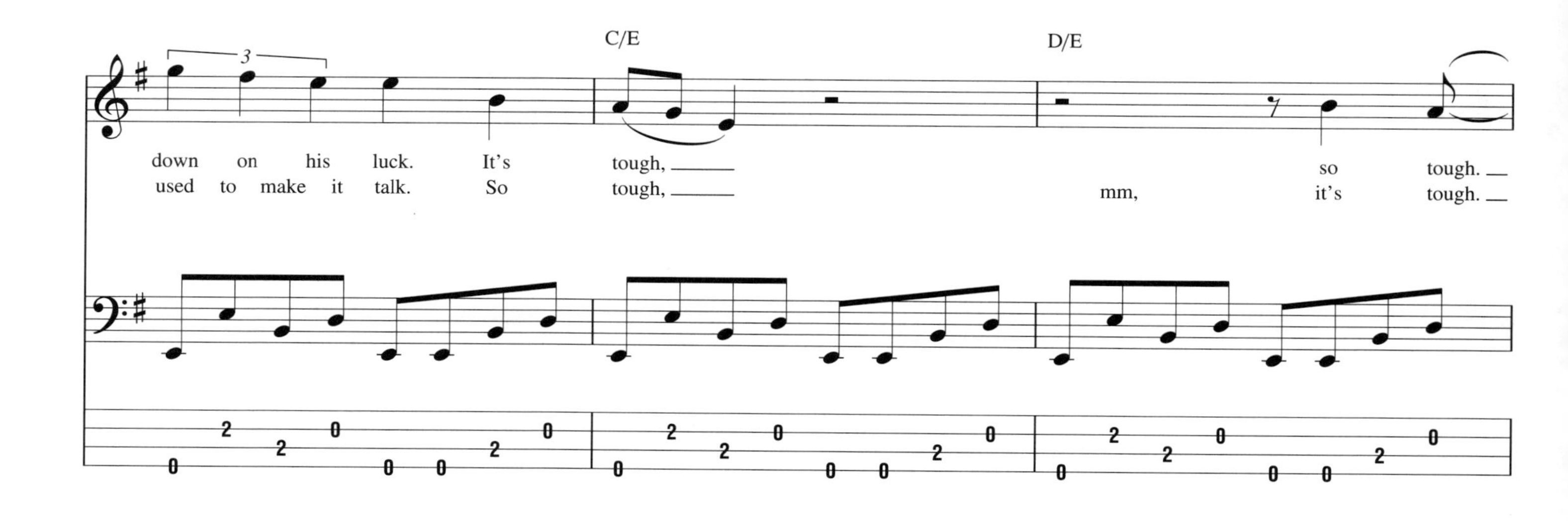
C/E
D/E
down on his luck. It's tough, so tough.
used to make it talk. So tough, mm, it's tough.

Em
2nd time, Bass: w/ Bass Fill 1
Gi - na works the din - er all day.
Gi - na dreams of run - ning a - way,

Work - ing for her man, she brings home her pay for
when she cries in the night, Tom - my whis - pers, "Ba - by, it's O.

Bass Fill 1

C/E
D/E
(Em)
love, mm, for love.
K. some - day."
Pre-Chorus
C5
D5
E5
She says, "We've got to
"We've got to
hold on to what we got. It
C5
D5
E5
C5
D5
does - n't make a dif - f'rence if we make it or not. We've got each oth - er and
E5
D5
C5
D5
that's a lot for love. We'll give it a shot."

Chorus
E5 C5 D5 G5 C5 D5
Whoa, we're half - way there. Whoa, liv - in' on a prayer.
0 2 3 3 2 3 4 5 5 5 5 5 5 2 4 5 0 2 3 2 3 5 5 5 5 5 5 0 3 2

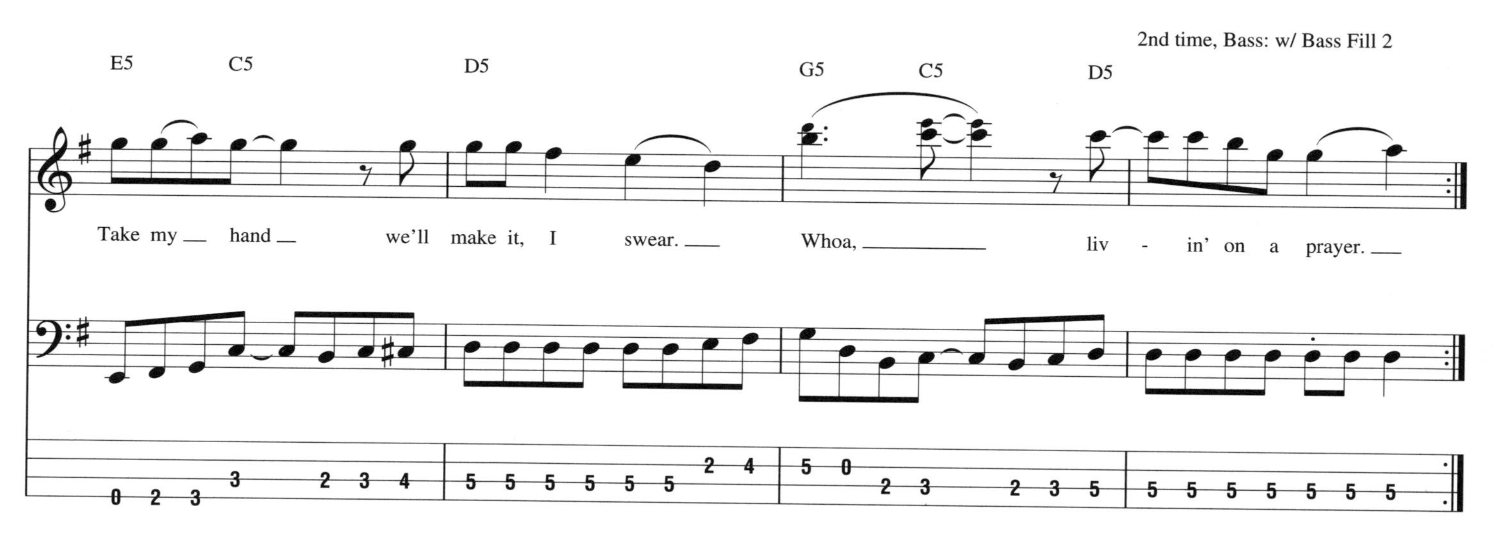
2nd time, Bass: w/ Bass Fill 2
E5 C5 D5 G5 C5 D5
Take my hand we'll make it, I swear. Whoa, liv - in' on a prayer.
0 2 3 3 2 3 4 5 5 5 5 5 5 2 4 5 0 2 3 2 3 5 5 5 5 5 5 5 5

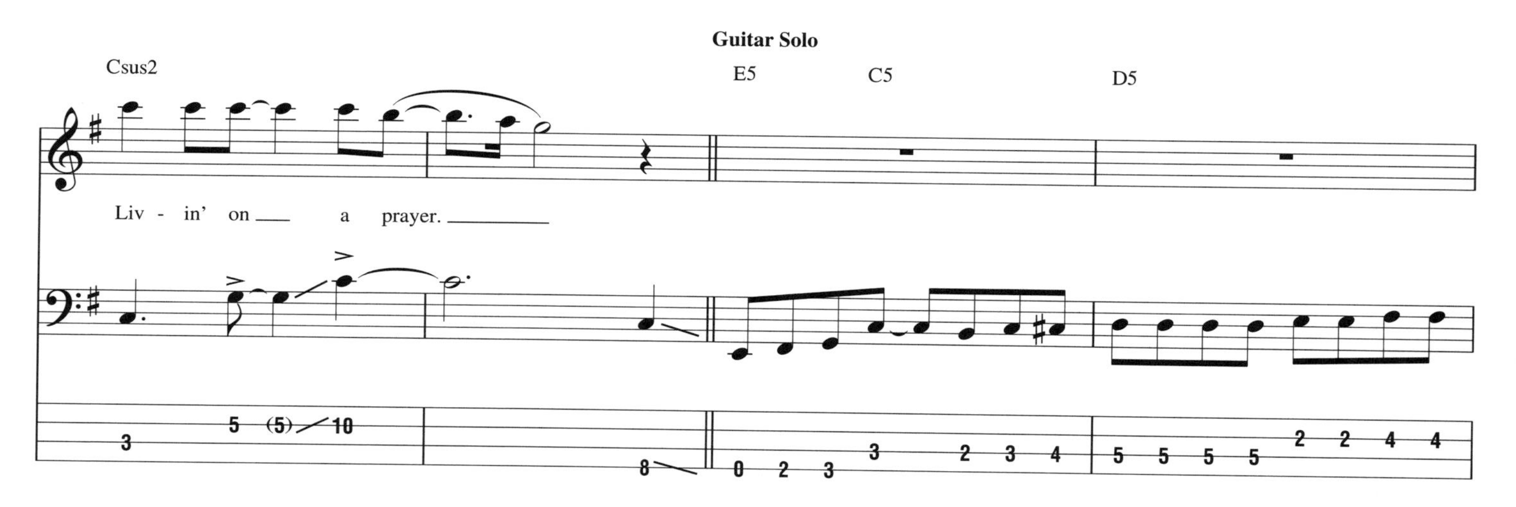
Guitar Solo
Csus2 E5 C5 D5
Liv - in' on a prayer.
3 5 (5) 10 8 0 2 3 3 2 3 4 5 5 5 5 2 2 4 4

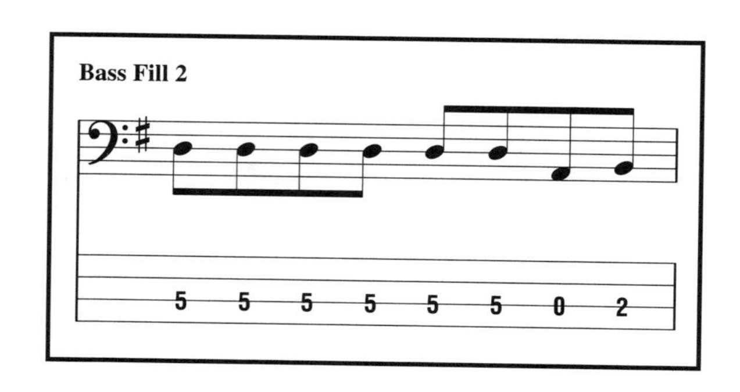
Bass Fill 2
5 5 5 5 5 5 0 2

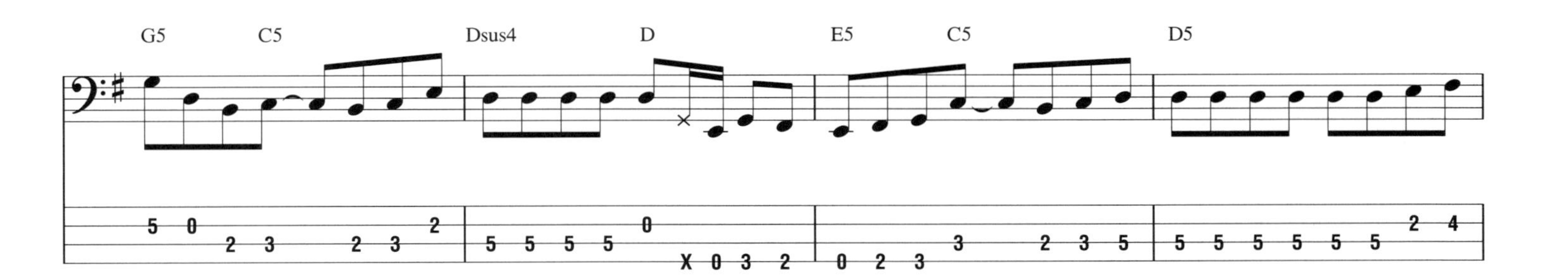
G5
C5
Dsus4
D
E5
C5
D5
5 0 2 3 2 3 2
5 5 5 5 0 X 0 3 2
0 2 3 3 2 3 5
5 5 5 5 5 5 2 4

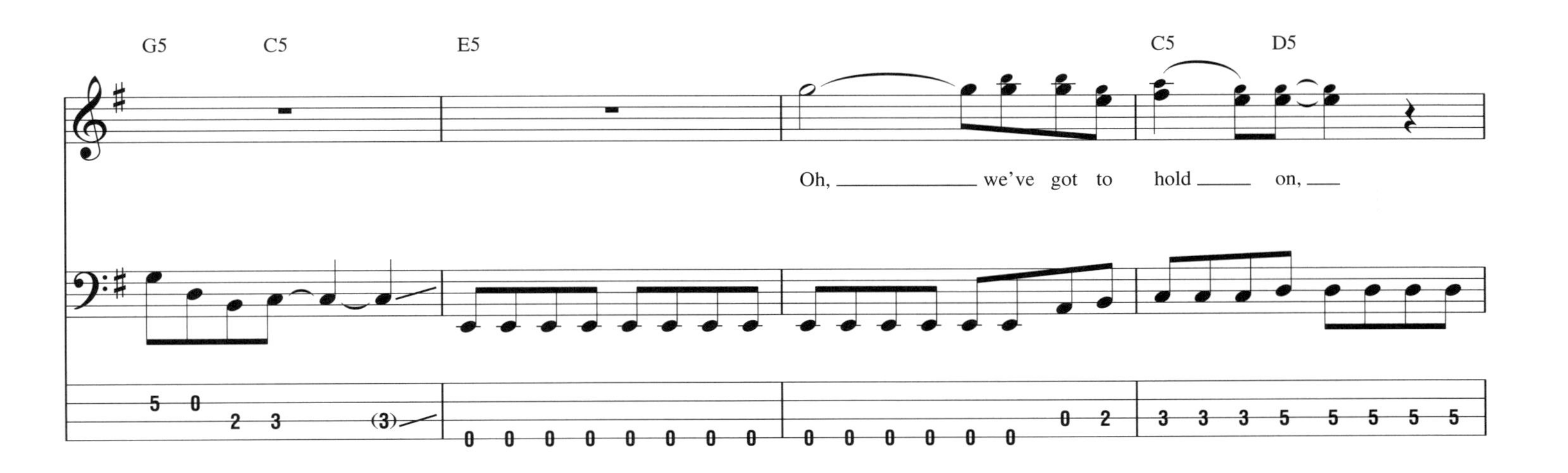
G5
C5
E5
C5
D5
Oh, we've got to hold on,
5 0 2 3 (3)
0 0 0 0 0 0 0 0
0 0 0 0 0 0 0 2
3 3 3 5 5 5 5 5

E5
D5
C5
D5
read - y or not, you live for the fight when it's all that you've got.
5 5 5 5 7 7 5
3 3
5 5 5 5

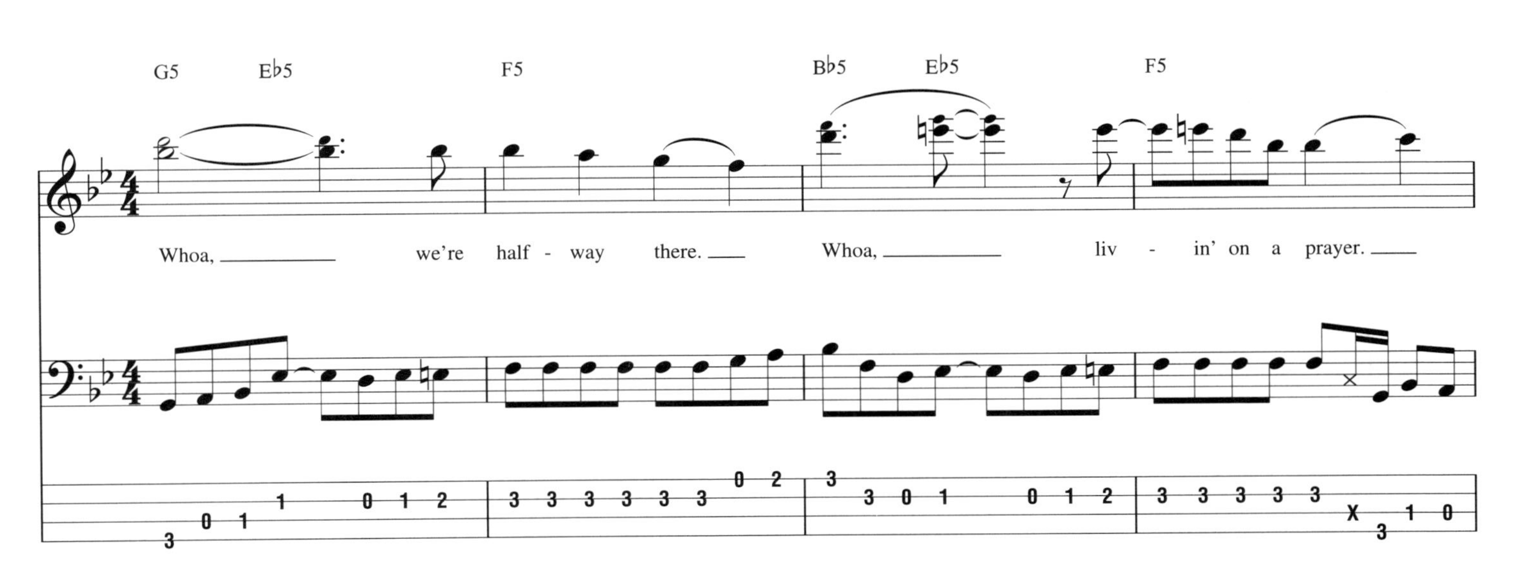
G5
E♭5
F5
B♭5
E♭5
F5
Whoa, we're half - way there. Whoa, liv - in' on a prayer.
3 0 1 1 0 1 2
3 3 3 3 3 3 0 2
3 3 0 1 0 1 2
3 3 3 3 3 X 3 1 0

G5
E♭5
F5
B♭5
E♭5
F5
Take my hand and we'll make it, I swear. Whoa, liv - in' on a prayer.
Whoa, we're half - way there. Whoa, liv - in' on a prayer.
Take my hand and we'll make it, I swear. Whoa, liv - in' on a prayer.
Begin fade
Fade out
Whoa, we're half - way there. Whoa, liv - in' on a prayer.

Mississippi Queen

Words and Music by Leslie West, Felix Pappalardi, Corky Laing and David Rea

D5 E5
Verse
G5 A5
she taught me ev - 'ry - thing.
1. Way down
2. This la -
G5 A5
a - round Vicks - burg,
- dy she asked me
a - round Lou - i - si - an - a way,
if I would be her man.
D5 E5
D5 E5
lived a Ca - jun la - dy
You know that I told her
called the
I'd do
A5 B5
Mis - sis - sip - pi Queen.
what I can
You know she was a danc - er,
to keep her look - in' pret - ty.
You know she was a danc - er,

G5 A5
N.C.(E5)
she moved better on wine. While the rest of them dudes was a'
Buy her dress-es that shine. While the rest of them dudes was a'
she moved better on wine, While the rest of them dudes was a'
1/2
N.C.
1., 2.
get-tin' their kicks; bud-dy, beg your par-don I was get-tin' mine.
mak-in' their bread; bud-dy, beg your par-don I was los-in' mine.
get-tin' their kicks; broth-er beg your par-don, I was
3.
get-tin' mine. Hey, Mis-sis-sip-pi Queen.

Mr. Brownstone

Words and Music by W. Axl Rose, Slash, Izzy Stradlin', Duff McKagan and Steven Adler

Tune down 1/2 step:
(low to high) E♭-A♭-D♭-G♭

Intro
Moderate Rock ♩ = 105

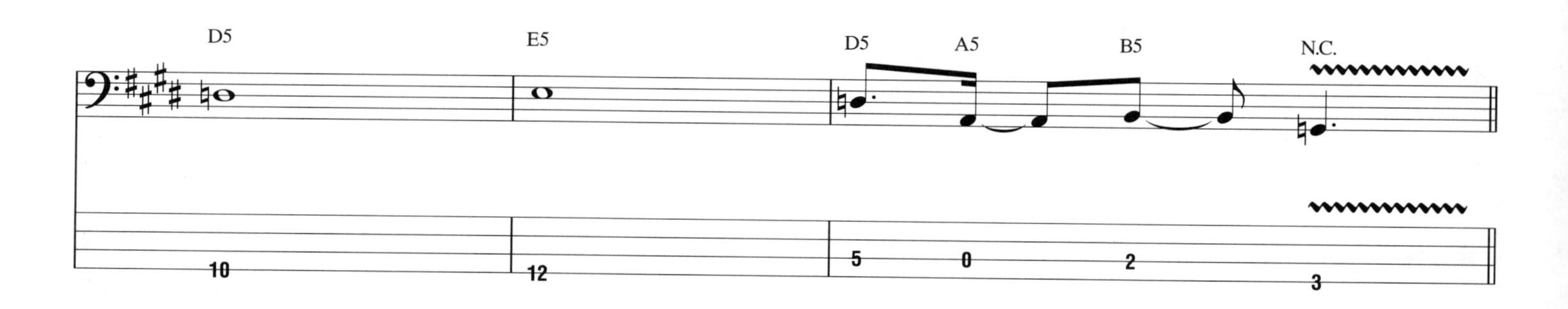

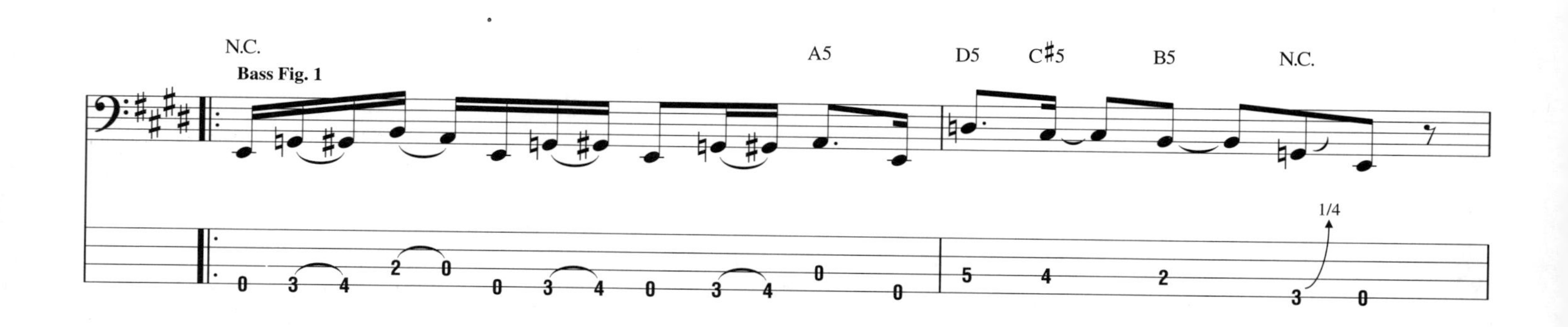

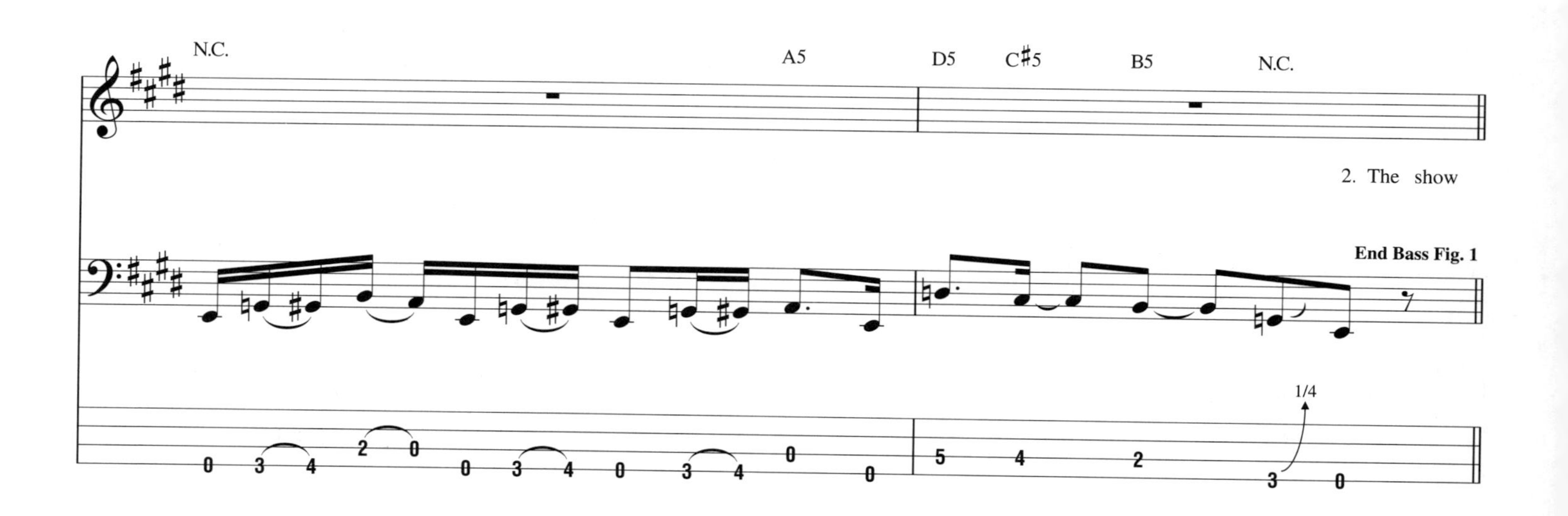

Verse
E5
A5
E5
1. I get up __ a - round sev - en,
get out - ta bed __ a - round nine.
And
u - su - al - ly starts a - round sev - en,
we go on stage __ a - round nine.
0 0 0 3 5
5 5 5 3 0
A5
1.
G5 E5
I don't wor - ry a - bout noth - in', no, __ be - cause
wor - ry - ing's a waste __ of my time.
Get on the bus __ a - bout e - lev - en, sip - pin' a
0 0 0 3 5
5 5 5 3 0
2.
G5 E5
Chorus
G5 F5 G5
drink and feel - in' fine. __
We've __ been danc - in' __ with
5 5 5 3 0 7
3 1 3 1 2 3 1 2
C5 B♭5 C5
D C D
Mis - ter Brown - stone. __
He's __ been knock - in'.
3 1 3 1 2 3 0
5 3 5 3 4 5 0

N.C.
E5
He won't have me a - lone.
To Coda 1
To Coda 2
N.C.
No, no, no. He won't leave me a - lone. I
Bass Fig. 2
End Bass Fig. 2
Bridge
B5 A5 B5 A5 G5 A5
used to do a lit - tle, but a lit - tle would - n't do, and so the lit - tle got more and more. I
Bass Fig. 3
B5 A5 B5
1.
A5 G5 A5
just keep try - in' to get a lit - tle bet - ter, said a lit - tle bet - ter than be - fore. I
End Bass Fig. 3

2.
D.S. al Coda 1
A5
G5
A5
lit - tle bet - ter than be - fore.
Coda 1
N.C.
Guitar Solo
F♯5
B5
E5
A5
1.
2.
D5
E5/B
G5
F5
C5
B♭5
C♯5
Interlude
Bass: w/ Bass Fig. 1
4

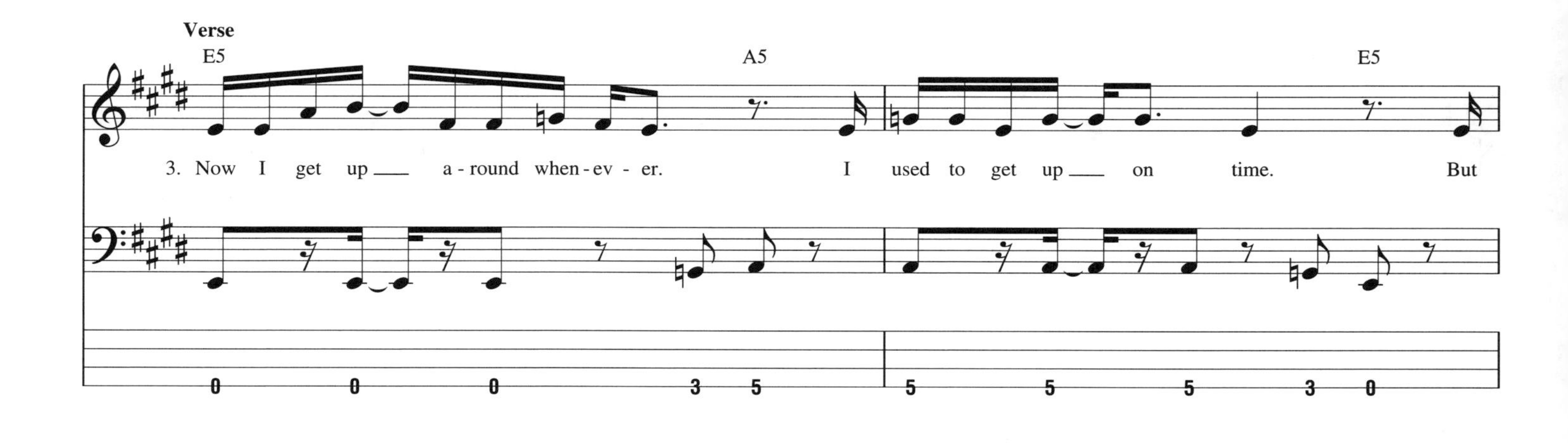
Verse
E5
A5
E5
3. Now I get up ___ a - round when - ev - er. I used to get up ___ on time. But
0 0 0 3 5 5 5 5 3 0

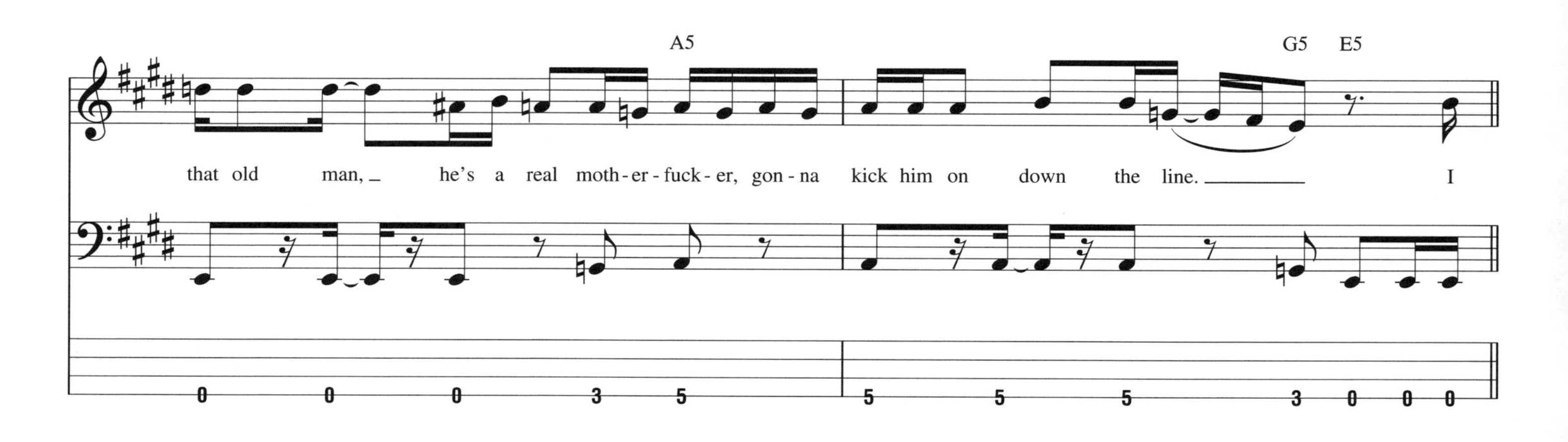
A5
G5 E5
that old man, _ he's a real moth - er - fuck - er, gon - na kick him on down the line. ___ I
0 0 0 3 5 5 5 5 3 0 0 0

Bridge
Bass: w/ Bass Fig. 3 (1 1/2 times)
B5 A5 B5 A5 G5 A5
used to do a lit - tle, but a lit - tle would-n't do, and so the lit - tle got more and more. ___ I

1.
B5 A5 B5 A5 G5 A5
just keep try - in' to get ___ a lit - tle bet - ter, said a lit - tle bet - ter than be - fore. ___ I

2.
D.S. al Coda 2
B5 A5 B5 A5 G5 A5/E
just keep try - in' to get ___ a lit - tle bet - ter, said a lit - tle bet - ter than be - fore. ___
7 5 7 X 5 6 7 0 0 7 7 7 5 5 5 7 5 8 (8)

Coda 2
Interlude
Bass: w/ Bass Fig. 2
Bass: w/ Bass Fig. 1
N.C.
N.C.
A5
D5
C♯5
B5
N.C.
Ooh, won't leave me a - lone.
A5
D5
C♯5
B5
N.C.
Outro
E5
Stuck it in the mid-dle, and I shot it in the mid-dle, and it
it drove me out - ta my mind.
A5
I
should-'ve known bet - ter, said I wish I nev - er met her, said I,
I leave it all
E
be - hind.
Free time
E7
Yow - sa!

No One Like You

Words and Music by Klaus Meine and Rudolf Schenker

F/A Am F
for a man who needs love. I miss you since I've been a -
all my long - ing for love. I don't want my feel - ings re -
C/A E7 Am F
way. Babe, was - n't eas -
strained. Ooh, babe, I just need
Am F
- y to leave you a - lone. It's get - ting hard -
you like nev - er be - fore, just im - ag -
Am F
- er now that I'm gone; if I had the choice I would stay.
- ine you'd come through this door; you'd take all my sor - row a -

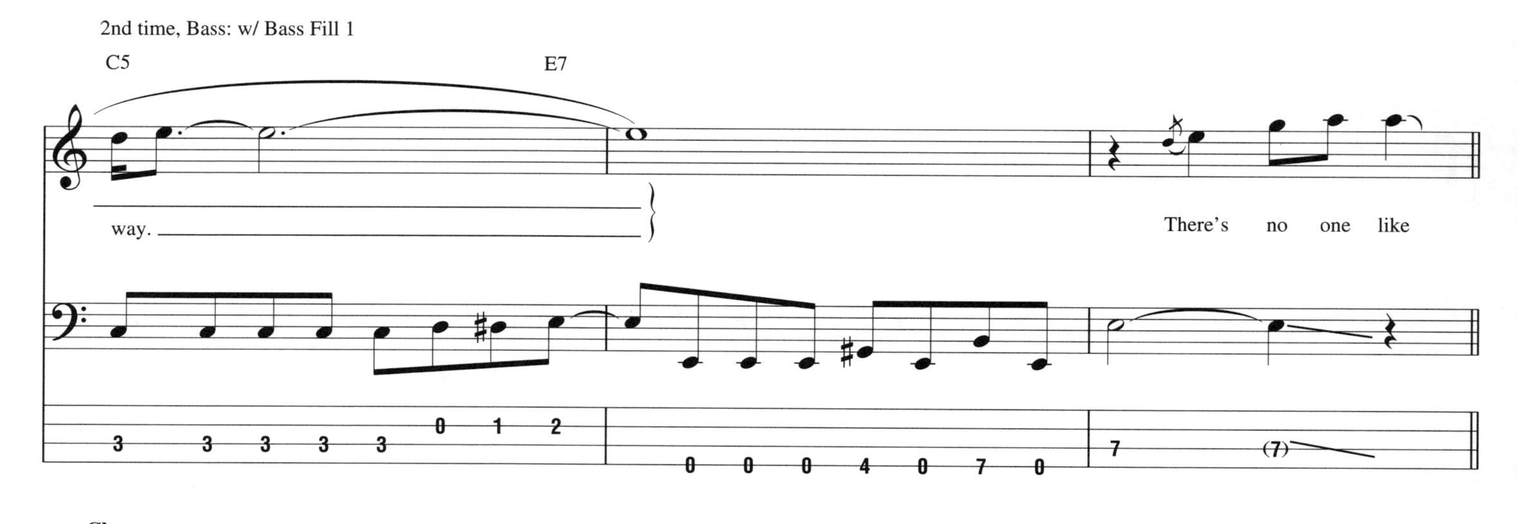
2nd time, Bass: w/ Bass Fill 1
C5
E7
way.
There's no one like
3 3 3 3 3 0 1 2
0 0 0 4 0 7 0
7 (7)

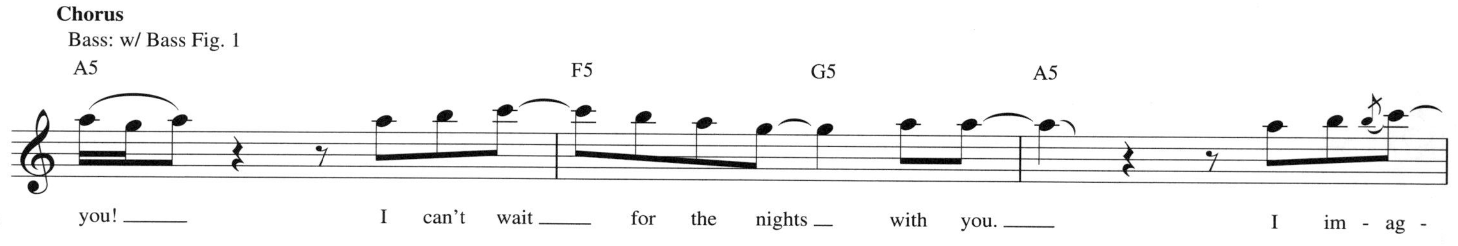
Chorus
Bass: w/ Bass Fig. 1
A5
F5
G5
A5
you! I can't wait for the nights with you. I im - ag -

F5
G5
A5
F5
G5
- ine the things we do. I just wan - na be loved by you.

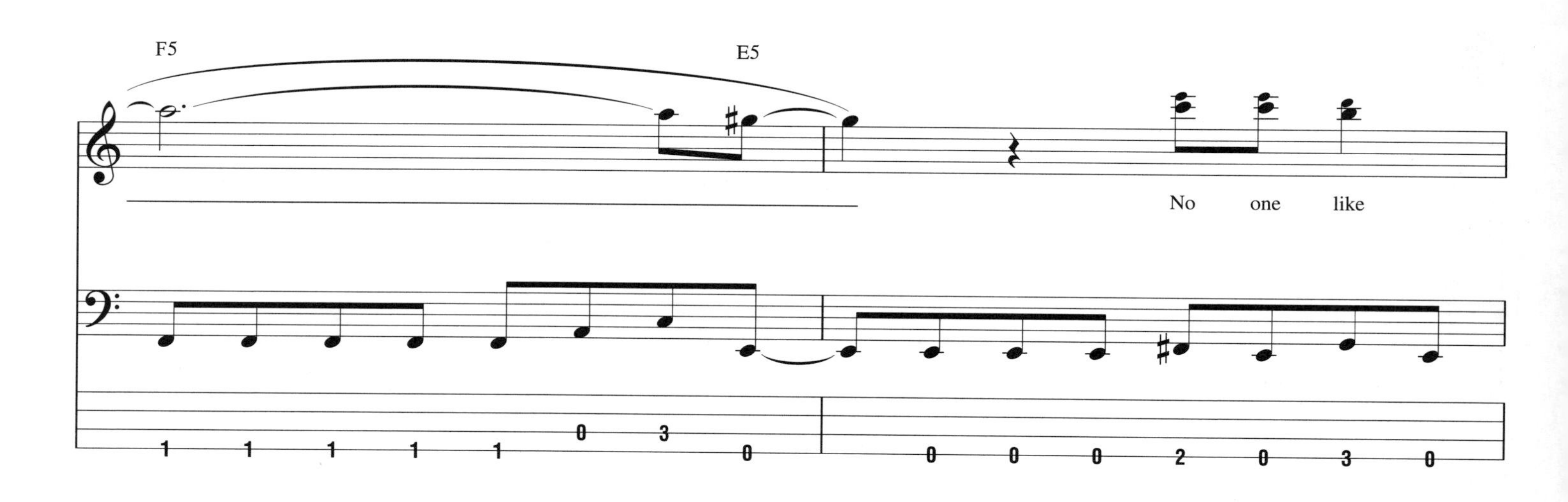
F5
E5
No one like
1 1 1 1 1 0 3 0
0 0 0 2 0 3 0

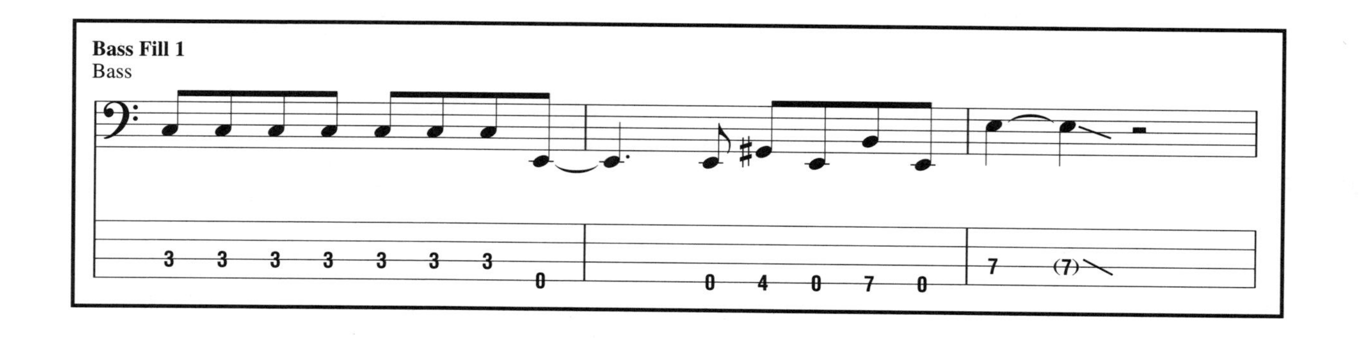
Bass Fill 1
Bass
3 3 3 3 3 3 3 0
0 4 0 7 0
7 (7)

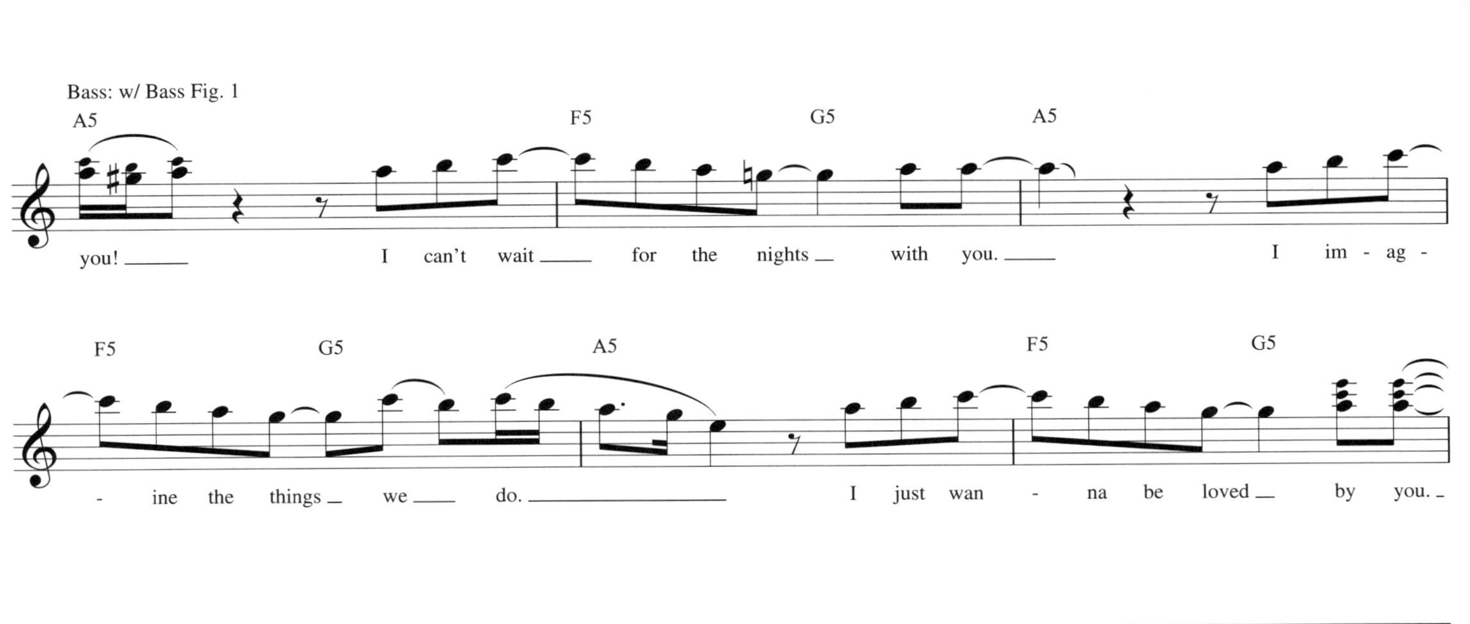
Bass: w/ Bass Fig. 1
A5
F5
G5
A5
you! I can't wait for the nights with you. I im - ag -

F5
G5
A5
F5
G5
- ine the things we do. I just wan - na be loved by you.

1.
F5
E5
1 1 1 1 1 1 1 0
0 0 0 4 0 7 0
7 (7)
2.
F5
E5
1 1 1 1 1 0 3 0
0 0 0 2 0 3 0

A5
F5
G5
A5
F5
G5
5 5 0
1 0 3 3 2 5
5 5 (5)
1 0 3 3 2 5

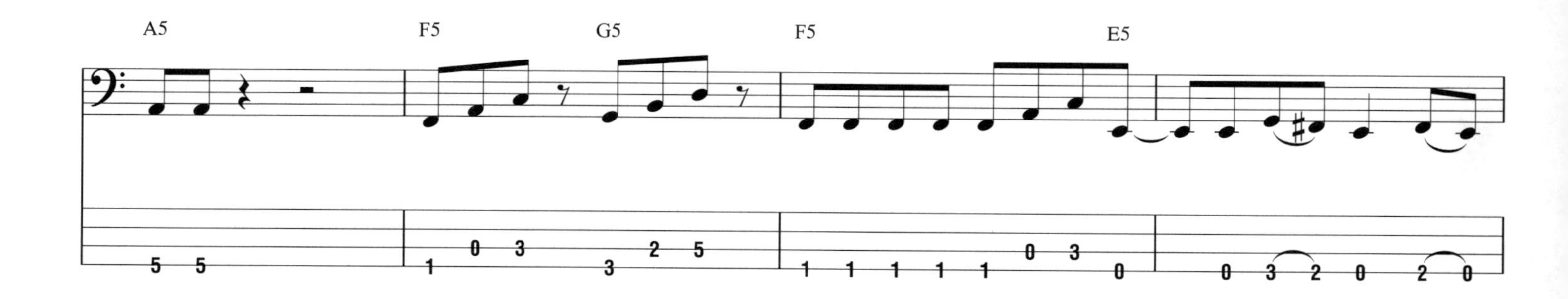
A5
F5
G5
F5
E5

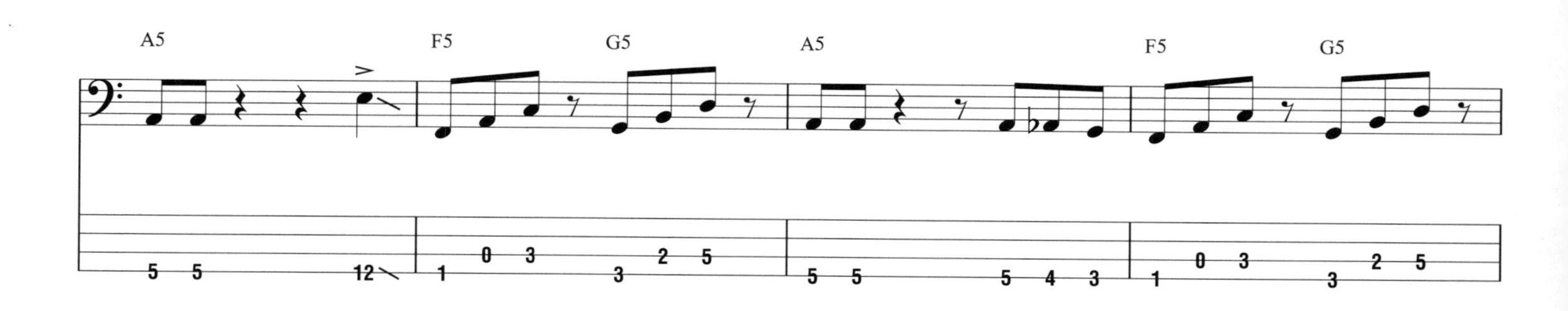
A5
F5
G5
A5
F5
G5

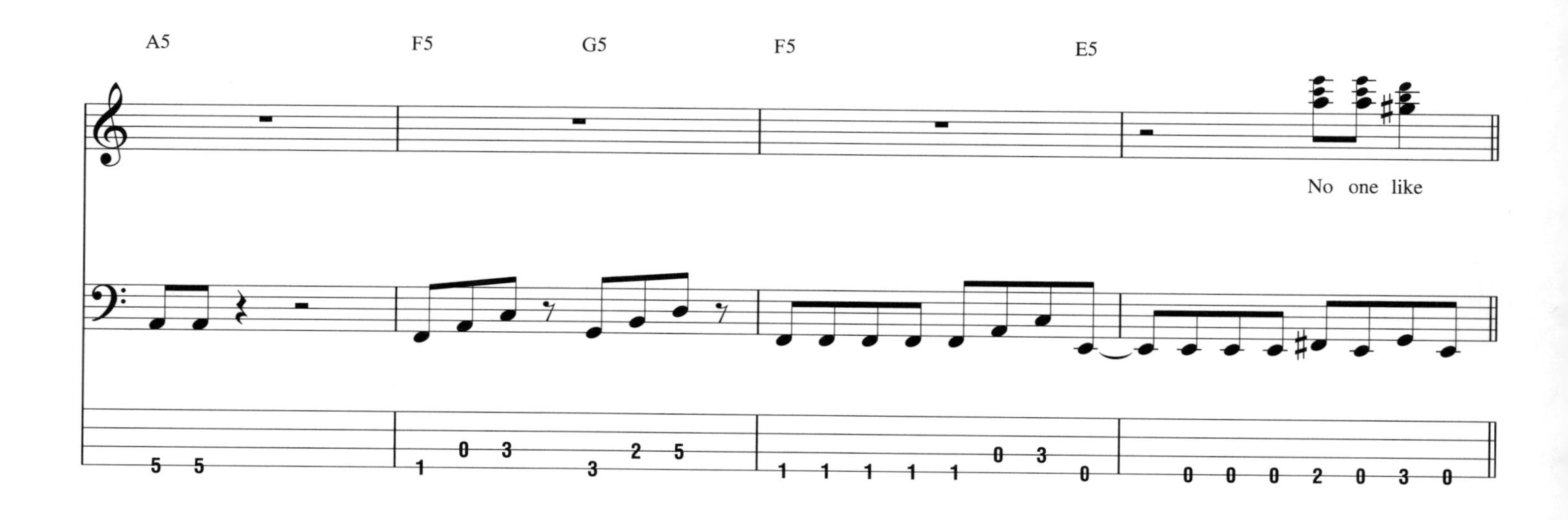
A5
F5
G5
F5
E5
No one like

Chorus

A5
F5
G5
A5
you! I can't wait for the nights with you. I im - ag -

F5 G5 A5 F5 G5
- ine the things we do. I just wan - na be loved by you.
F5 E5 A5
No one like you! I can't wait
Begin fade
F5 G5 A5 F5 G5
for the nights with you. I im - ag - ine the things we do.
Fade out
A5 F5 G5 F5 E5
I just wan - na be loved by you!

Peace Sells

Words and Music by Dave Mustaine

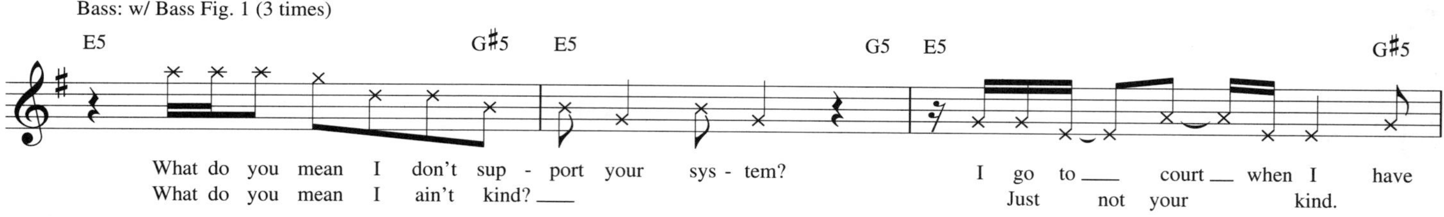

E5
Bb5 A5
G#5
G5
to.
What do you mean I can't get to work on time?
What do you mean I could-n't be the Pres - i - dent
Got noth - ing bet - ter to do.
of the U - nit - ed States of A - mer - i - ca?
What do you mean I don't pay
Tell me some - thing,
my bills?
it's still "We
Why do you think I'm broke?
The Peo - ple," right?
Huh?
Chorus
D5
F#5
If there's a new way,
well, I'll be the first in line.
1.
F5 C5
But it bet - ter work this time.
Interlude
Bass: w/ Bass Fig. 1

2.
Interlude
G5
F#5
F5
C5
E5
But it bet - ter work this time.
*Sing 1st time only.
1.
2.
G#5
G5
Oh.
Guitar Solo
F#5
G5
F#5
G5
F#5
E5
**Sing 1st time only.
G#5
G5
Play 3 times
F#5
G5
F#5
D5
D#5

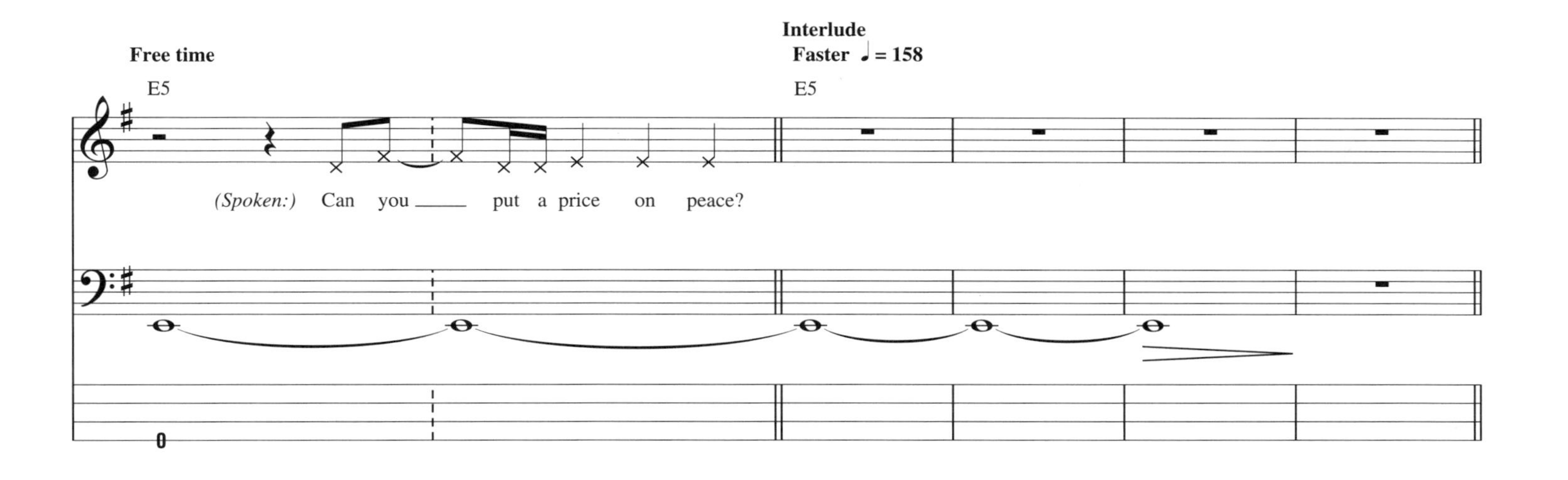
Free time
E5
(Spoken:) Can you put a price on peace?
Interlude
Faster ♩ = 158
E5

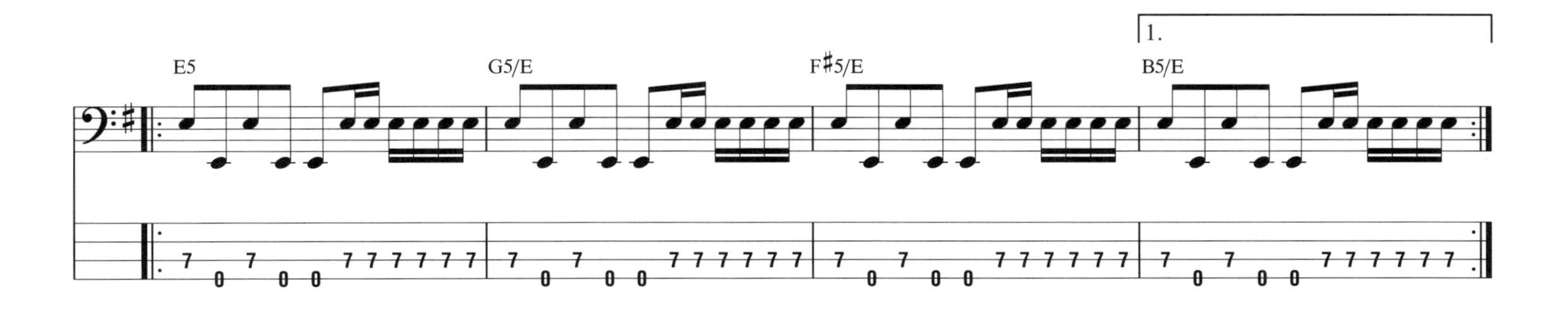
E5
G5/E
F♯5/E
1.
B5/E

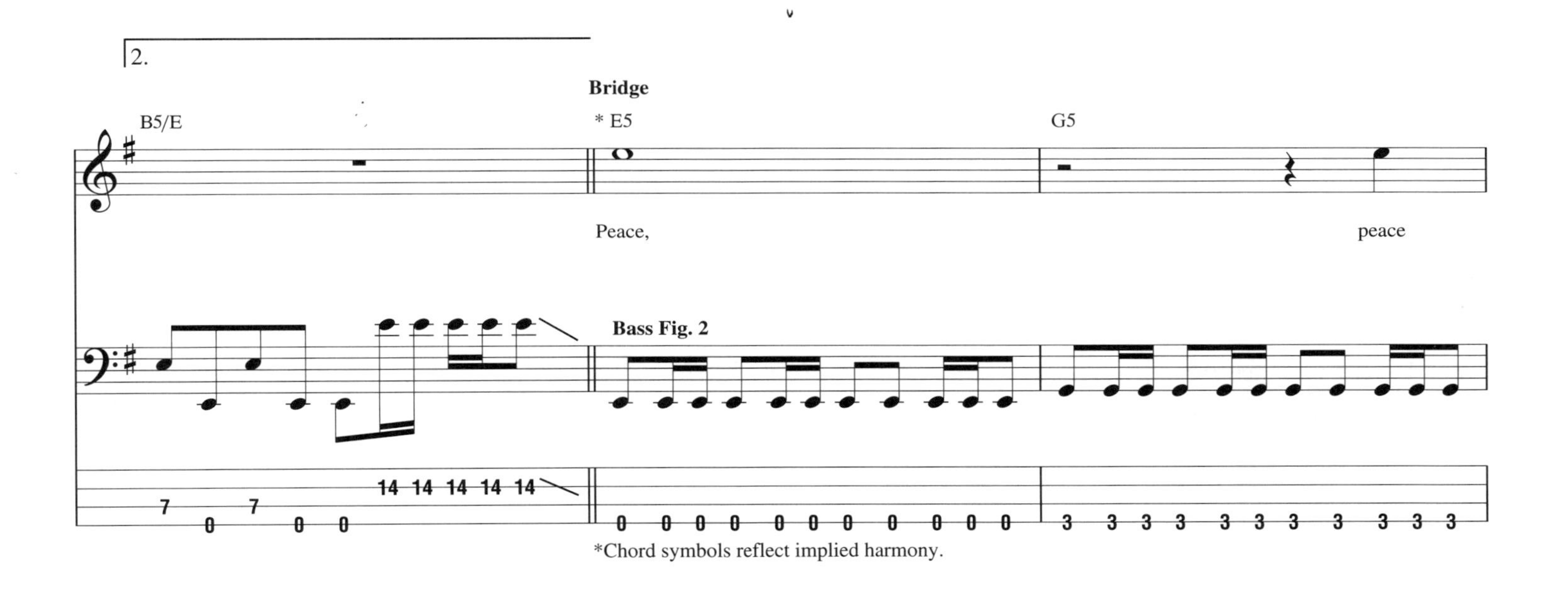
2.
B5/E
Bridge
* E5
G5
Peace,
peace
Bass Fig. 2
*Chord symbols reflect implied harmony.

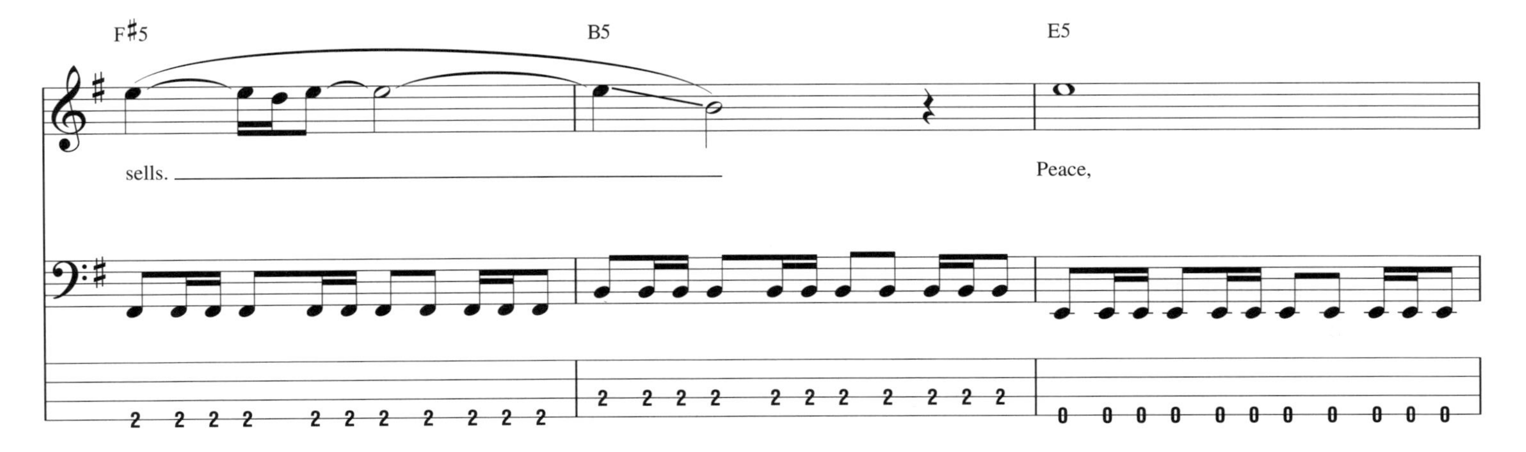
F♯5
B5
E5
sells.
Peace,

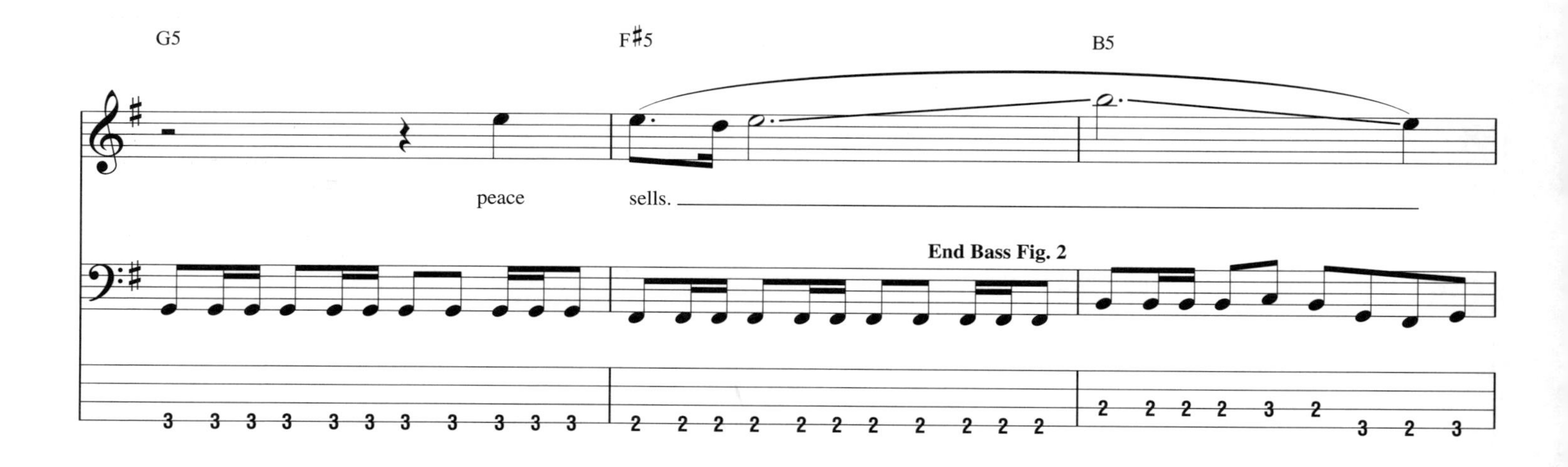
G5
F#5
B5
peace
sells.
End Bass Fig. 2
3 3 3 3 3 3 3 3 3 3 3
2 2 2 2 2 2 2 2 2 2 2
2 2 2 2 3 2 3 2 3

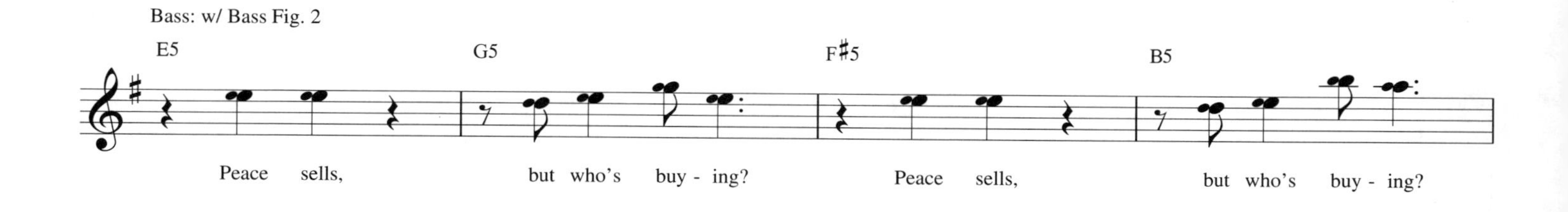
Bass: w/ Bass Fig. 2
E5
G5
F#5
B5
Peace sells, but who's buy - ing? Peace sells, but who's buy - ing?

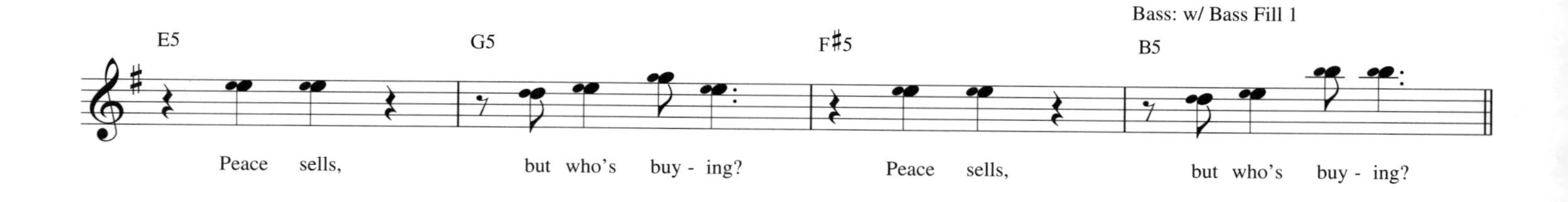
Bass: w/ Bass Fill 1
E5
G5
F#5
B5
Peace sells, but who's buy - ing? Peace sells, but who's buy - ing?

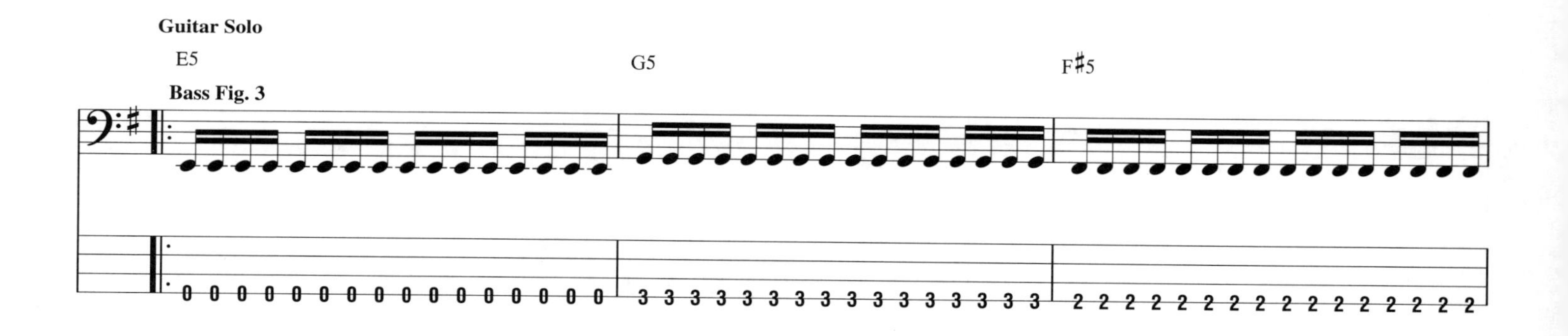
Guitar Solo
E5
G5
F#5
Bass Fig. 3
0 0 0 0 0 0 0 0 0 0 0 0 0 0 0 0
3 3 3 3 3 3 3 3 3 3 3 3 3 3 3 3
2 2 2 2 2 2 2 2 2 2 2 2 2 2 2 2

Bass Fill 1
2 2 2 2 2 2 2 4 4 4 4 4 4

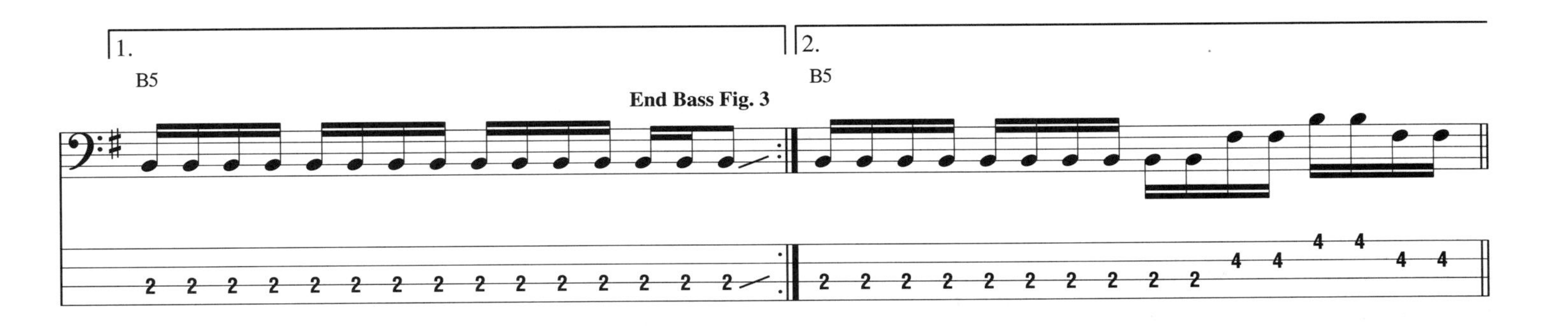
1.
2.
B5
End Bass Fig. 3
B5

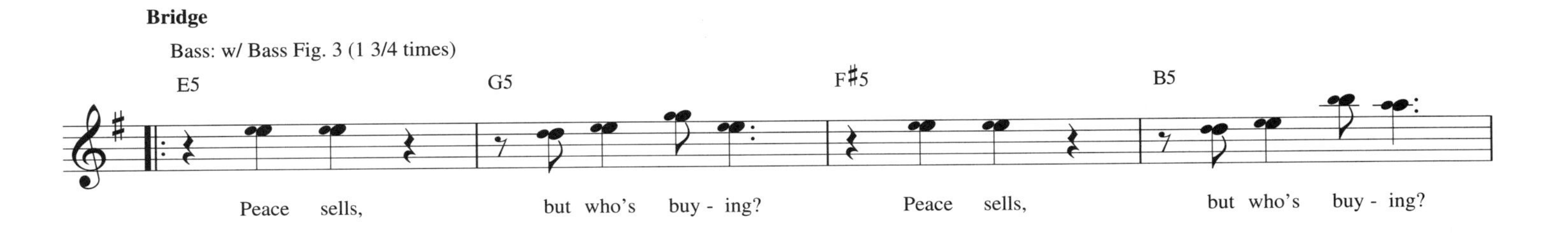
Bridge
Bass: w/ Bass Fig. 3 (1 3/4 times)
E5
G5
F#5
B5
Peace sells, but who's buy - ing? Peace sells, but who's buy - ing?

E5
G5
F#5
Peace sells, but who's buy - ing? Peace sells,

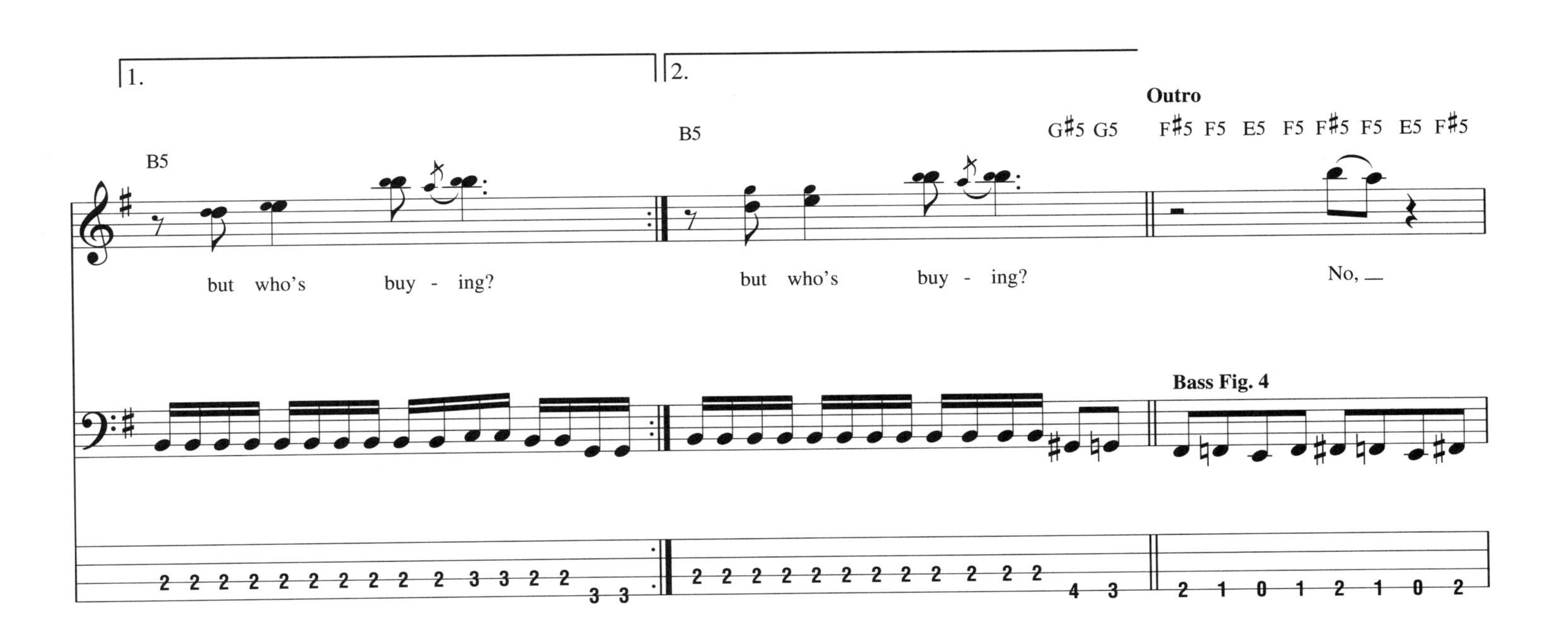
1.
2.
Outro
B5
B5
G#5 G5
F#5 F5 E5 F5 F#5 F5 E5 F#5
but who's buy - ing? but who's buy - ing? No, __
Bass Fig. 4

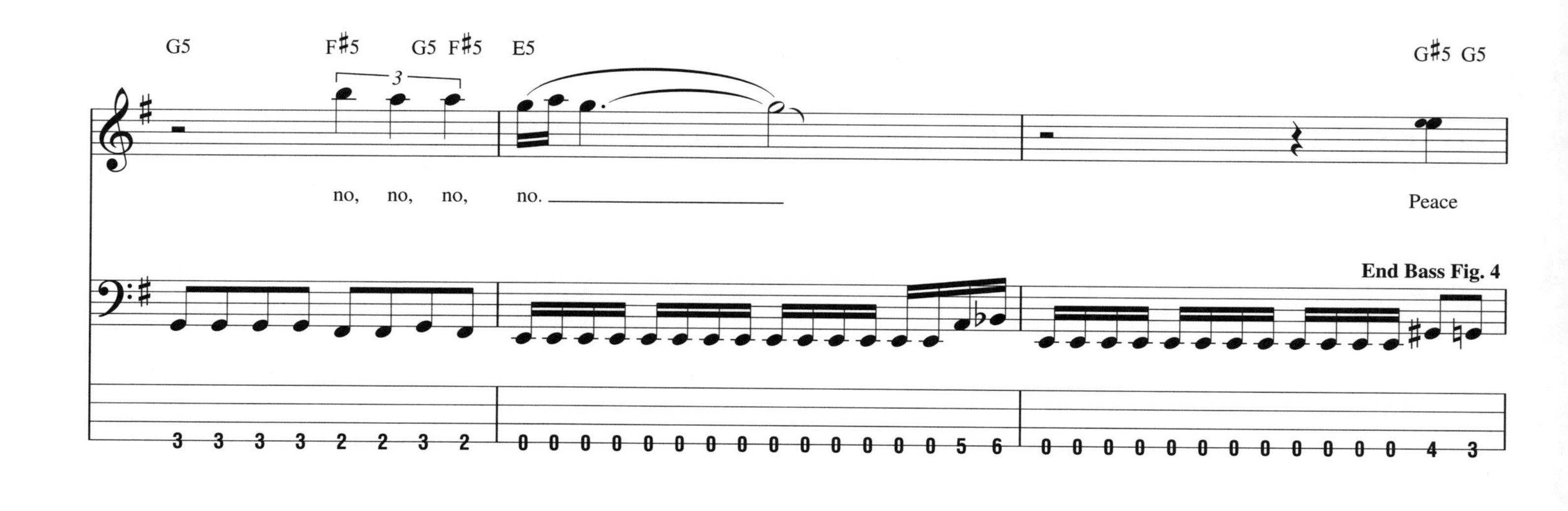
G5 F#5 G5 F#5 E5 G#5 G5
no, no, no, no.
Peace
End Bass Fig. 4

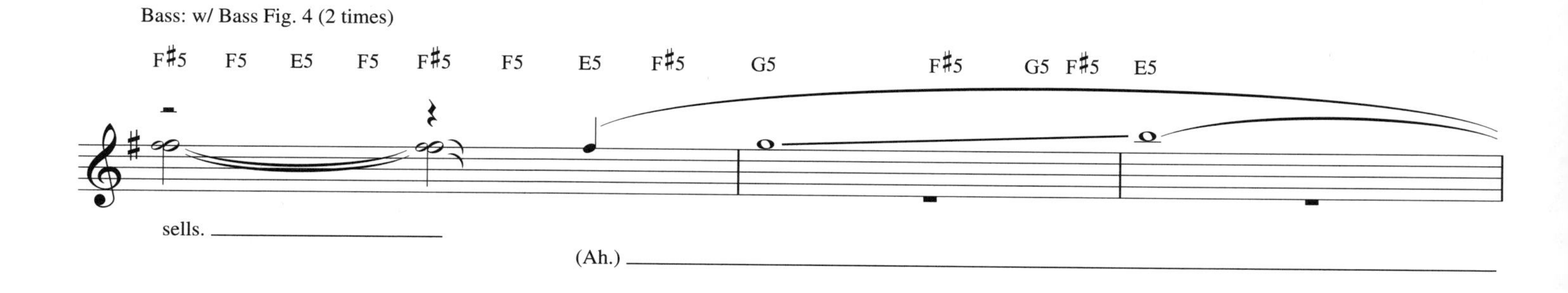
Bass: w/ Bass Fig. 4 (2 times)
F#5 F5 E5 F5 F#5 F5 E5 F#5 G5 F#5 G5 F#5 E5
sells.
(Ah.)

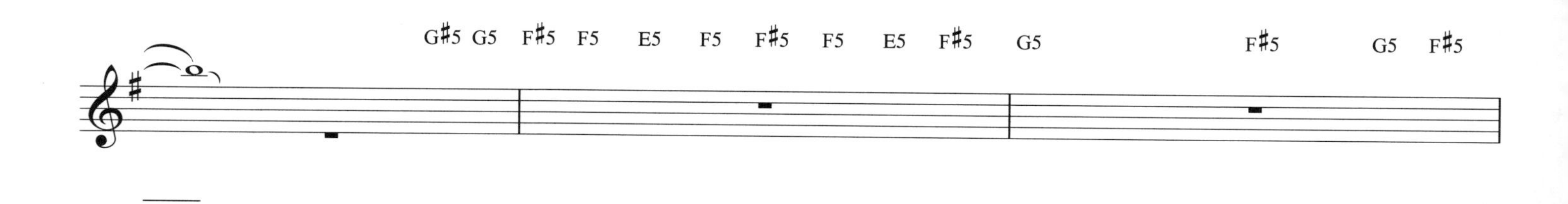
G#5 G5 F#5 F5 E5 F5 F#5 F5 E5 F#5 G5 F#5 G5 F#5

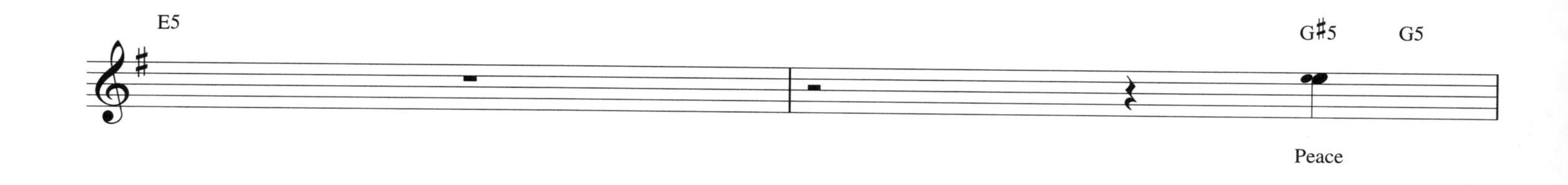
E5 G#5 G5
Peace

F#5 F5 E5 F5 F#5 F5 E5 F#5 G5 F#5 G5 F#5 E5
sells.
Ah!

Rainmaker

Words and Music by David Murray, Steven Harris and Bruce Dickinson

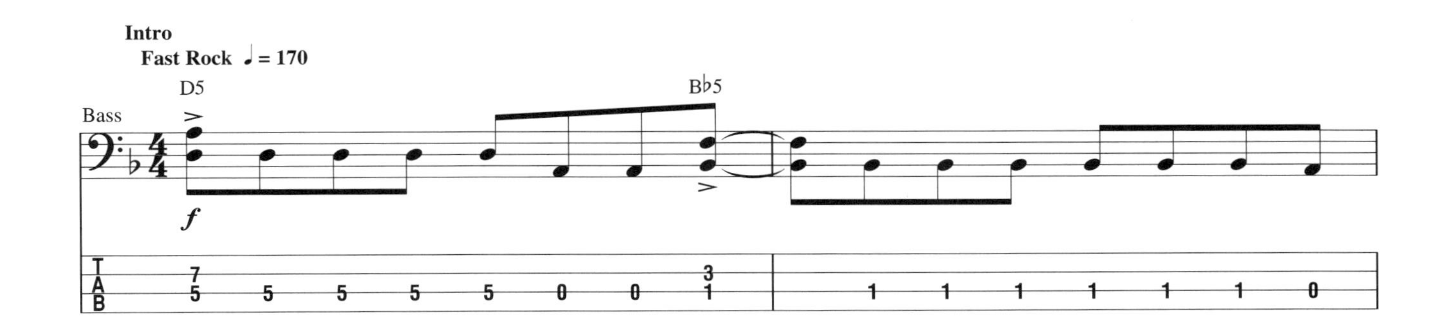

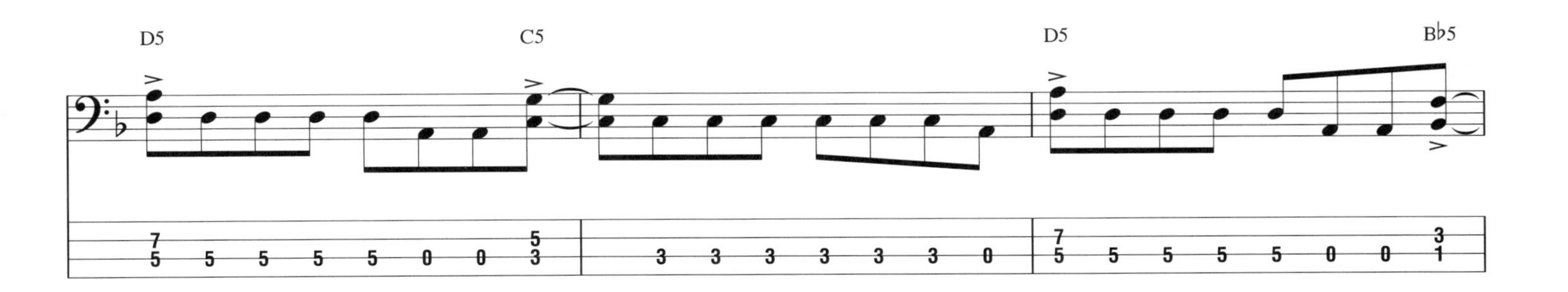

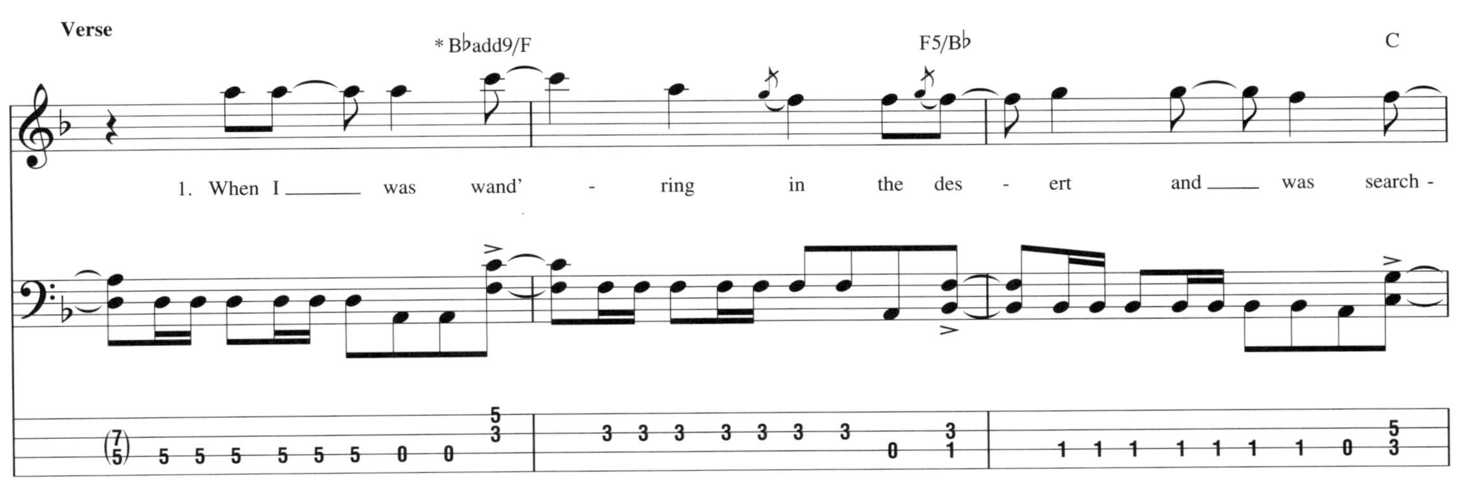

*Chord symbols reflect overall harmony.

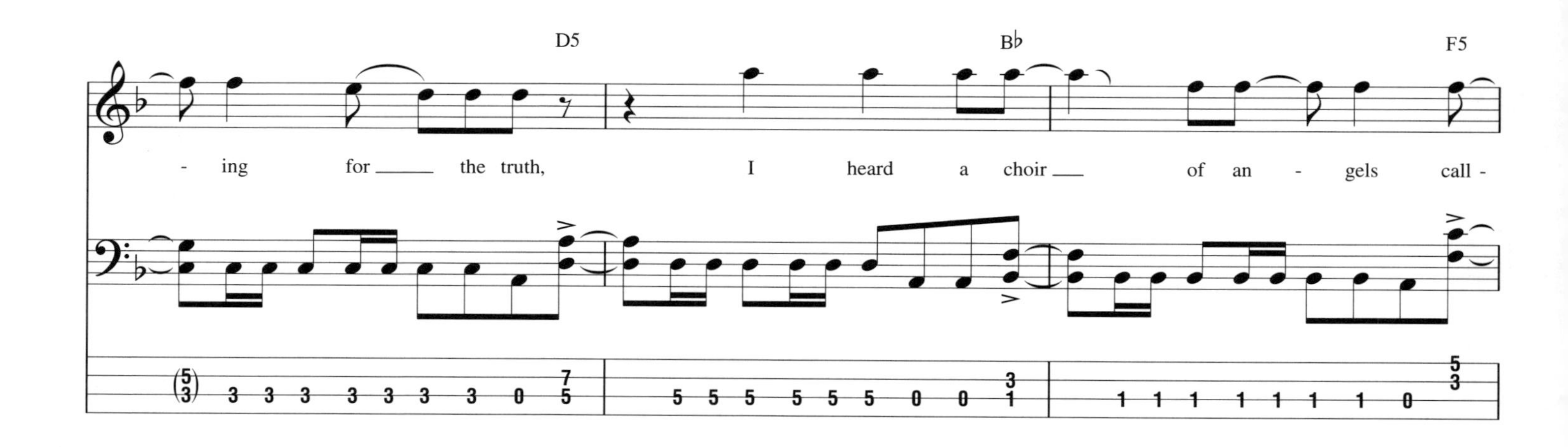
D5
B♭
F5
- ing for the truth, I heard a choir of an - gels call -

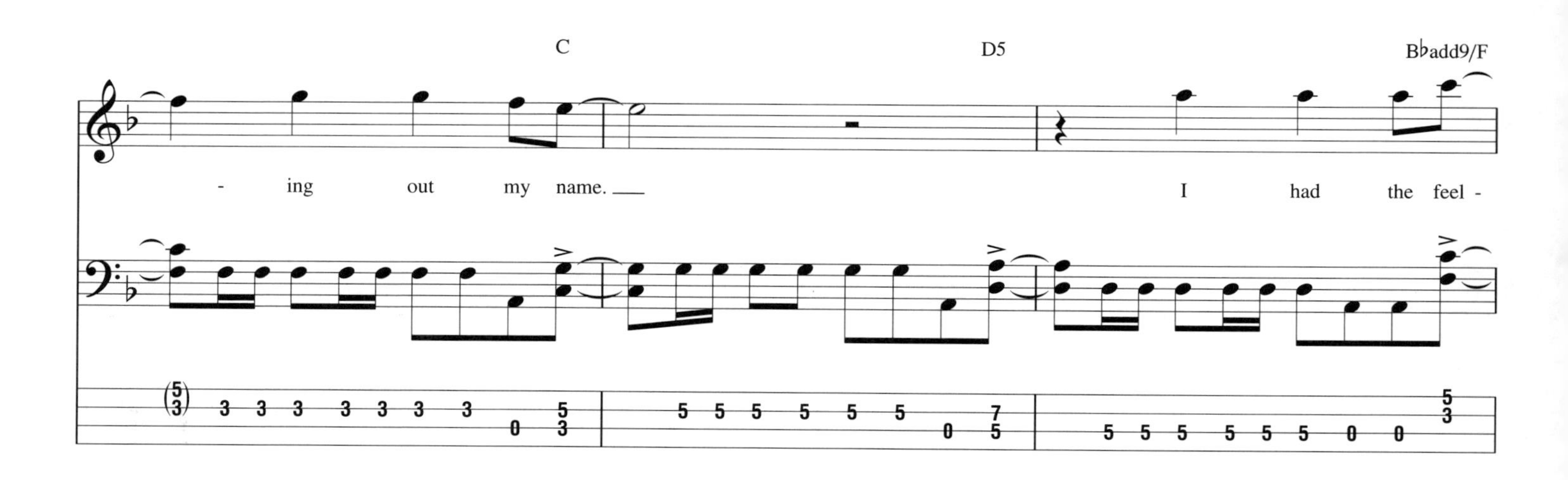
C
D5
B♭add9/F
- ing out my name. I had the feel -

F5/B♭
C
B♭5
- ing that my life would nev - er be the same a - gain.

C5
I turned my face to - wards the bar - ren sun.

Pre-Chorus
D5
F5
B♭5
And I know of the pain that you feel
C5
G5
B♭5
the same as me.
And I dream of the rain
F5
C5
D5
as it falls upon the leaves.
1. And the cracks
2., 3. And the cracks
F5
B♭5
C5
on our lives, like the cracks upon the ground,
in the ground, like the cracks are in our lives,

To Coda
G5
B♭5
C5
they are sealed
they are sealed
and are now
and are now
washed a - way.
far a - way.

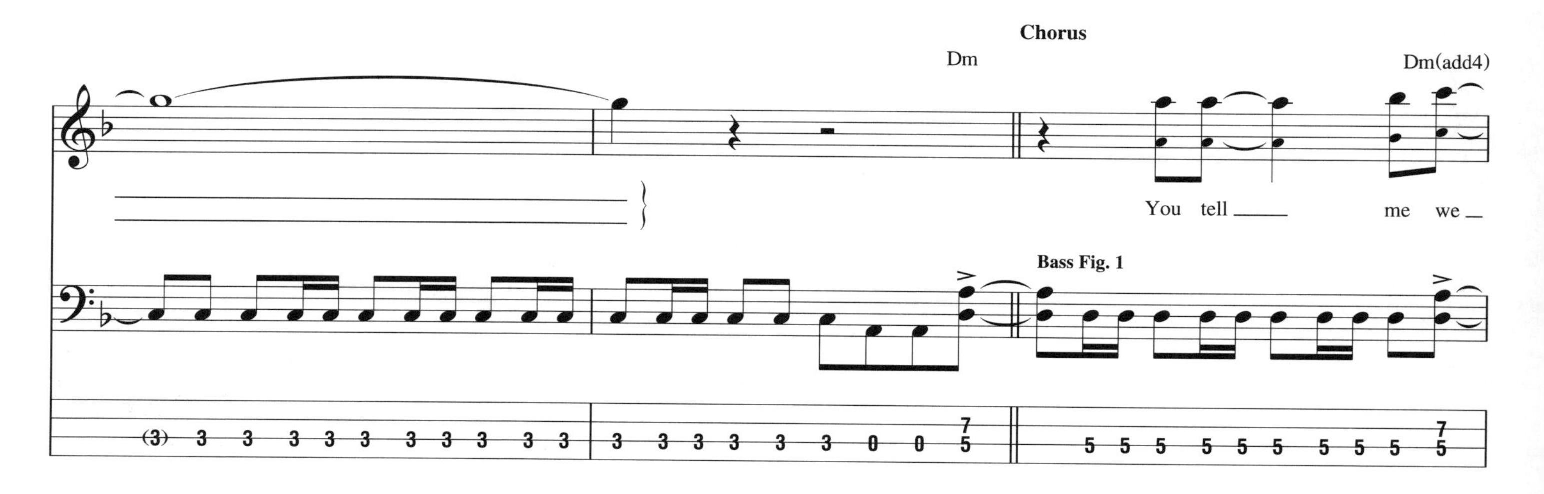
Chorus
Dm
Dm(add4)
You tell me we
Bass Fig. 1

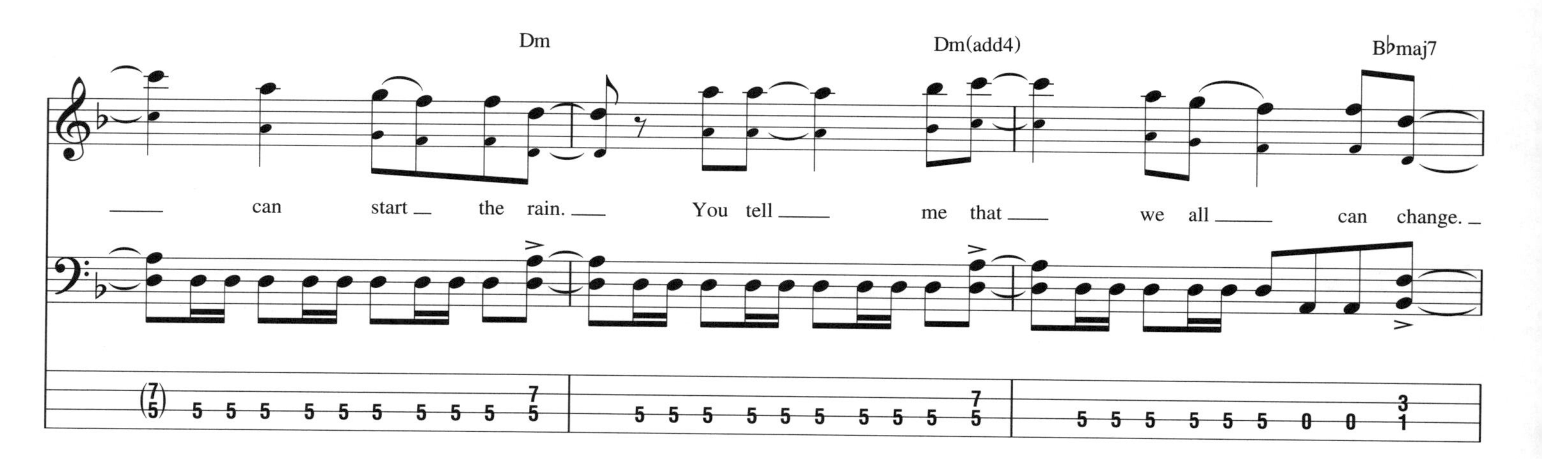
Dm
Dm(add4)
B♭maj7
can start the rain.
You tell me that
we all can change.

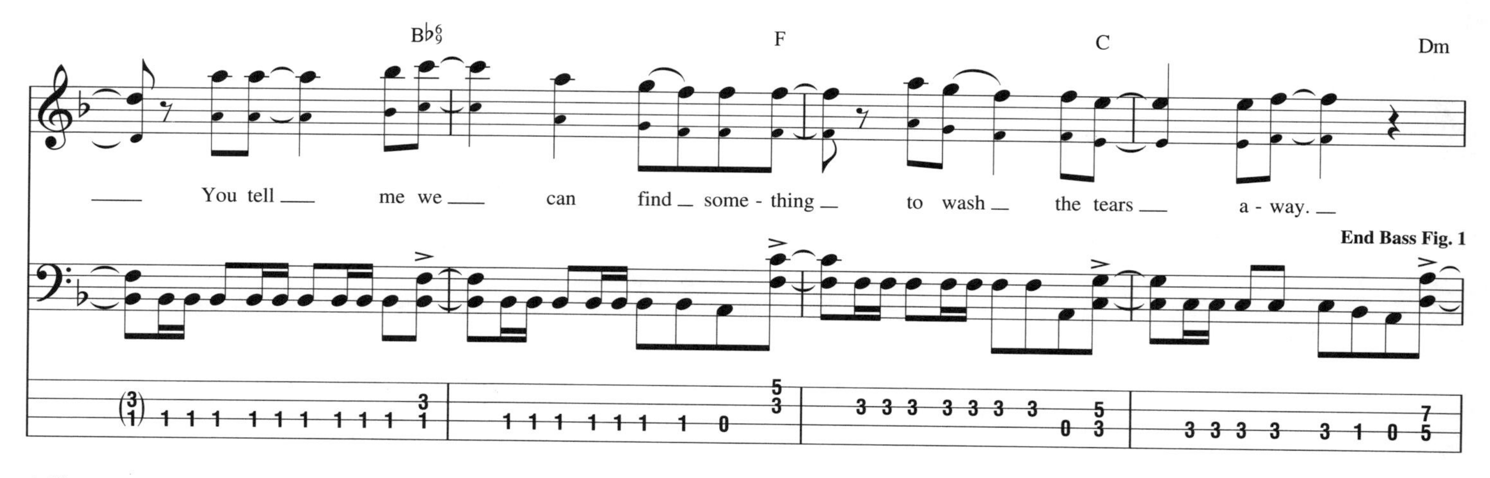
F
C
Dm
You tell me we
can find some - thing
to wash the tears
a - way.
End Bass Fig. 1

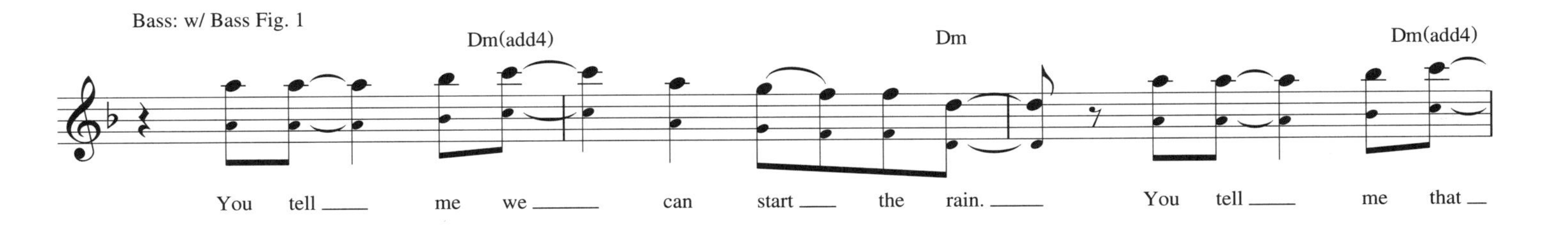
Bass: w/ Bass Fig. 1
Dm(add4)
Dm
Dm(add4)
You tell me we can start the rain. You tell me that

B♭maj7
B♭6/9
F
we all can change. You tell me we can find some - thing

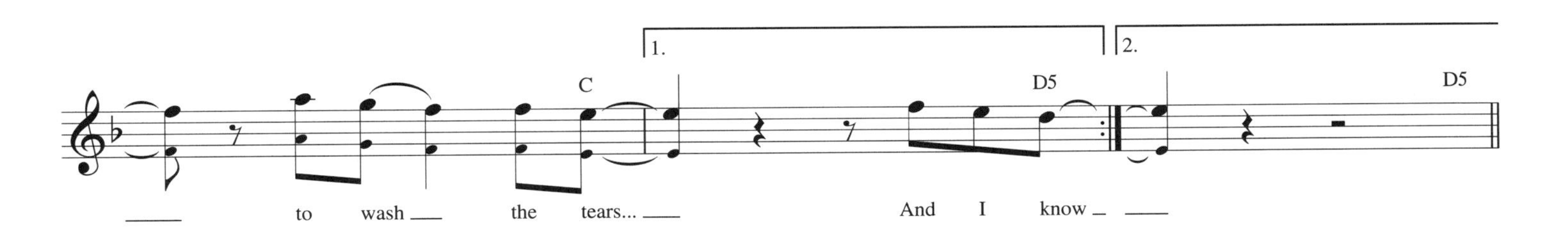
1.
2.
C
D5
D5
to wash the tears... And I know

Guitar Solo
B♭5
C5
F5

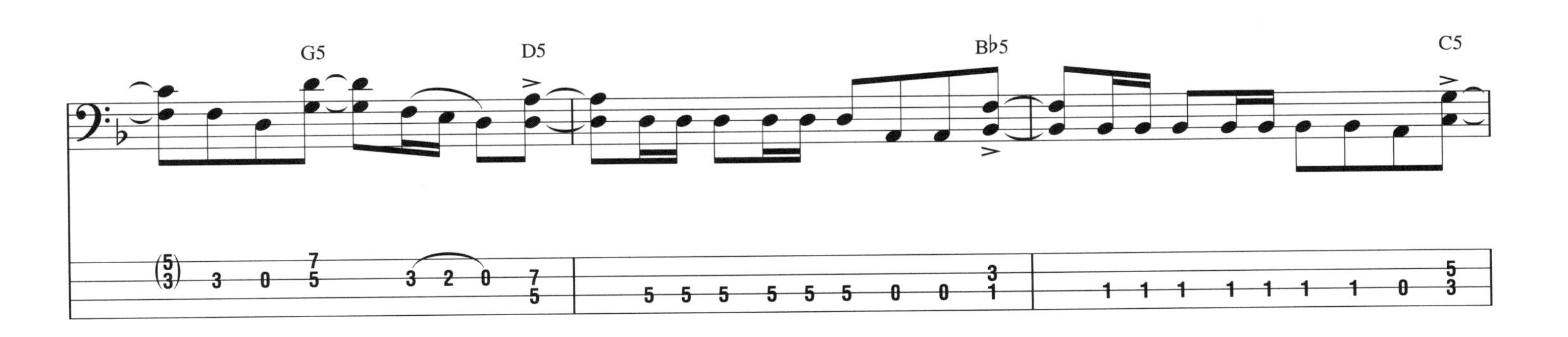
G5
D5
B♭5
C5

1.
2.
D5
B5

D/F♯
G5
A5
D5
E5
B5
D/F♯
G5
A5
1.
2.
B5
Dm
Chorus
Bass: w/ Bass Fig. 1 (2 times)
Dm(add4)
Dm
Dm(add4)
You tell me we can start the rain. You tell me that
we all can change. You tell me we can find some - thing
B♭maj7
B♭6/9
F
1.
2.
C
Dm
C
D.S. al Coda
D5
to wash the tears a - way.
to wash the tears...
And I know

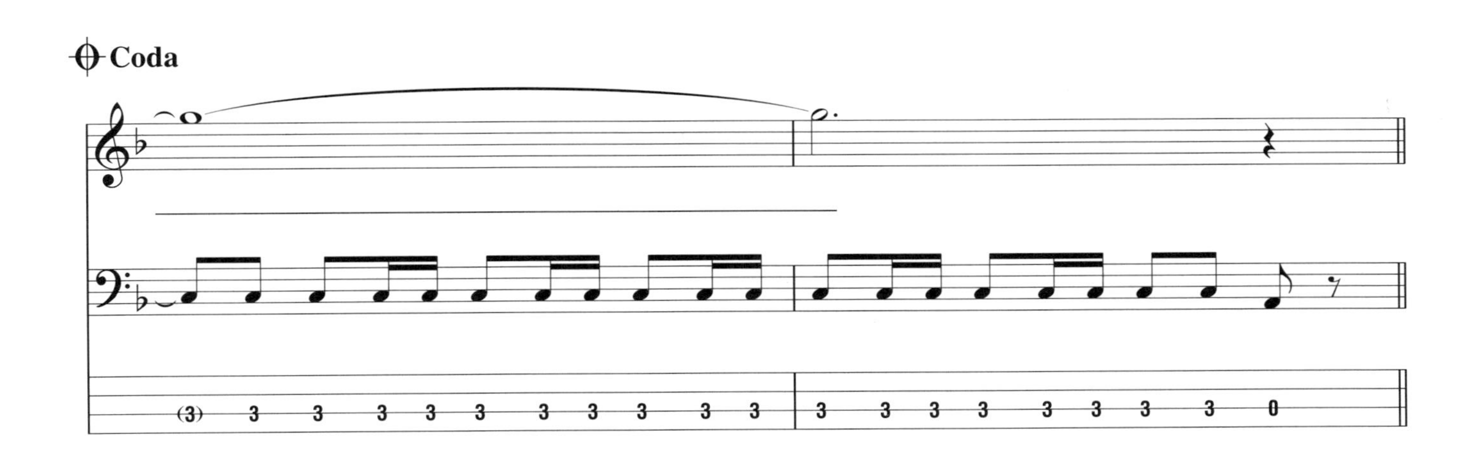
Coda

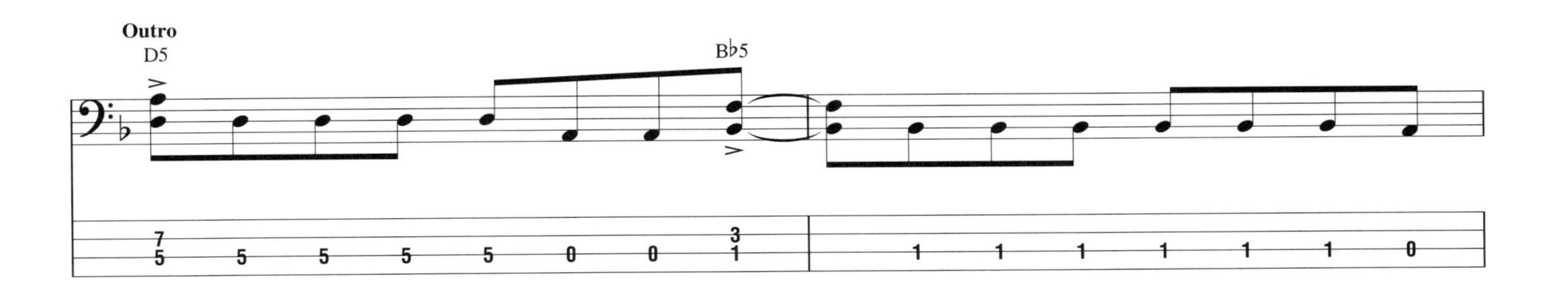
Outro
D5
B♭5

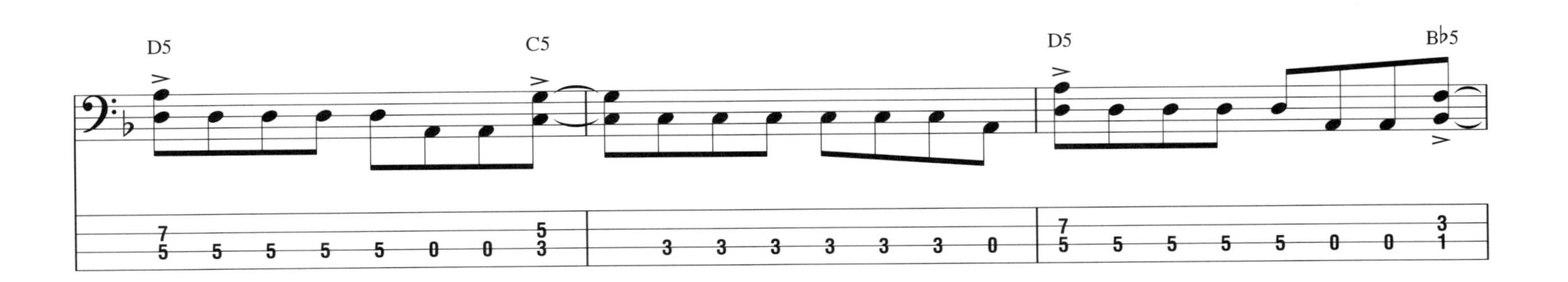
D5
C5
D5
B♭5

C5

D5

Runnin' with the Devil

Words and Music by David Lee Roth, Edward Van Halen, Alex Van Halen and Michael Anthony

Tune down 1/2 step:
(low to high) E♭-A♭-D♭-G♭

Intro
Moderate Rock ♩ = 95

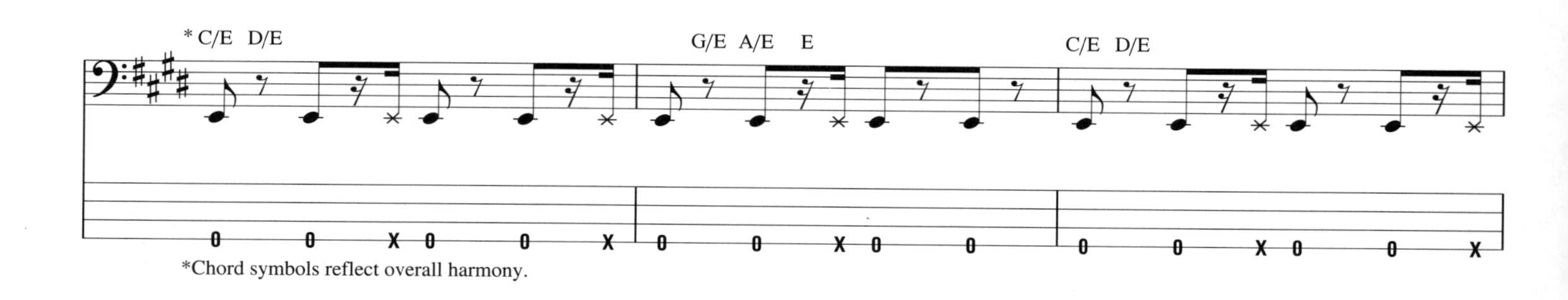

*Chord symbols reflect overall harmony.

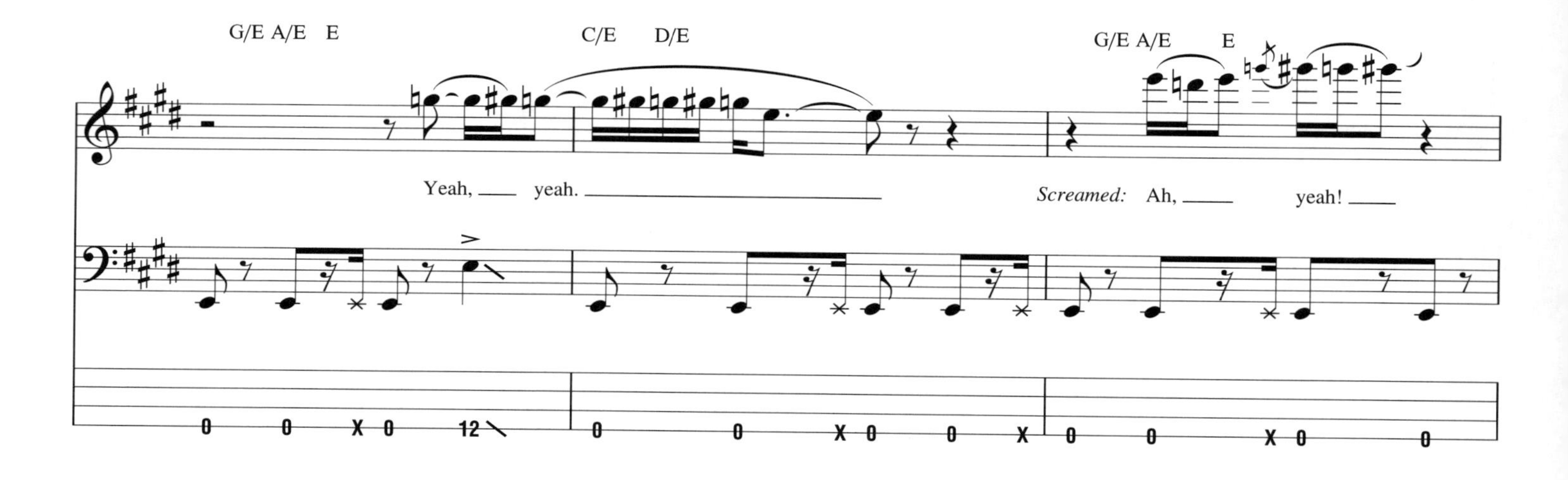

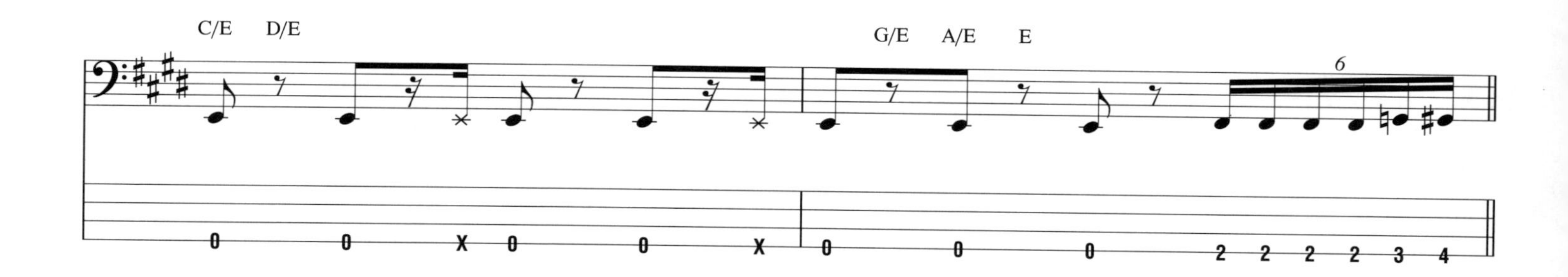

Verse
A5
G/A
F♯m/A
Em/A
1. I live my life like there's
2., 3. I found the simple life
no to - mor - row,
ain't so sim - ple
what's so sim - ple
no
and all I've got I had to steal.
when I jumped out on that road.
Em
Least I don't need to
I got no love, no
beg or borrow.
love you'd call real.
Yes, I'm liv - in' at a pace that kills.
Ain't got no - bod - y wait - in' at home.
1st time, Bass: w/ Bass Fig. 1
2nd & 3rd times, Bass: w/ Bass Fig. 1 (1st 7 meas.)
C/E D/E
G/E A/E
E
Ooh, yeah.
Screamed: Ah,
ah, ha,
Run - nin' with the dev - il.

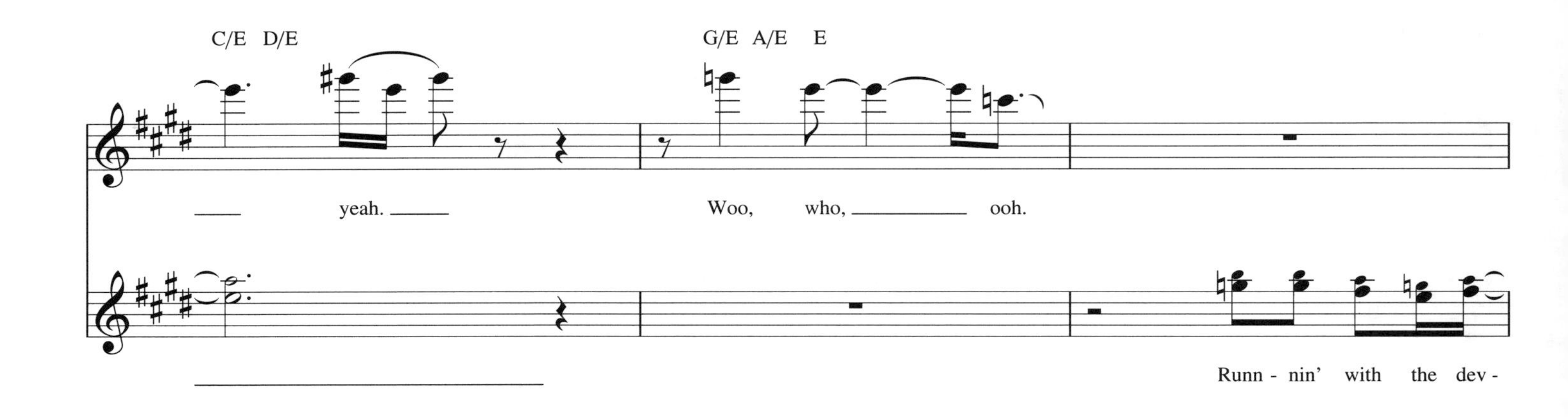
C/E D/E
G/E A/E E
yeah.
Woo, who, ooh.
Runn - nin' with the dev -

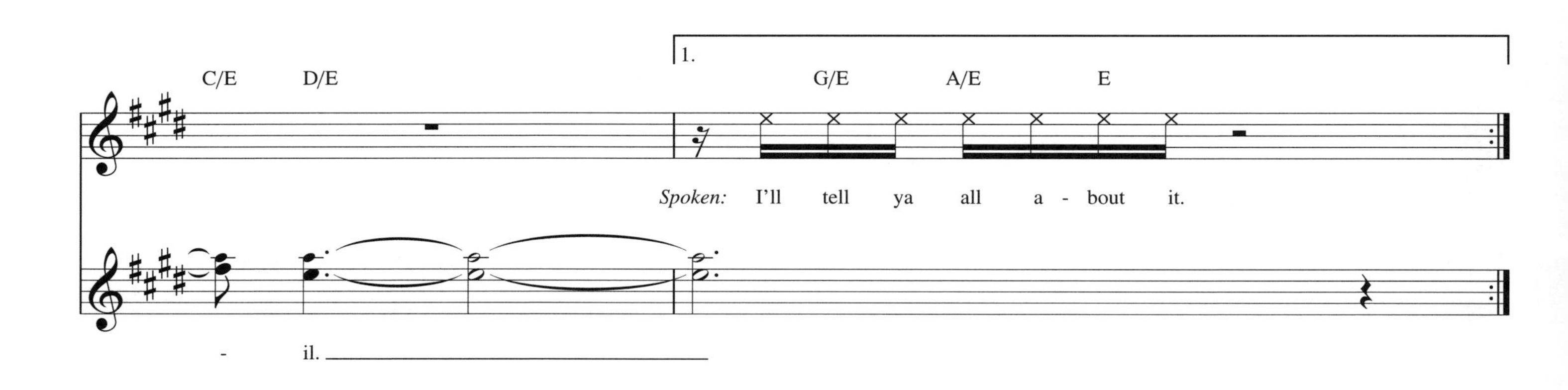
C/E D/E
1.
G/E A/E E
Spoken: I'll tell ya all a - bout it.
- il.

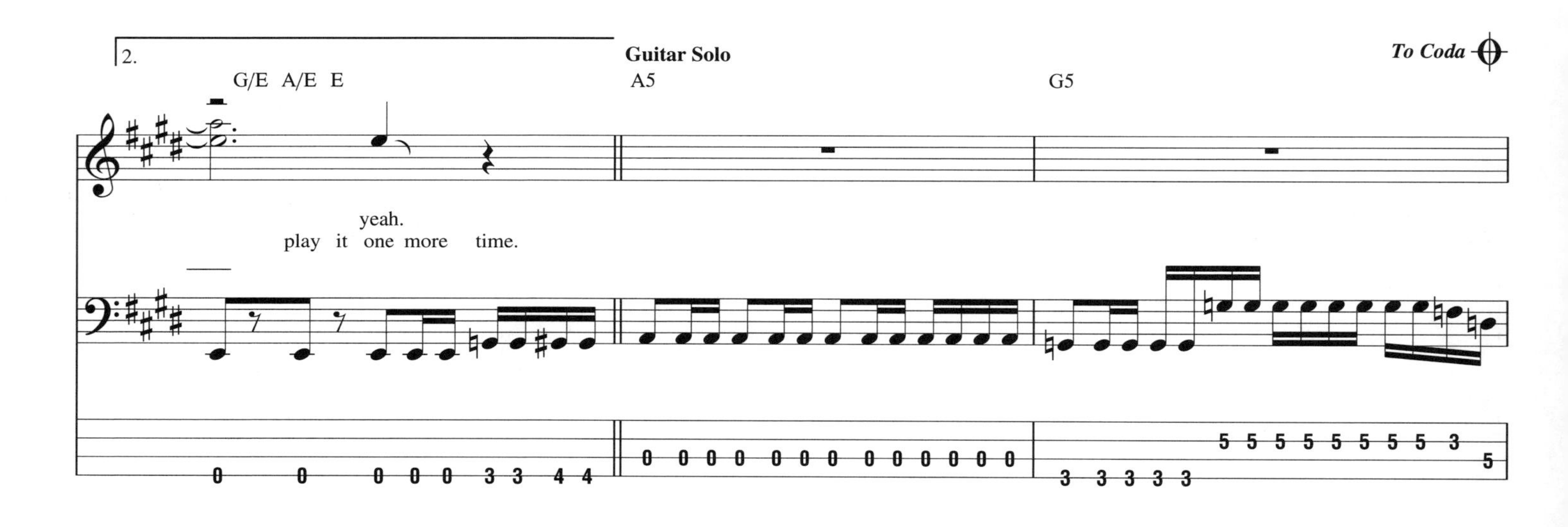
2.
Guitar Solo
To Coda
G/E A/E E
A5
G5
yeah.
play it one more time.

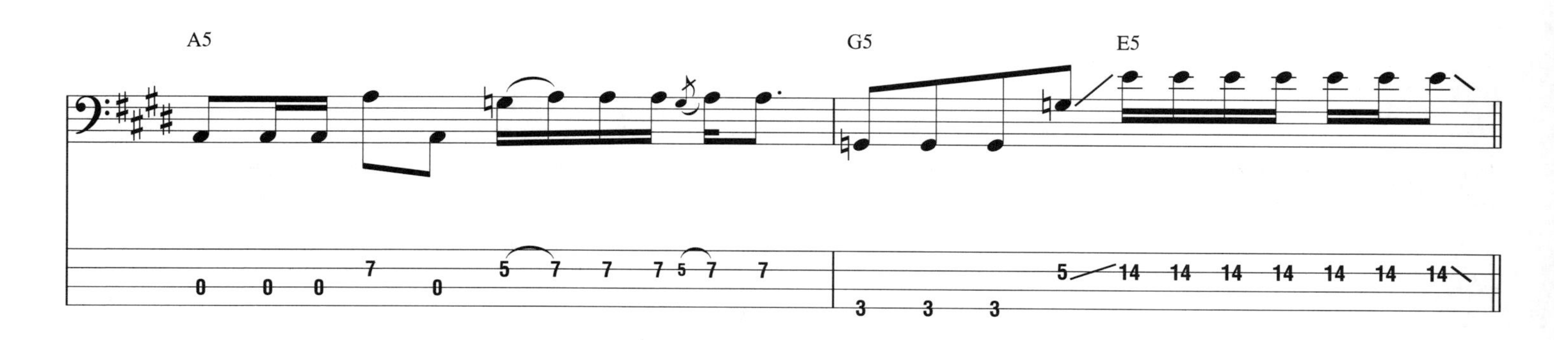
A5
G5
E5

Interlude
C/E D/E
G/E A/E E
Whoo!
0 0 X 0 0 X 0 0 X 0 12
C/E D/E
G/E A/E E
D.S. al Coda
(take 2nd ending)
Spoken: You know, I,
6
0 0 X 0 0 X 0 0 0 2 2 2 2 3 4
Coda
A5
G5
E5
0 0 0 7 0 5 7 0 0 12 14 (14)
3 3 3 3 3 3 0 2 14
Outro-Chorus
C/E D/E
G/E A/E E
Ha,
yeah.
Run - nin' with the dev -
0 0 0 0 0 0 0 0

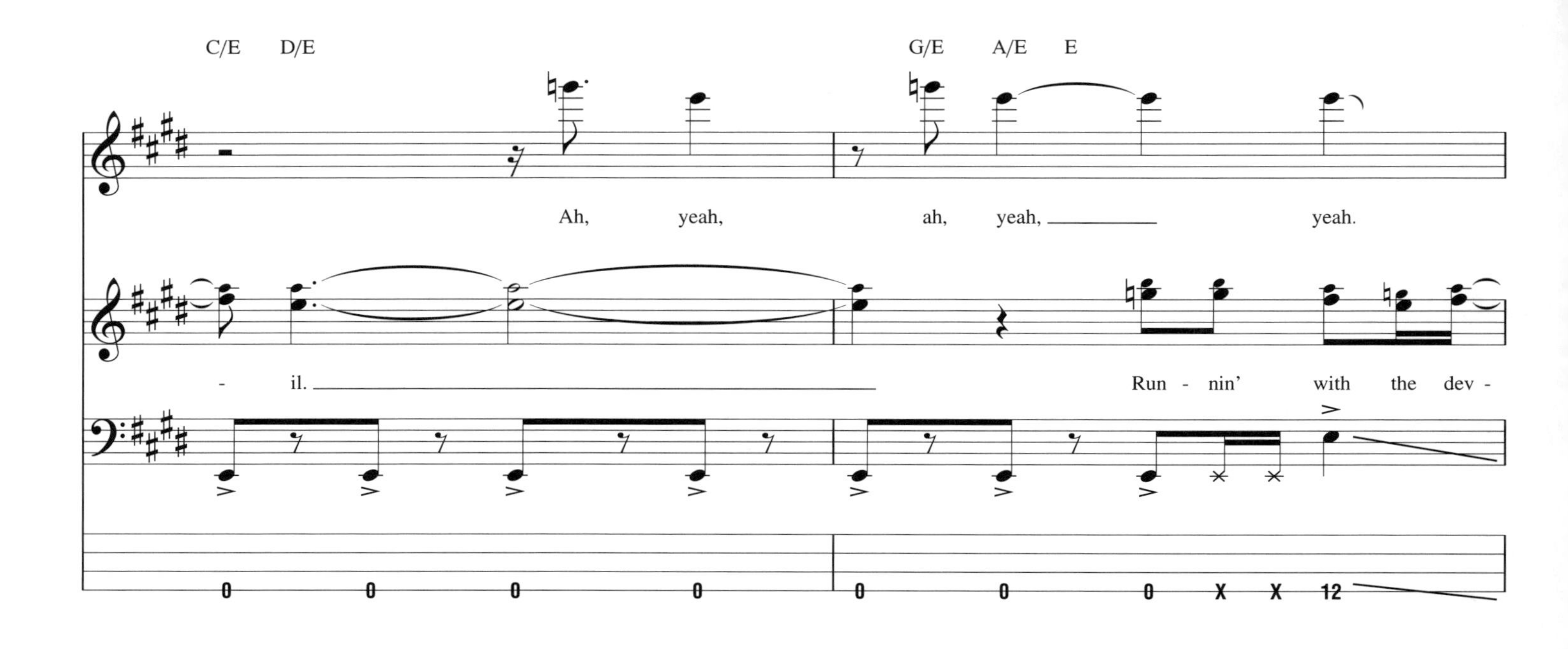
C/E D/E
G/E A/E E
Ah, yeah, ah, yeah, yeah.
- il.
Run - nin' with the dev -
0 0 0 0 0 0 0 X X 12

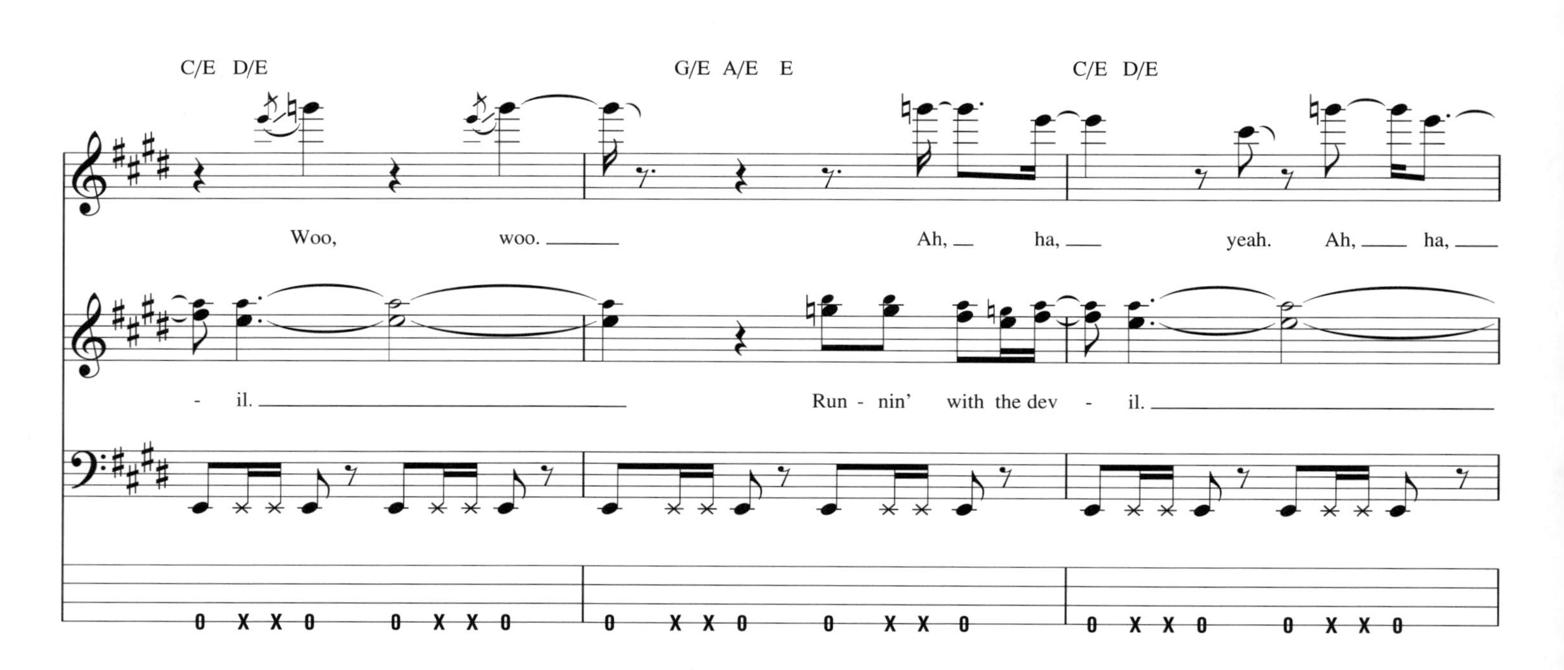
C/E D/E
G/E A/E E
C/E D/E
Woo, woo.
Ah, ha, yeah. Ah, ha,
- il.
Run - nin' with the dev - il.
0 X X 0 0 X X 0 0 X X 0 0 X X 0 0 X X 0 0 X X 0

G/E A/E E
C/E D/E
G/E A/E E
yeah. Ah, huh, yeah. Ooh.
Run - nin' with the dev - il.
0 X X 0 0 0 12 0 0 0 0 0 12 0

St. Anger

Words and Music by James Hetfield, Lars Ulrich, Kirk Hammett and Bob Rock

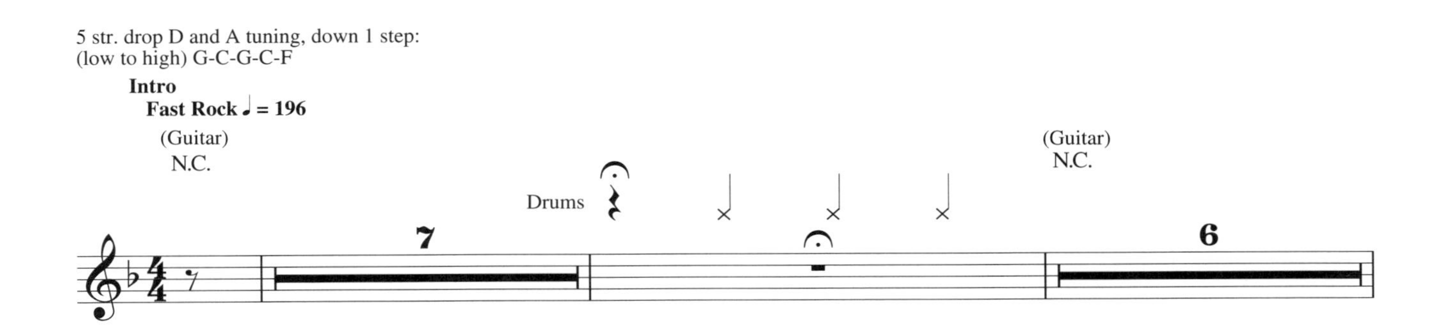

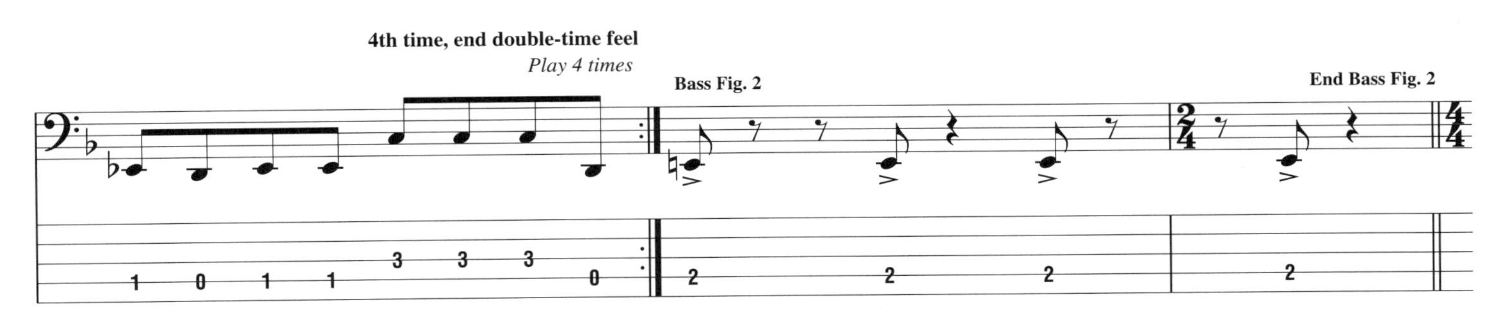

*Chord symbols reflect overall harmony.

D5
C5
E(♭5)/B♭
A5
He
nev - er gets re - spect.
You flush it out, you flush it out.
Saint
An - ger 'round my neck.
He
You flush it out, you flush it out.)
Interlude
Tempo I

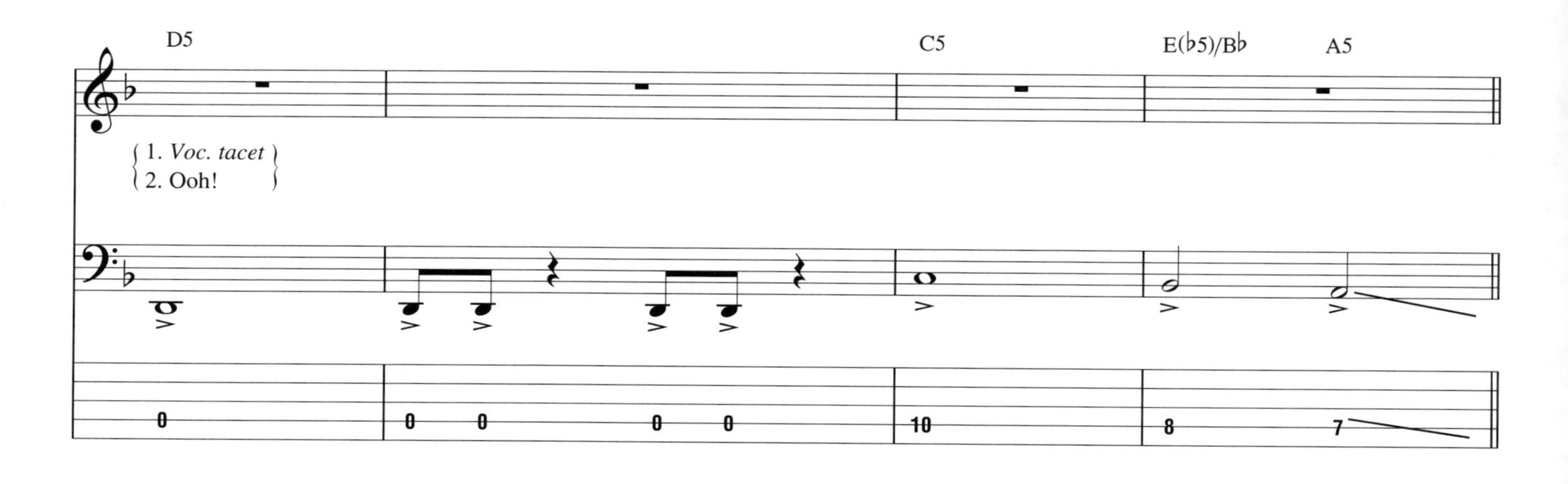
D5
C5
E(♭5)/B♭
A5
1. Voc. tacet
2. Ooh!
0
0 0 0 0
10
8 7

Chorus
Double-time feel
D5
Fuck it all and no re - grets, I hit
Bass Fig. 4
0 0 0 0 0 0 0 0
0 0 0 0 0 0 0 0

C5
E(♭5)/B♭
A5
the lights on these dark sets. I
End Bass Fig. 4
10 10 10 10 10 10 10 10
8 8 8 8 7 7 7 7

w/ Bass Fig. 4 (7 times)
D5
C5
need a voice to let my - self, to let my - self go free.

E(♭5)/B♭ A5 D5
Fuck it all and fuck-in' no re-grets, I hit
C5 E(♭5)/B♭ A5 D5
the lights on these dark sets. Me-dal-lion noose, I
C5 E(♭5)/B♭ A5
hang my-self, Saint An-ger 'round my neck. I
D5 C5 E(♭5)/B♭ A5
feel my world shake like an earth-quake.
D5 C5
Hard to see clear. Is it me? Is it
E(♭5)/B♭ A5 D5
fear? I'm mad-ly in an-ger with you. I'm
C5 E(♭5)/B♭ A5 D5
mad-ly in an-ger with you. I'm mad-ly in an-ger with you.
To Coda 2
C5 E(♭5)/B♭ A5
I'm mad-ly in an-ger with you.

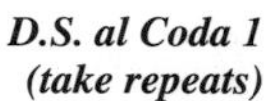
D.S. al Coda 1
(take repeats)

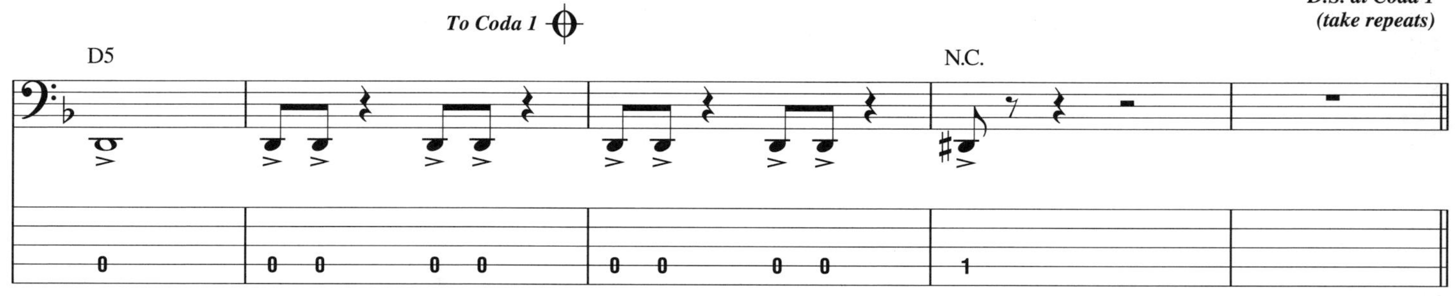
To Coda 1
D5
N.C.

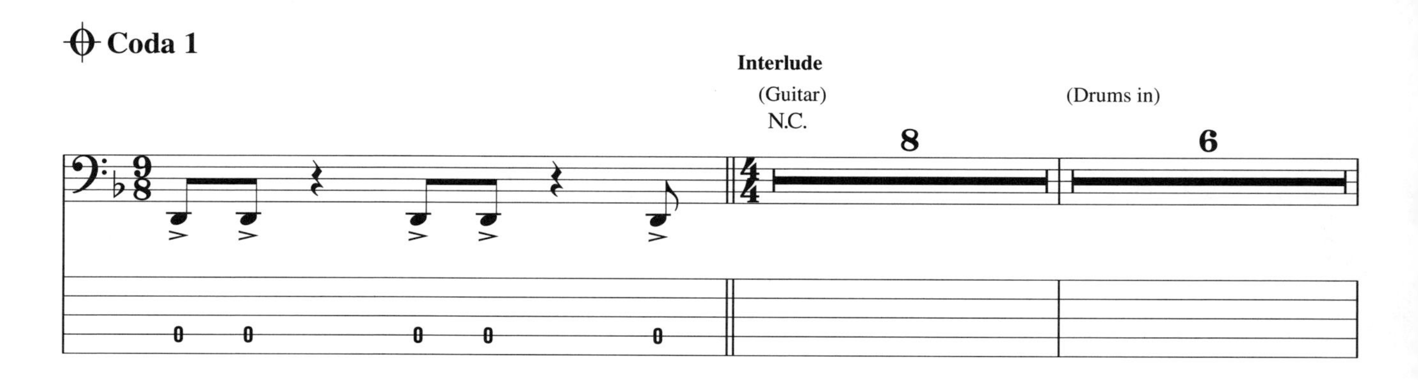
Coda 1
Interlude
(Guitar)
N.C.
8
(Drums in)
6

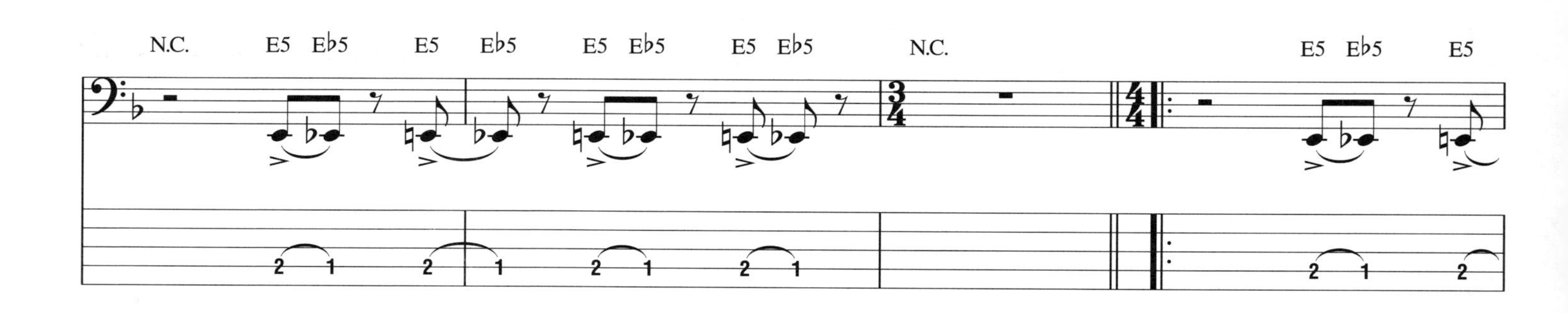
N.C.
E5 E♭5
E5 E♭5
E5 E♭5
E5 E♭5
N.C.
E5 E♭5 E5

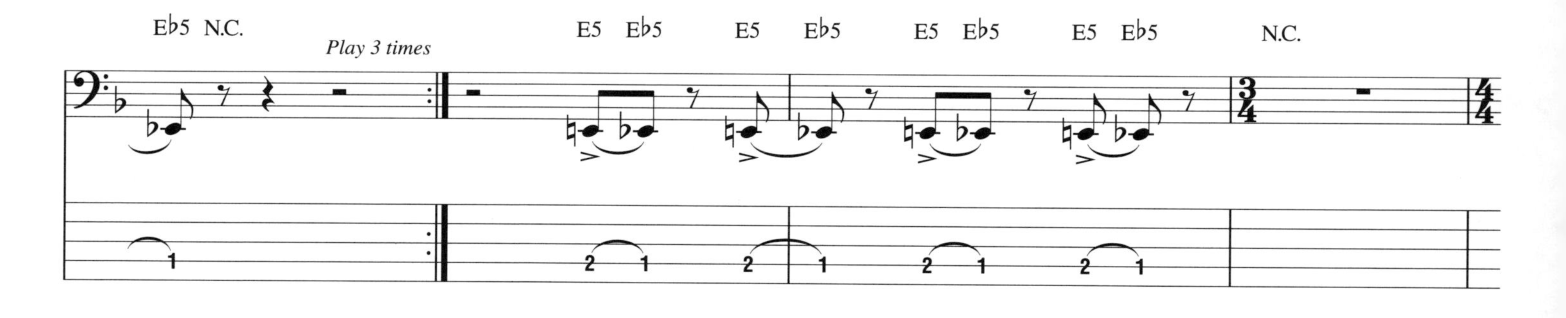
E♭5 N.C.
Play 3 times
E5 E♭5
E5 E♭5
E5 E♭5
E5 E♭5
N.C.

w/ Bass Fig. 1 (4 times)
N.C.
7
Bridge
w/ Bass Fig. 1 (10 times)
N.C.
And I want my

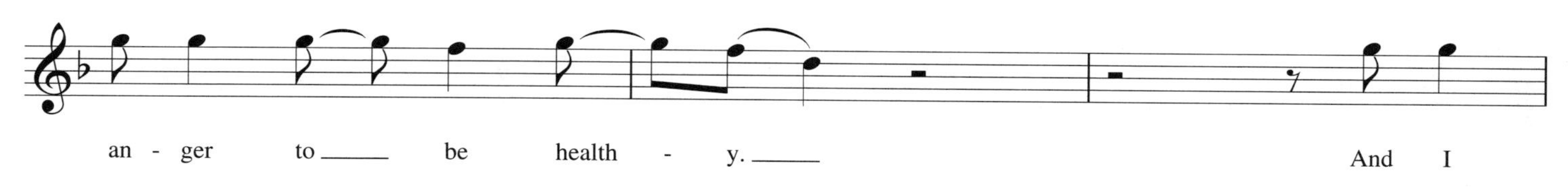
an - ger to be health - y.
And I

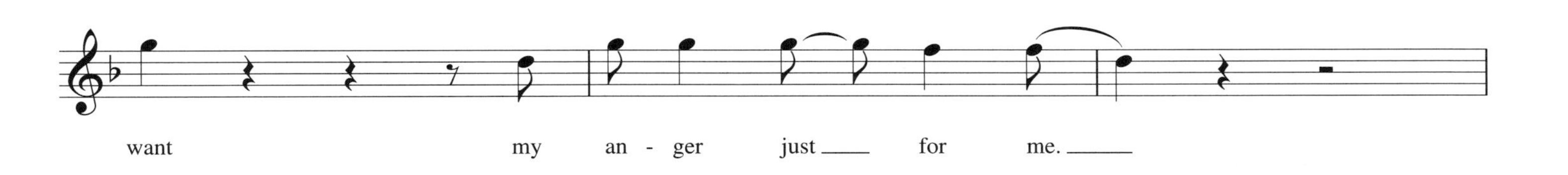
want my an - ger just ___ for me. ___

And I need my an - ger not ___ to con -

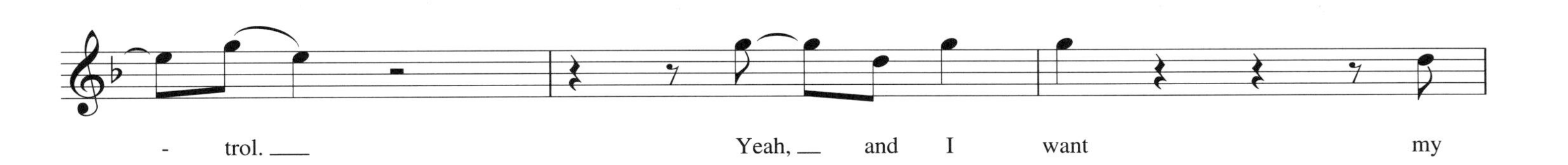
- trol. ___ Yeah, ___ and I want my
4

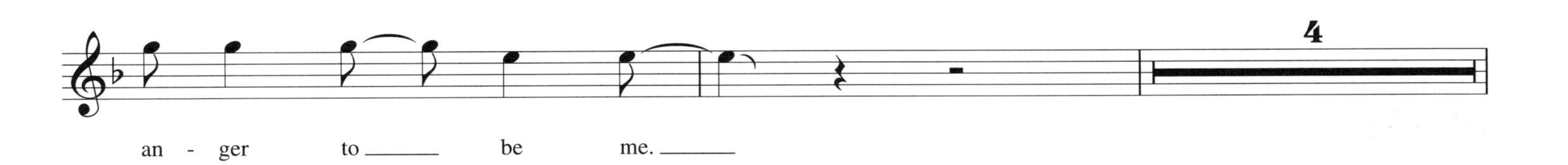
an - ger to ___ be me. ___
4

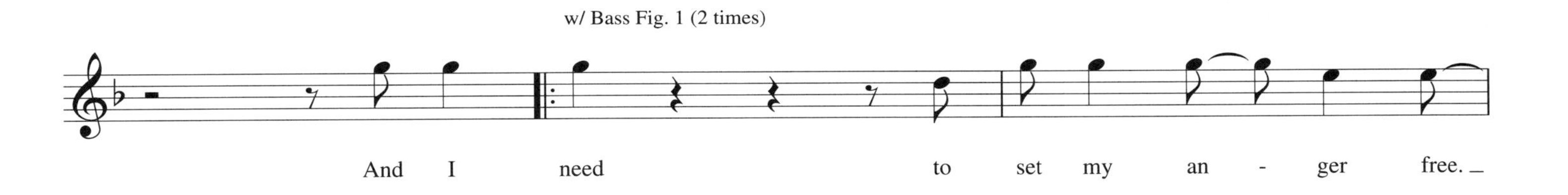
w/ Bass Fig. 1 (2 times)
And I need to set my an - ger free. ___

w/ Bass Fig. 1 (4 times)
___ And I need to

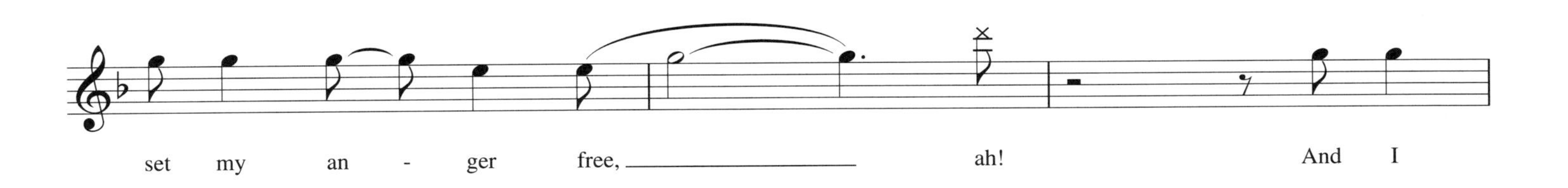
set my an - ger free, ___ ah! And I

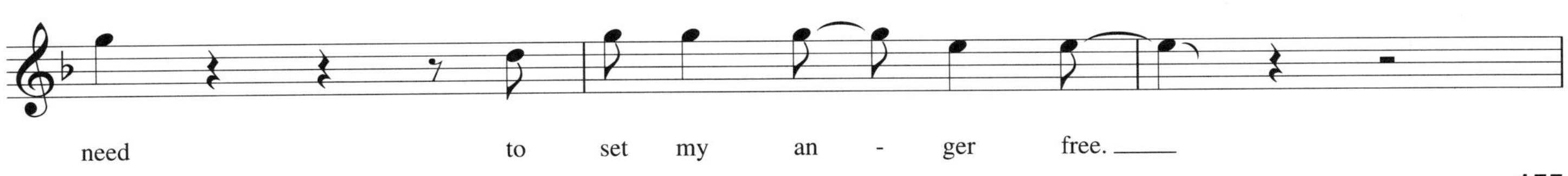
need to set my an - ger free. ___

D.S.S. al Coda 2
Interlude
Double-time feel
w/ Bass Fig. 1 (4 times)
N.C.
End double-time feel
w/ Bass Fig. 2
Set it free!
Coda 2
E(♭5)/B♭
A5
w/ Bass Fig. 4 (2 times)
D5
I'm mad - ly in an - ger with you.
I'm
C5
mad - ly in an - ger with you.
E(♭5)/B♭
A5
I'm
D5
mad - ly in an - ger with you.
C5
I'm mad - ly in an - ger with you.
E(♭5)/B♭
End double-time feel
A5
D5
N.C.
D5

School's Out

Words and Music by Alice Cooper and Michael Bruce

E5 A/E Em E5 A/E E5 Em7 E5 A/E Em E5 A/E E5 Em7
makin' all their noise, 'cause they found new toys.
E5 A/E Em
Pre-Chorus
C5 D5 E♭5
Well, we can't salute ya, can't find a flag. If that don't suit ya,
Chorus
G5 B♭5 C5 F5 G5
that's a drag. School's out for summer!
F5 G5 B♭5 C5 F5 G5 F5 G5
School's out for ever
Bass Fig. 1
End Bass Fig. 1

w/ Bass Fig. 1
B♭5
C5
F5
G5
F5
G5
School's been blown to piec - es!
Bridge
C
Csus2♯11
C
Csus2♯11
C
Csus2♯11
C
Csus2♯11
No more pen - cils, no more books,
Dsus4
D
D9
D
Dsus4
D
no more teach - er's dir - ty looks. Yeah!
(No more teach - er's dir - ty looks.)
Guitar Solo
E5
A/E
N.C.
Em
E5
A/E
Em
Play 3 times
E5
A/E
E5
Em
E5
A/E
Em
2. Well, we got

Verse
E5 A/E E5 Em7 E5 A/E Em E5 A/E E5 Em7 E5 A/E Em
no class, and we got no prin - ci - ples, and we got
sim.
E5 A/E E5 Em7 E5 A/E Em E5 A/E E5 Em7 E5 A/E Em
no in - no-cence. We can't e-ven think of a word that rhymes!
Chorus
w/ Bass Fig. 1 (2 times)
G5 B♭5 C5 F5 G5 F5 G5 B♭5 C5 F5 G5 F5 G5
School's out for sum-mer! School's out for ev-er! My
G5 F C/G
school's been blown to piec - es!
Bridge
C Csus2♯11 C Csus2♯11
No more pen - cils,
C Csus2♯11 C Csus2♯11 Dsus 2/4 D D9 D Dsus 2/4 D
w/ children's laughter & talking
no more books, no more teach - er's dir - ty

D9 D C Csus2#11 C Csus2#11 C Csus2#11 C Csus2#11
looks Out for sum - mer, out til fall.
Dsus2/4 D D9 D Dsus2/4 D N.C.
We might not go back at all!
Chorus
w/ Bass Fig. 1 (3 times)
G5 B♭5 C5 F5 G5 F5 G5 G5 B♭5 C5
School's out for ev - er! School's out for
F5 G5 F5 G5 B♭5 C5 F5 G5 F5 G5
sum-mer! School's out with fe - ver!
w/ school bell
w/ children's cheers & tape effects
Gm F C
School's out com - plete - ly!

Smokin' in the Boys Room

Words and Music by Michael Koda and Michael Lutz

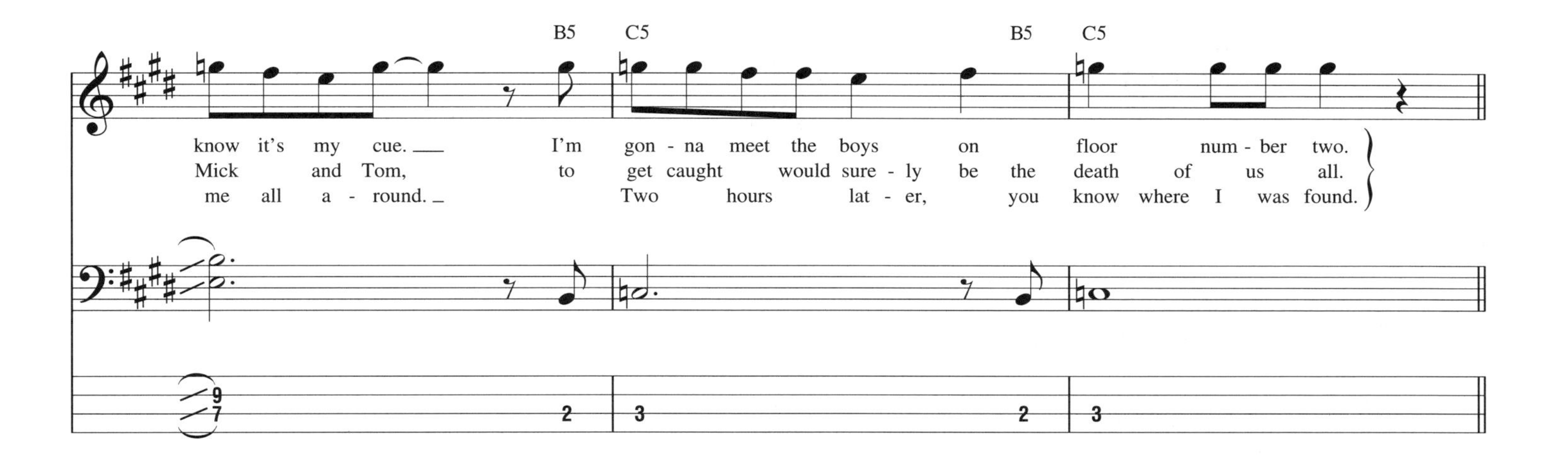

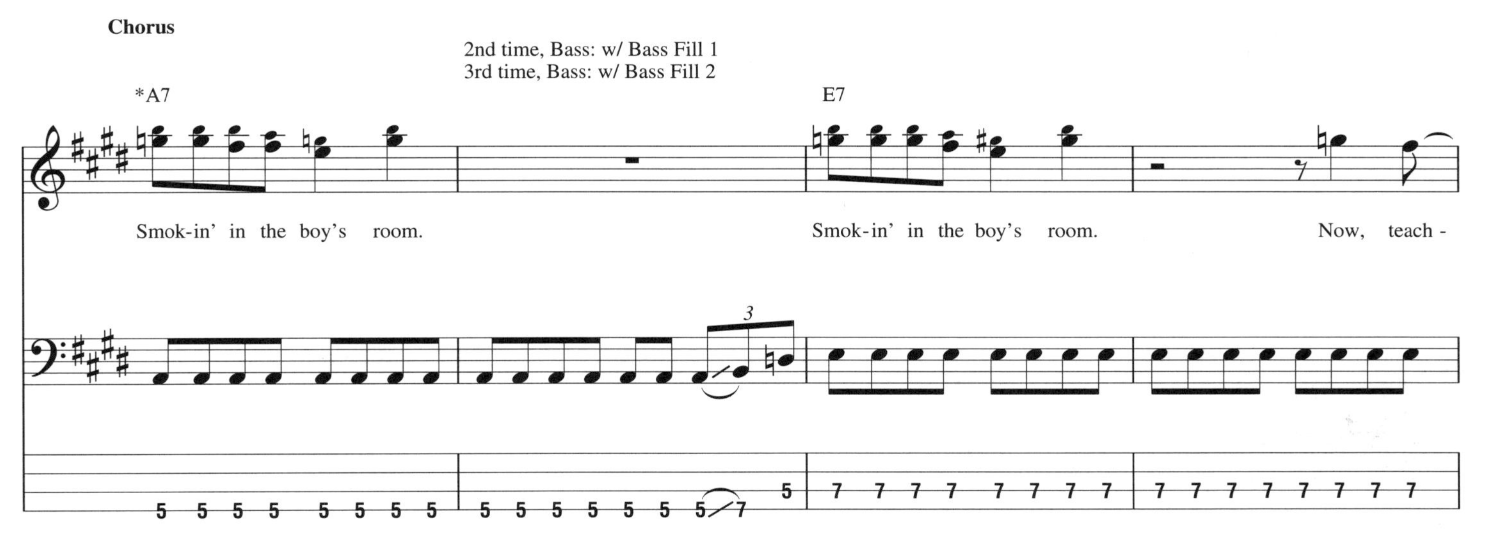

*Chord symbols reflect overall harmony.

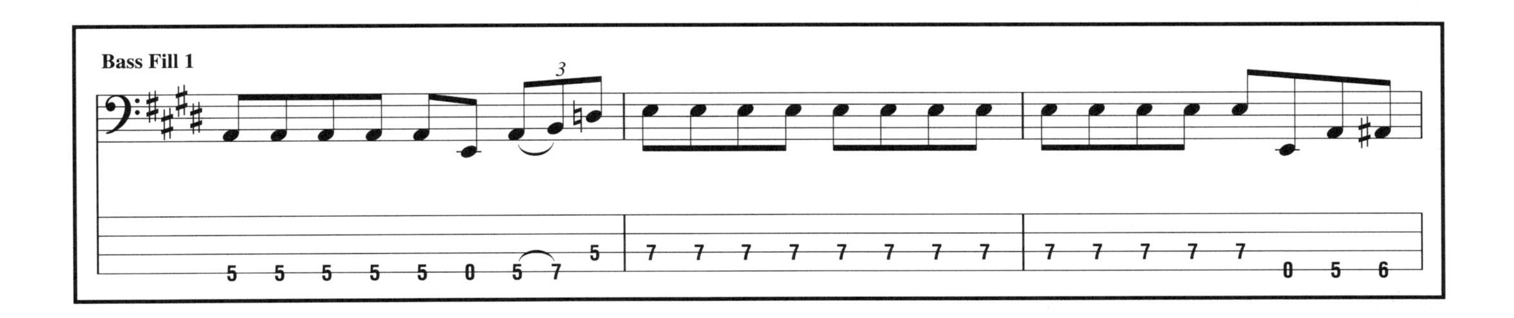

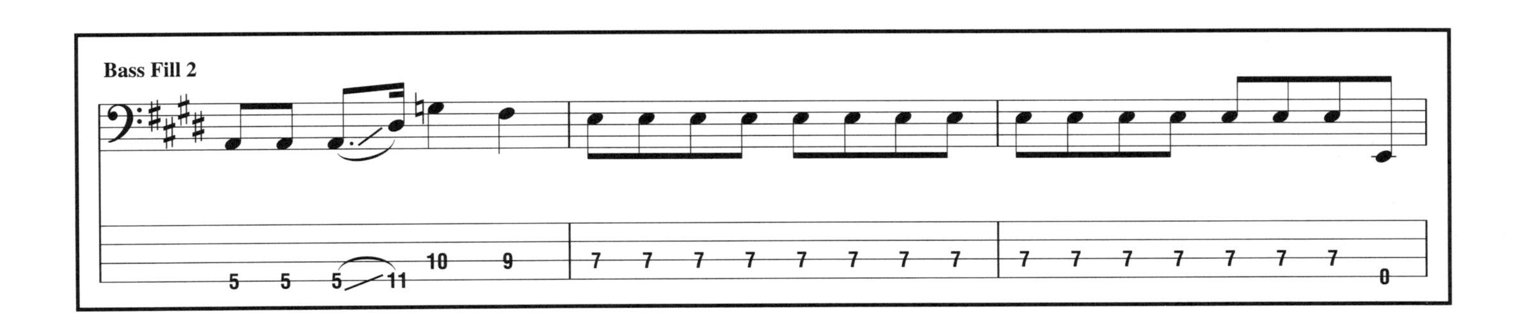

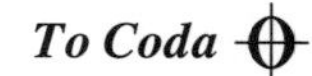
To Coda

B7
A7
B7
- er, don't fill me up with your rule, 'cause ev - 'ry - bod - y knows that
1.
A7
D♯5
E5
D♯5
E5
D♯5
smok - in' ain't al - lowed in school.
2.
A7
D♯5
E5
smok - in' ain't al - lowed in school.
(Spoken:) Hey, can I be excused?
Harmonica Solo
A7
E7

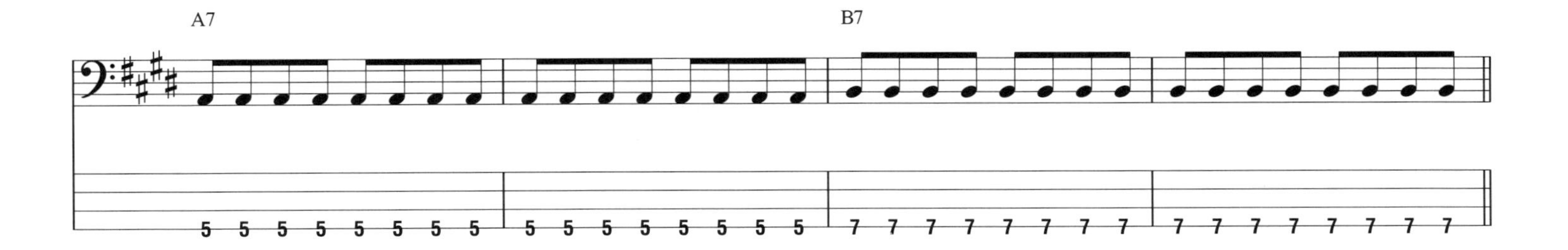
A7
B7

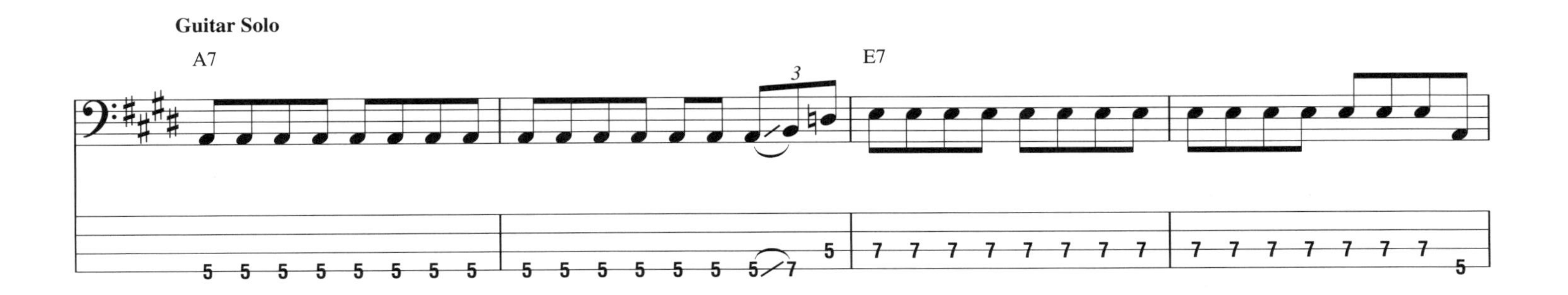
Guitar Solo
A7
E7

A7
B7

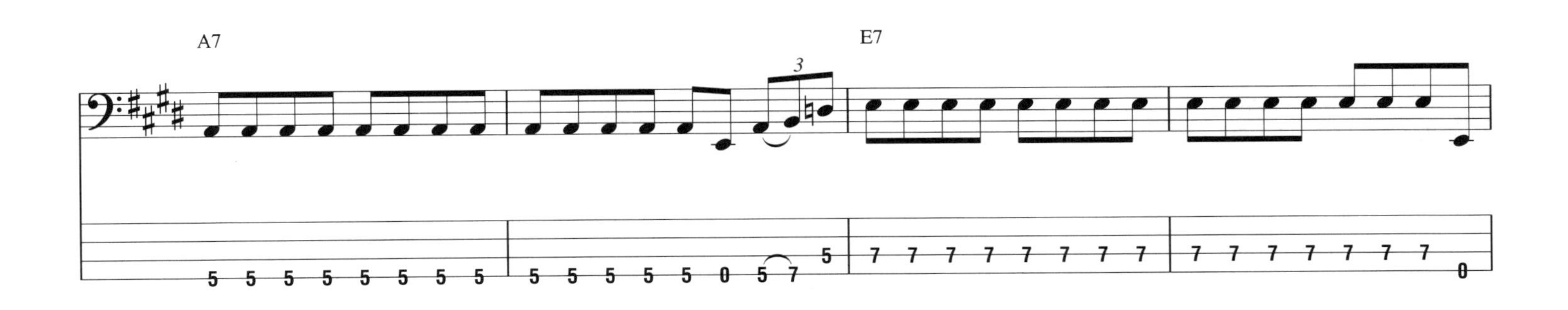
A7
E7

D.S. al Coda
A7
F♯7
B7
D♯5
3. Well,

Coda
A5
D♯5
E5
E5
F♯5
G
G♯5
smok - in' ain't al - lowed in school. Ev - 'ry - bod - y.
5 0 0 0 2 3 4
Interlude
Bass tacet
N.C.
1.
2.
Smok-in' in the boy's room. (Oo.) Smok-in' in the boy's room. I tell you, I was Hey, teach -
*1st time only.
B7
A7
B7
- er, don't ya fill me up with your rule, 'cause ev - 'ry - bod - y knows that
7 7 7 7 7 7 7 0 5 5 5 5 5 5 5 0 7 7 7 7 7 7 7 0
A7
D♯5
E5
E5
F♯5
G
G♯5
smok - in' ain't al - lowed in school. One more.
5 0 0 0 2 3 4

Outro-Chorus
A7
E7
Smok - in' in the boy's room.
Smok - in' in the boy's room.
B7
A7
Now teach - er, I ain't fool - in' a - round with your rule, 'cause
B7
A5 N.C.
rit.
ev - 'ry - bod - y knows that smok - in' ain't al - lowed in school.
rit.
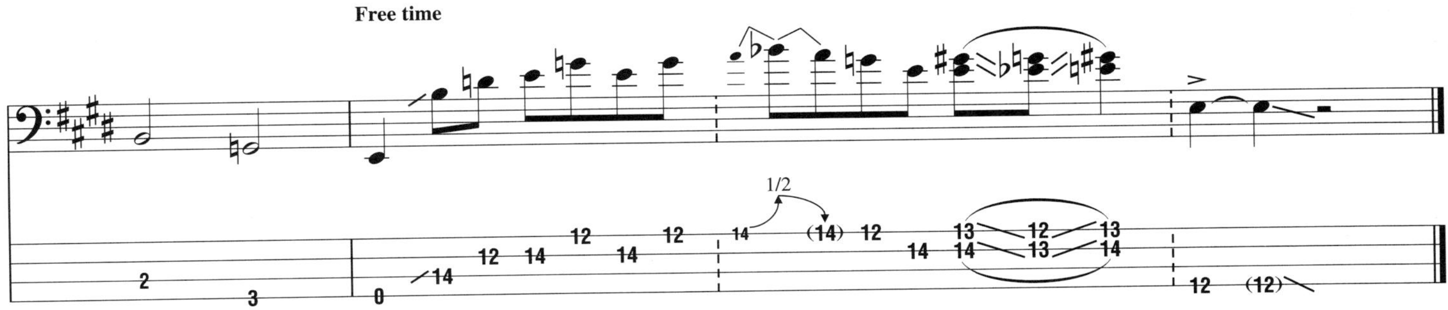
Free time
1/2

Sweet Leaf

Words and Music by Frank Iommi, John Osbourne, William Ward and Terence Butler

A5
D5
D♭5
C5
me
to my
mind
and left me
now,
my life is
clear.
I love you
a new be - lief.
And soon the
want - ing
you and your
kind.
Oh,
yeah.
sweet leaf
though you can't
hear.
world
will love you
sweet leaf.
yeah, ba - by.
Interlude
G5
E5
To Coda
1.
2.
Bridge
Faster ♩ = 173
B
accel.

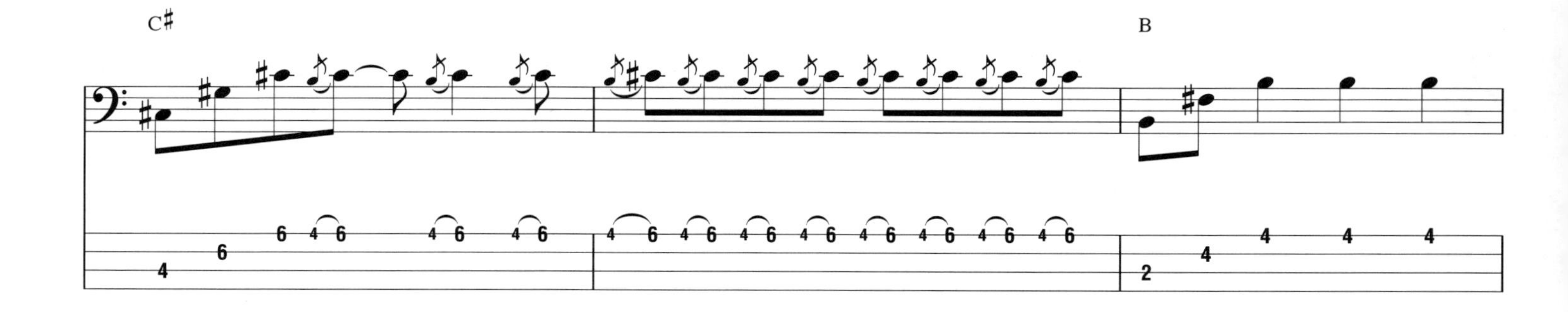
C♯
B

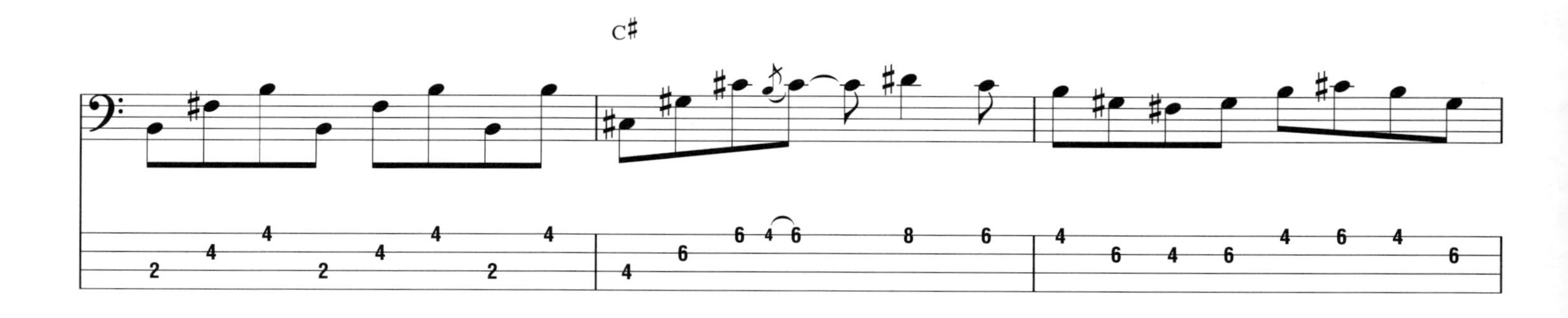
C♯

B
C♯

Guitar Solo
N.C.

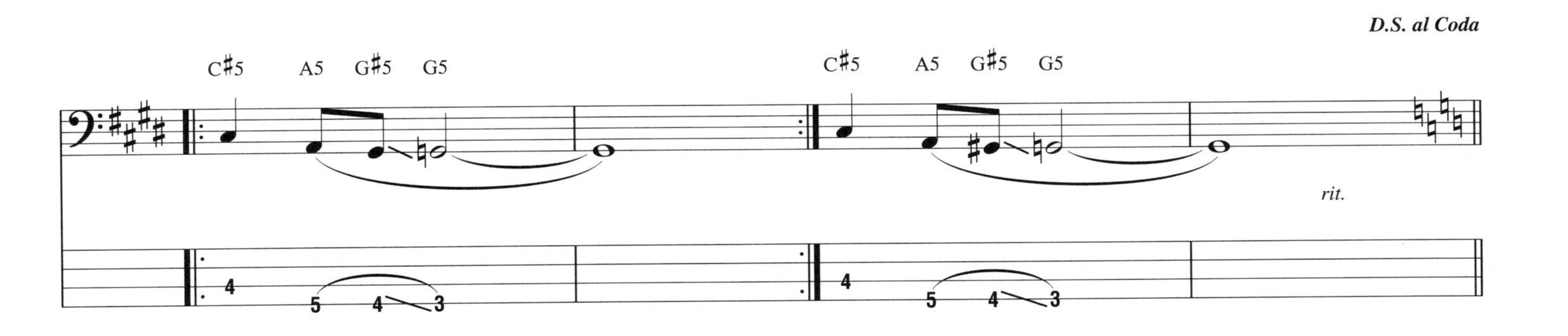
D.S. al Coda
C♯5
A5
G♯5
G5
C♯5
A5
G♯5
G5
rit.

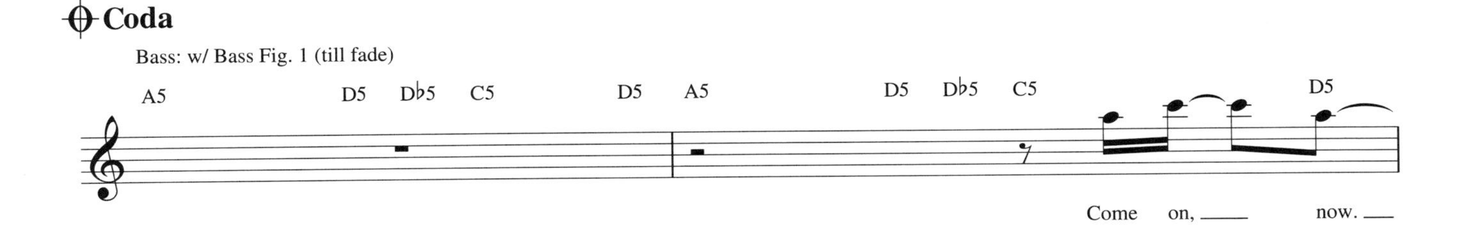
Coda
Bass: w/ Bass Fig. 1 (till fade)
A5
D5
D♭5
C5
D5
A5
D5
D♭5
C5
D5
Come on, now.

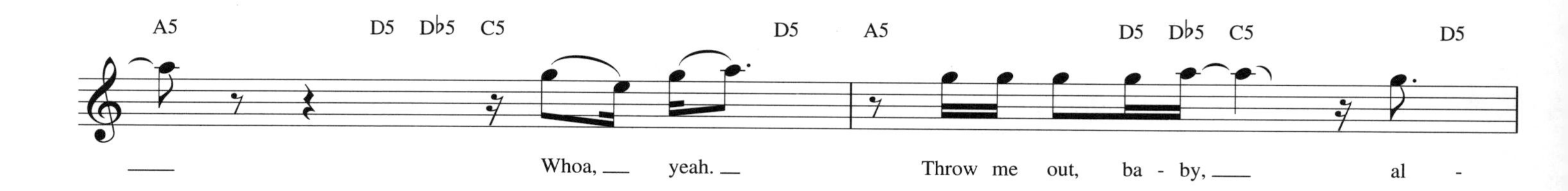
A5 D5 D♭5 C5 D5 A5 D5 D♭5 C5 D5
Whoa, yeah. Throw me out, ba - by, al -

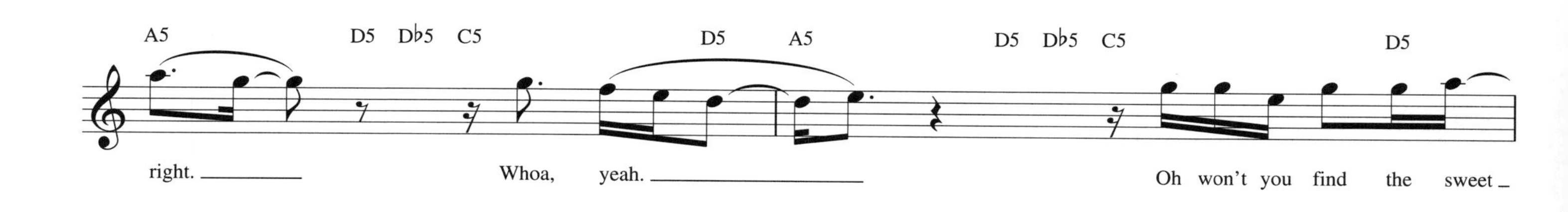
A5 D5 D♭5 C5 D5 A5 D5 D♭5 C5 D5
right. Whoa, yeah. Oh won't you find the sweet

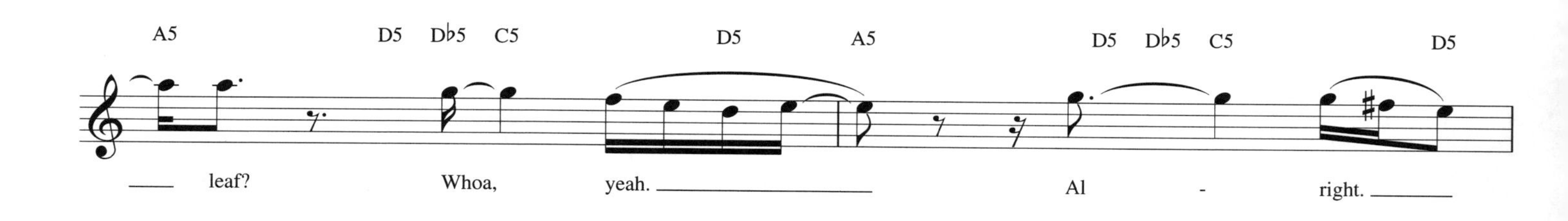
A5 D5 D♭5 C5 D5 A5 D5 D♭5 C5 D5
leaf? Whoa, yeah. Al - right.

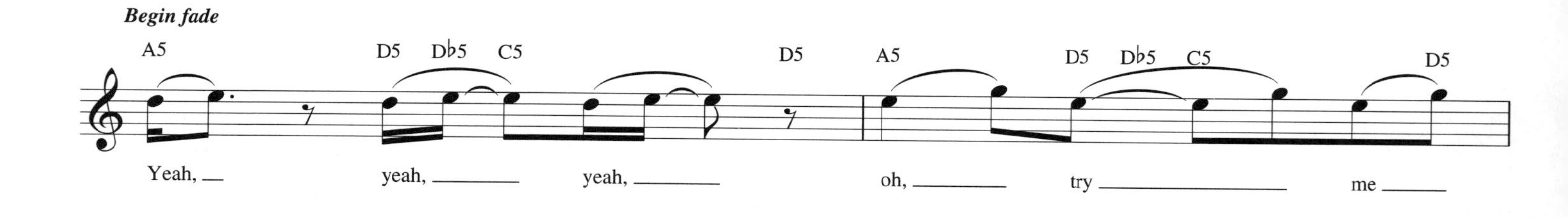
Begin fade
A5 D5 D♭5 C5 D5 A5 D5 D♭5 C5 D5
Yeah, yeah, yeah, oh, try me

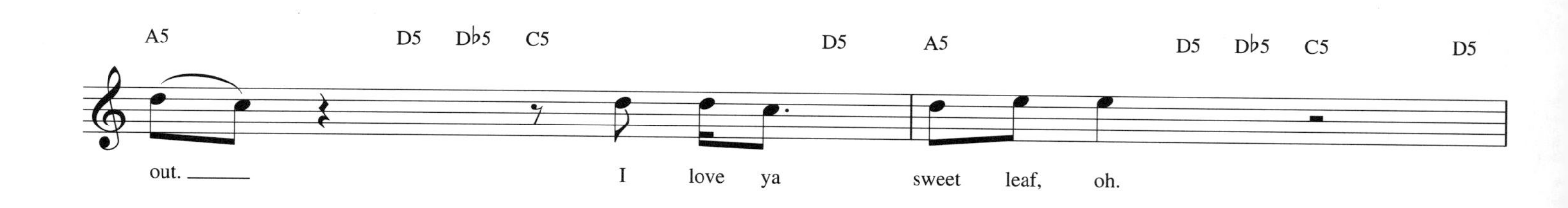
A5 D5 D♭5 C5 D5 A5 D5 D♭5 C5 D5
out. I love ya sweet leaf, oh.

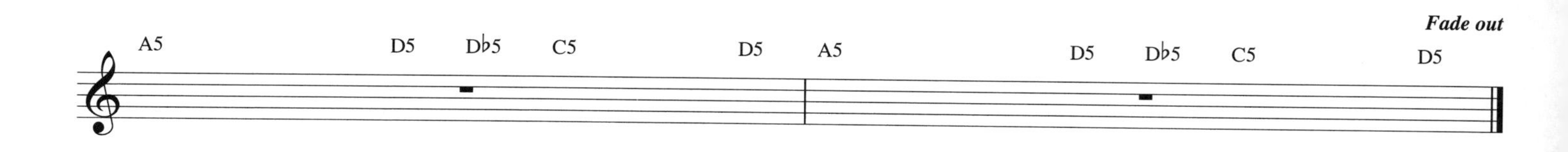
Fade out
A5 D5 D♭5 C5 D5 A5 D5 D♭5 C5 D5

Up All Night

Words and Music by Mark Slaughter and Dana Strum

Tune down 1 step:
(low to high) D-G C-F

Intro

Moderate Rock ♩ = 104

(sound effects)

20 sec.

N.C.

Up all night,

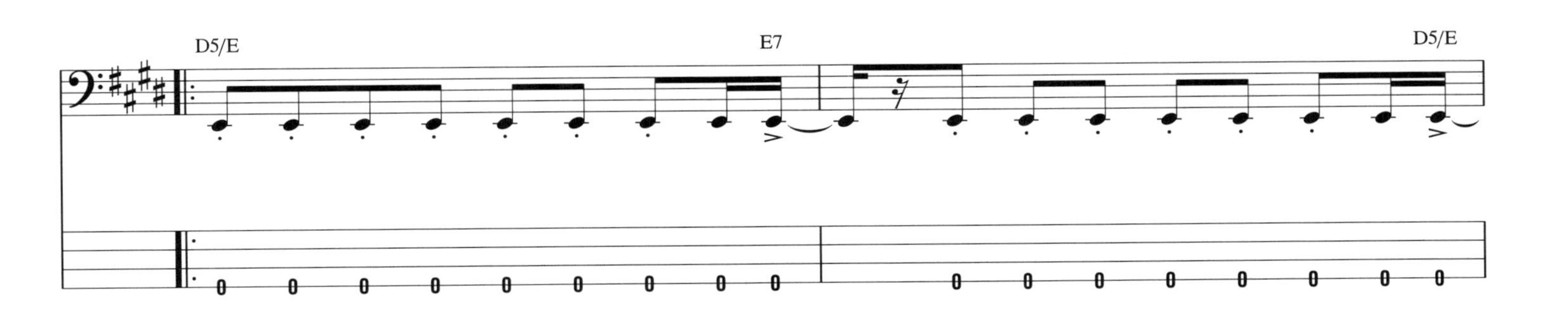

Verse
2nd time, Bass: w/ Bass Fill 1
D5/E
E7
D5/E
E7
1. When eve - nin' comes I am a - live. I love to prowl a - round in the streets.
2. Driv - in' down the boul - e - vard all a - lone, the ne - on signs are call - ing my name.

N.C.
D5/E
E7
D5/E
3
It's the moon - light that con - trols my mind. Now
Find me in the cor - ner hav - ing the time of my life. You'd

E7
N.C.
Pre-Chorus
F5
C5
G5
I've got the pow - er to speak, yeah.
think you'd want to do the same.

Bass Fill 1

F5 C5 G5 F5
(A - wake from dusk to dawn.
Watch - in' the cit - y lights.
Stars are shin - ing down.
C5 G5 F5 C5 G5
They'll be shin - in' down on you and I.
And I'll hold you till the morn - in' light.
And when morn - ing comes.)
Chorus
A5 Dsus2 G5 N.C.
Ev - 'ry-bod - y sing it now.
Up all night, sleep all day.
A5 Dsus2
1. G5 N.C.
2. G5 N.C.
Up all night, sleep all day. That's right.
sleep all day. That's right.
1/2

A5
Dsus2
G5
N.C.
A5
Dsus2
Up all night, sleep all day. Come on, come on. Up all night. Oh,
1/2

G5
may - be we could just stay up twen - ty - four hours a day, uh.

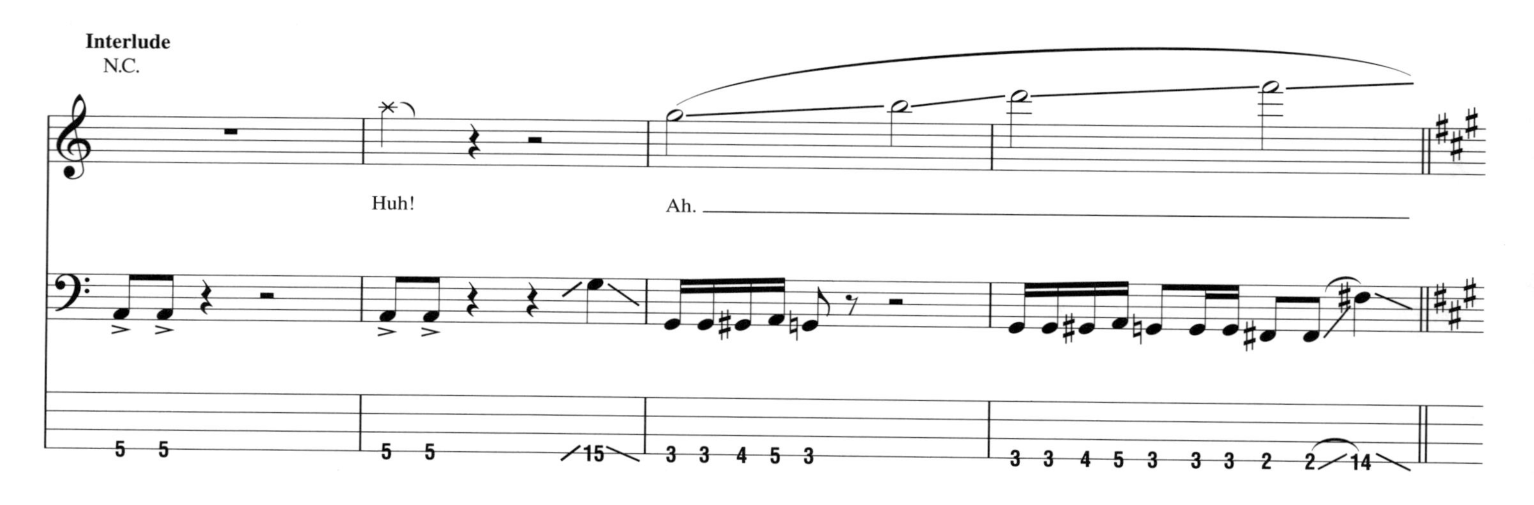
Interlude
N.C.
Huh!
Ah.

Guitar Solo
F♯m

Fmaj7(♯11)
G6
3
1 1 1 1 3 1 1 1 0
3 3 3 3 3 3 3 3 3 3 0

B
7 7 7 7 7 7 7 7 7
7 7 7 7 7 7 7 7 7

A
G♯m
3
5 5 5 5 5 5 5 5 5 5
5 5 5 5 5 5 5 5 5 5 0
4 4 4 4 4 4 4 4

G5
A5
4 4 4 4 4 4 4 0
3 3 3 3 5 5 7
5 5 5 5 7 9 7 9 7 9 7

Pre-Chorus
G5
D5
A5
G5
D5
A5
Watch - in' the cit - y lights.
(A - wake from dusk to dawn.
3 3 3 5 5 5 5 7 5
5 5 5 5 5 4 5 3
3 3 3 5 5 5 7 5

G5
D5
A5
F5
Stars are shin - ing down. They'll be shin - in' down on you and I. And I'll
And when morn - ing comes.)
D5
A5
hold you till the morn - in' light. Ev - 'ry - bod - y sing it now.
Chorus
B5
E5
A5
N.C.
Up all night, sleep all day. Up all night,
1/2
A5
N.C.
B5
sleep all day. Up all night.
1/2

Walk This Way

Words and Music by Steven Tyler and Joe Perry

Interlude
N.C. (E5)
Bass Fig. 2
A5
End Bass Fig. 2
Verse
Bass: w/ Bass Fig. 1 (3 times)
N.C. (C7)
2., 4. See - saw swing - in' with the boys in the school and your feet fly - in' up in the air, I sing,
"Hey did - dle did - dle" with your kit - ty in the mid - dle of the swing like you did - n't care. So I
took a big chance at the high school dance with a mis - sy who was read - y to play, was a
*Sing harmony 1st time only.
me she was fool - in' 'cause she knew what she was do - in' and I know'd love was here to stay when she told me to...
when she told me how to walk this way. She told me to...

Chorus
C7
F7
(Walk this way, talk this way,
Bass Fig. 3
End Bass Fig. 3
1st time, Bass: w/ Bass Fig. 3 (3 times)
2nd time, Bass: w/ Bass Fig. 3 (2 times)
C7
F7
C7
walk this way, talk this way, walk this way,
To Coda
F7
C7
F7
talk this way, walk this way, talk this way.) Uh, just gim - me a kiss.
Guitar Solo
N.C. (C7)
Interlude
Bass: w/ Bass Fig. 2
D.S. al Coda
A5
N.C. (E5)
A5
A - like this! Oo, Uh.

Coda
C7
F7
walk this __ way, __
talk this __ way.) __
Uh, just gim - me a kiss. __
3 3 3 6 10 10 8 10
1 1 1 3 1 2 3 1 2

Guitar Solo
N.C. (C7)
3 3 1 3 0 1 3 0 3
3 3 10 8 10 8 9 10 8 9

A5
Like this!
3 3 1 3 0 1 3 0 3
3 3 1 3 0 3 5

N.C.
Play 12 times and fade
0 3 4 7 5 6 7 7 0
0 3 4 7 5 6 7 7 0

White Wedding

Words and Music by Billy Idol

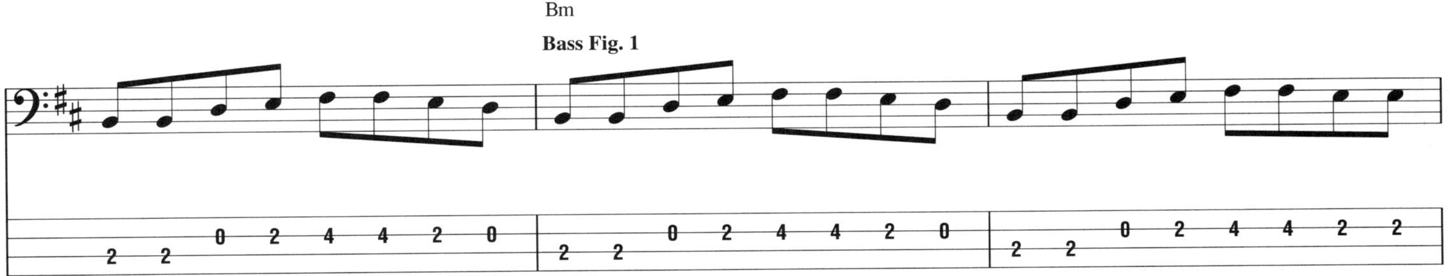

Verse
2nd & 3rd time, Bkgd. Voc.: w/ Voc. Fill 1
B5
A5
E5
1. Hey, lit - tle sis - ter, what have you done?
2. Hey, lit - tle sis - ter, who is it you're with?
3. Hey, lit - tle sis - ter, what have you done?
Bass Fig. 3
End Bass Fig. 3
Bass: w/ Bass Fig. 3
3rd time, Bkgd. Voc.: w/ Voc. Fill 2
Hey, lit - tle sis - ter, who's the on - ly one?
Hey, lit - tle sis - ter, what's your fas - ci - na (tion)?
Hey, lit - tle sis - ter, who's the on - ly one?
3rd time, Bkgd. Voc.: w/ Voc. Fill 3
Hey, lit - tle sis - ter, who's your su - per - man? Hey, lit - tle sis - ter, who's
Hey, lit - tle sis - ter, shot - gun, oh, yeah. Hey, lit - tle sis - ter, who's
I've been a - way for so long. I've been a - way for so
Voc. Fill 1
Ooh.
Ooh.
Voc. Fill 2
On - ly one, on - ly one, on - ly one, on - ly one.
Voc. Fill 3
So long.
So long.

B5
the one you want? Hey, lit - tle sis - ter, shot - gun!
your su - per - man? Hey, lit - tle sis - ter, shot - gun! It's a
long. I let you go for so long.

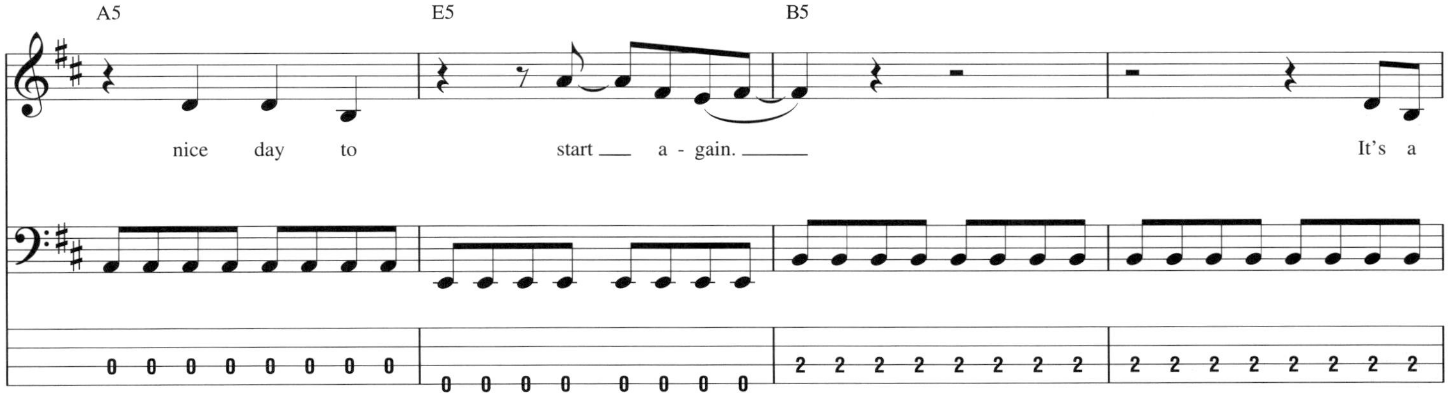
A5
E5
B5
nice day to start a - gain. It's a

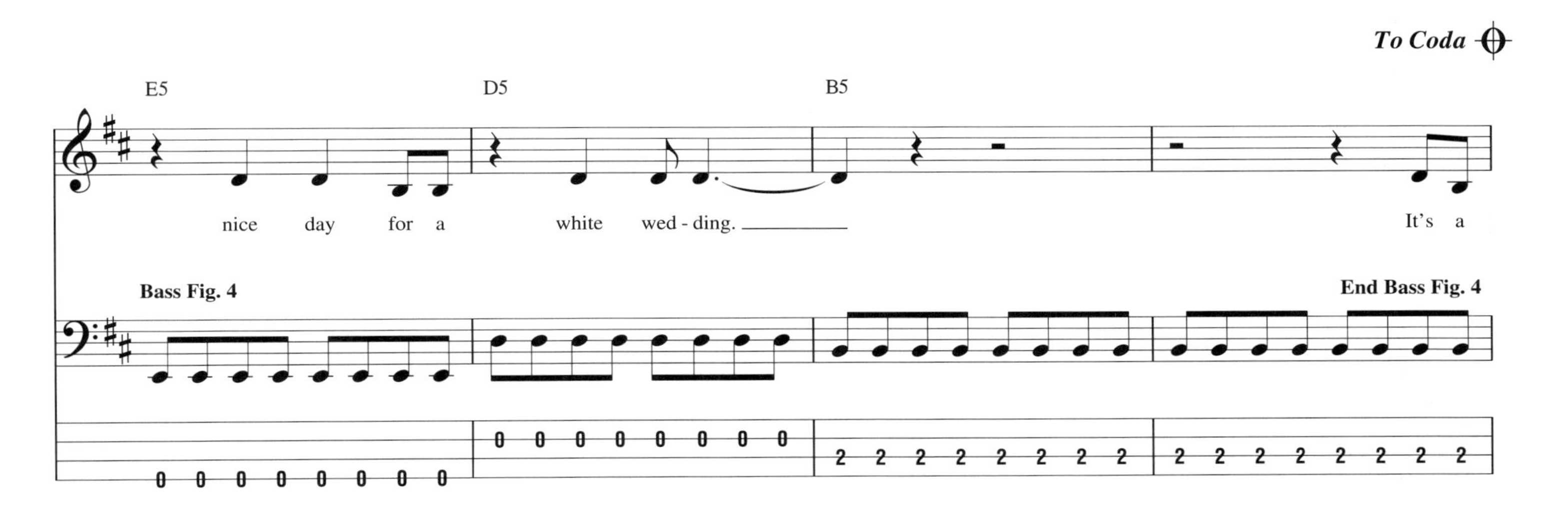
To Coda
E5
D5
B5
nice day for a white wed - ding. It's a
Bass Fig. 4
End Bass Fig. 4

1.
E5
D
Bm7
nice day to start a - gain.
Bass Fig. 5
End Bass Fig. 5

2.
Bass: w/ Bass Fig. 5
E5
D
Bm7
nice day to start a - gain, ow!
Interlude
Bass: w/ Bass Fig. 1
8
Bm
E9 (no 3rd)
Bm
D
E
Bass: w/ Bass Fig. 3 (1 1/2 times)
Bm7sus2
A5
E5
Pick it up. Take me back home, 'eah.
B5
D.S. al Coda
Coda
Bass: w/ Bass Fig. 4
E5
D
nice day to start a - gain,
Bm7
Bass: w/ Bass Fig. 2 (1st meas.)
B5
ow! There is

Bridge
Bass: w/ Bass Fig. 2 (3 1/2 times)
B5
Bm
noth - ing fair in this world, girl. There is
Bmadd4
noth - ing safe in this world. And there's
noth - ing sure in this world. And there's noth - ing pure in this
Bass: w/ Bass Fig. 4
E5
world. And if there's some-thing left in this world,
D5
B5
start a - gain. Come on, it's a
Outro-Chorus
D5
E5
Bm
nice day for a white wed - ding. Wow! It's a
Begin fade
Bass: w/ Bass Fig. 4 (till fade)
E5
D5
B5
nice day to start a - gain. It's a
Repeat and fade
E5
D5
B5
nice day to start a - gain. It's a

Won't Get Fooled Again

Words and Music by Pete Townshend

E
C/G
G5/D
A5
And the men who spurred us on
sit in judge - ment of all wrong,
they de -
cide and the shot - gun sings the song.
E
C/G
G5/D
Chorus
D
A5
D
A5
I'll tip my hat to the new con - sti - tu - tion,

D
A5
D
A5
D
A5
take a bow for the new rev - o - lu - tion. Smile and grin at the
D
A5
G
E
change all a - round, pick up my gui - tar and play,
G
E
G
just like yes - ter - day, then I'll get on my knees and
D
G5/D
D
pray
we

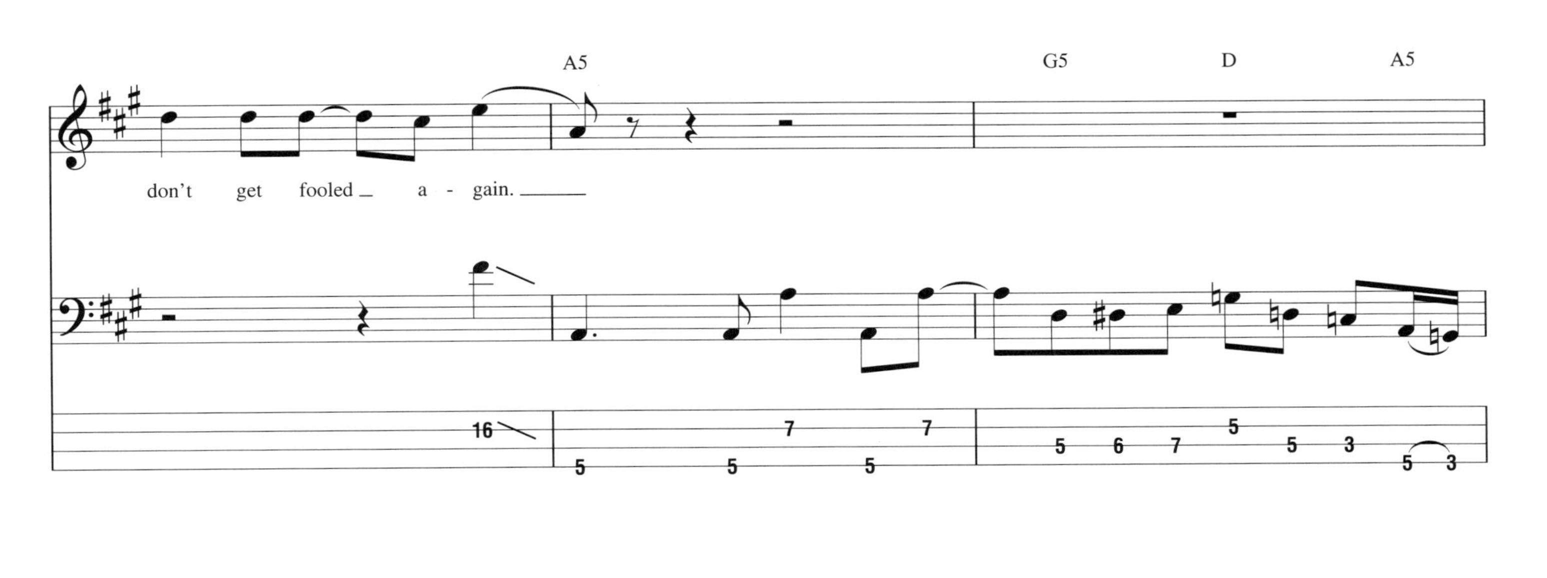
A5
G5
D
A5
don't get fooled a - gain.

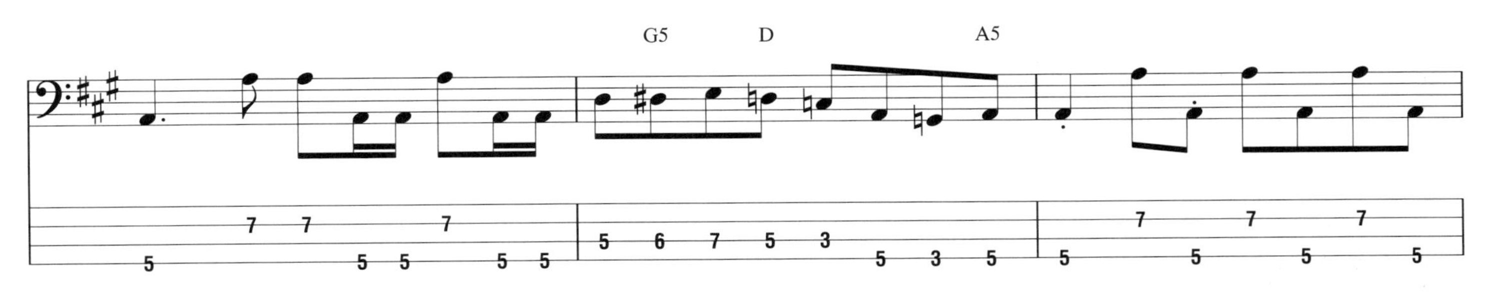
G5
D
A5

D
A5
D/A
2. A

Verse
A5
change, it had to come.
We knew it all a - long.

We were lib - er - at - ed from the fold, that's all.
E
C/G
G5/D
A5
And the world looks just the same,
and his - to - ry ain't changed,
'cause the
E
ban - ners, they are flown in the last war.

Chorus
C/G G5/D D A5 D5 A5
I'll tip my hat to the new con - sti - tu - tion,
D A5 D A5 D A5
take a bow for the new rev - o - lu - tion. Smile and grin at the
D A5 G E
change all a - round, pick up my gui - tar and play,
G E G
just like yes - ter - day, then I'll get on my knees and

D G5/D D G5/D Dm7
pray we
let ring
A5 G5 D
don't get fooled a - gain. No no!
A5 G5 A5
G5 D A5 G5 D
A5 G5 D A5

G5 D5 A5 D/A
5 5 6 7 5 8 7
7 5 5 5 5 5 7 5
7 5 6 7 5 5 7 5 3

A5 D/A A5
7 5 7 5 7 5 5
7 5 6 7 5 3 5 3
7 5 5 5 7 5 5 7 5 5

I'll
5 5 6 7 5 7 5 3
5 5 5 7 7 5 7 7
5 6 7 5 8 7 5

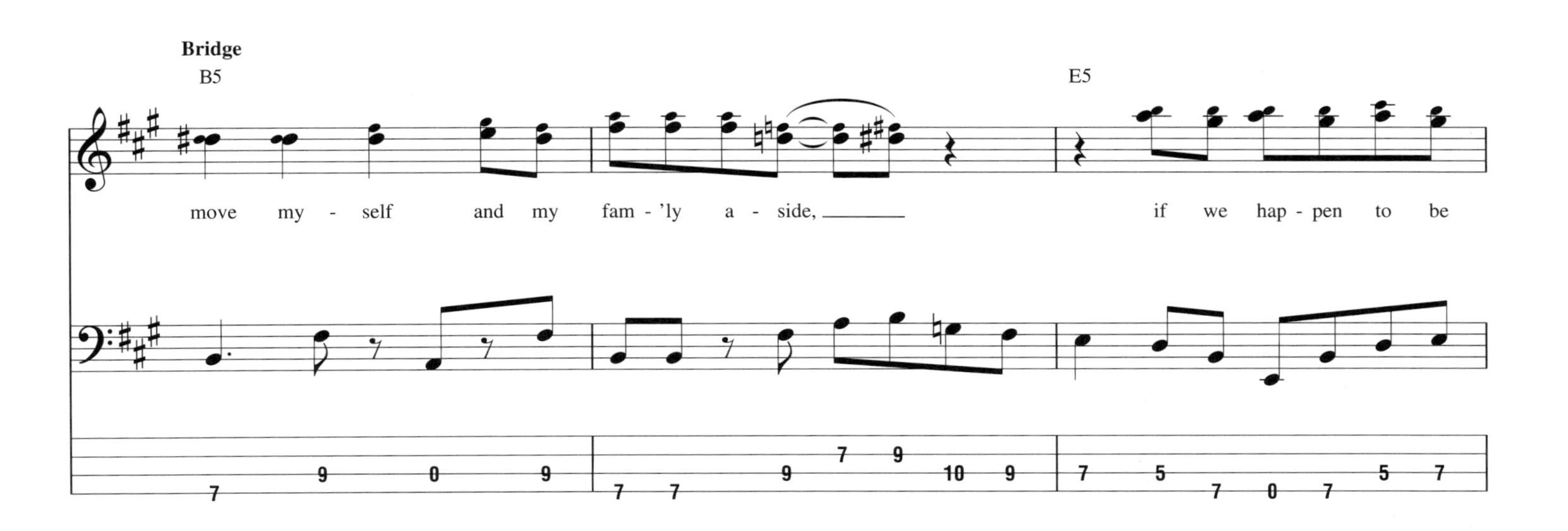
Bridge
B5
E5
move my - self and my fam - 'ly a - side,
if we hap - pen to be
7 9 0 9
7 7 9 7 9 10 9
7 5 7 0 7 5 7

A5
left half a - live. I'll get all my pa - pers and smile at the sky, oh, I
B5
know that the hyp - no - tized nev - er lie.
A E B A E

B A E B A E
Do ya?

Guitar Solo

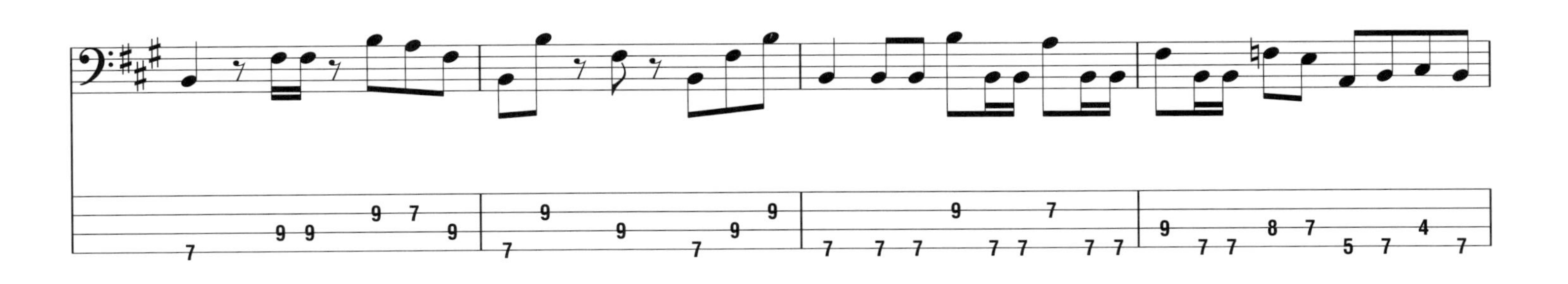

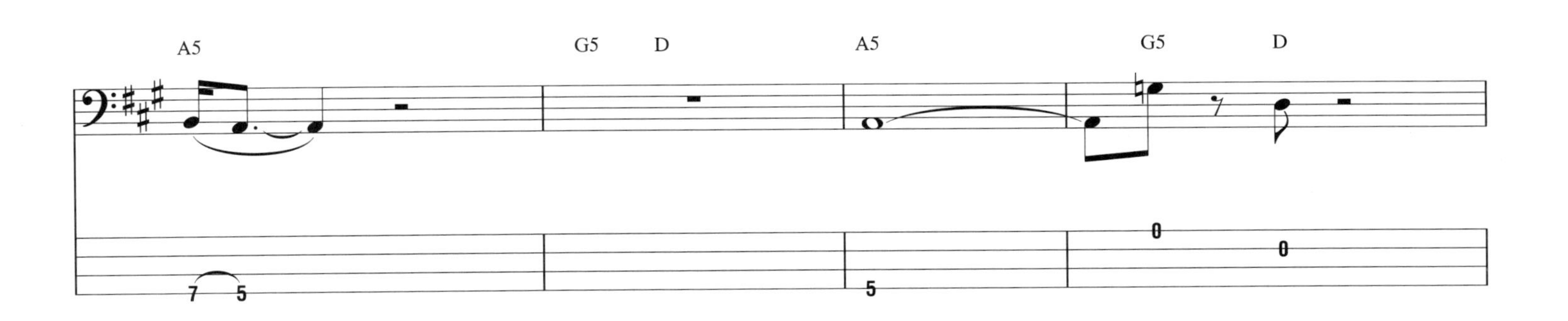

A5
G5
D
A5
G5
D
Yeah!
3. There's
Verse
A5
noth - ing in the street
looks an - y dif - fer - ent to me,
and the slo - gans are re - placed by the by.
E
C/G
G5/D
A5
And the part - ing on the left

is now parting on the right, and the
beards have all grown longer overnight.
E
Chorus
C/G G5/D
D A5
I'll tip my hat to the new constitution,
take a bow for the new revolution.
Smile and grin at the

D A5 G E
change all a - round, pick up my gui - tar and play,
G E G
just like yes - ter - day, then I'll get on my knees and
D
pray we
A5
don't get fooled a - gain.
Don't get fooled a - gain.

N.C. (A)

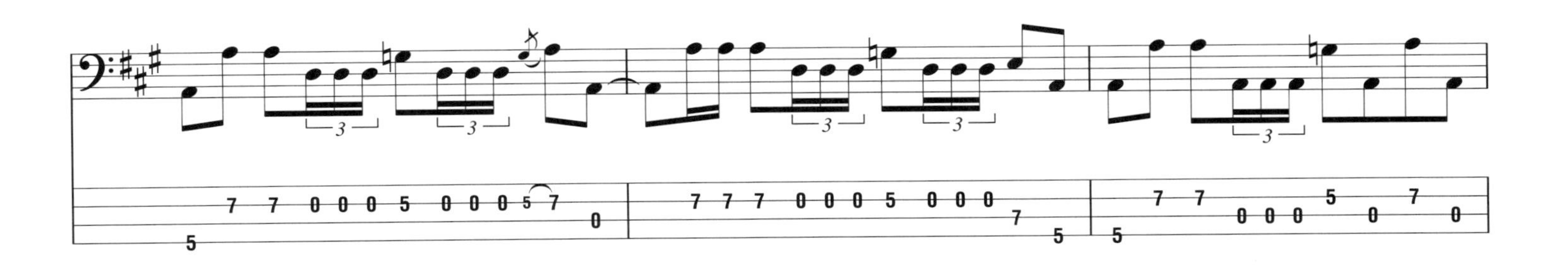

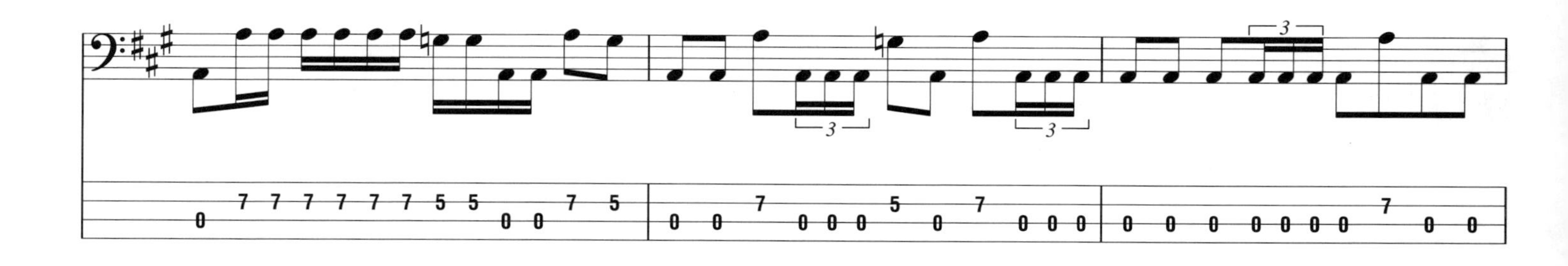

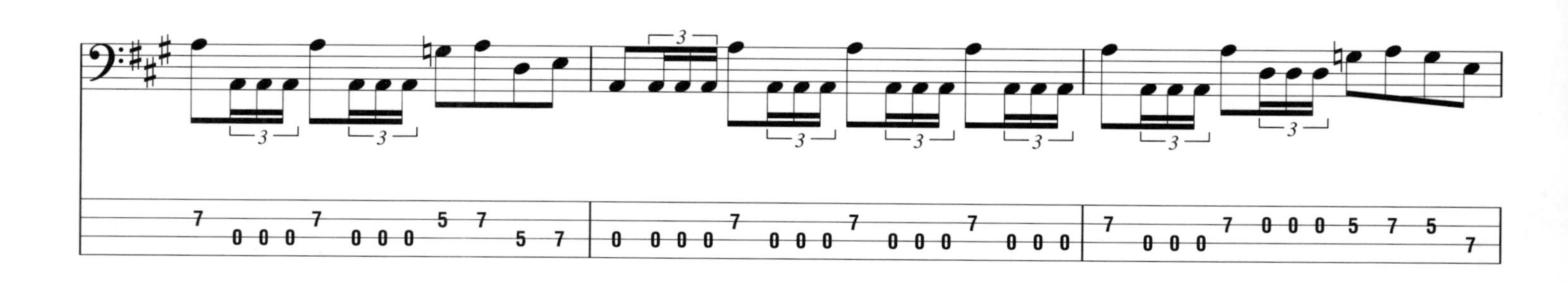

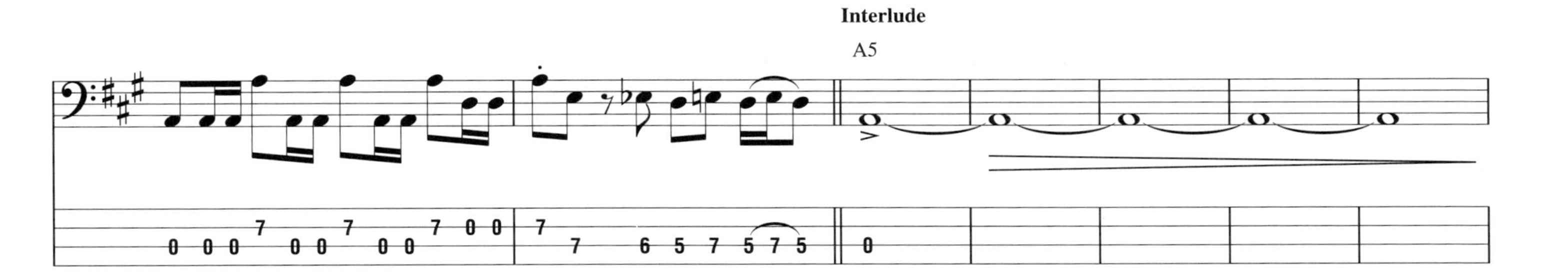
Interlude
A5
7 0 0 0 7 0 0 7 0 0 7 0 0 7 7 6 5 7 5 7 5 0

Bass tacet
(Arp. synth.)
18
14
Yeah!

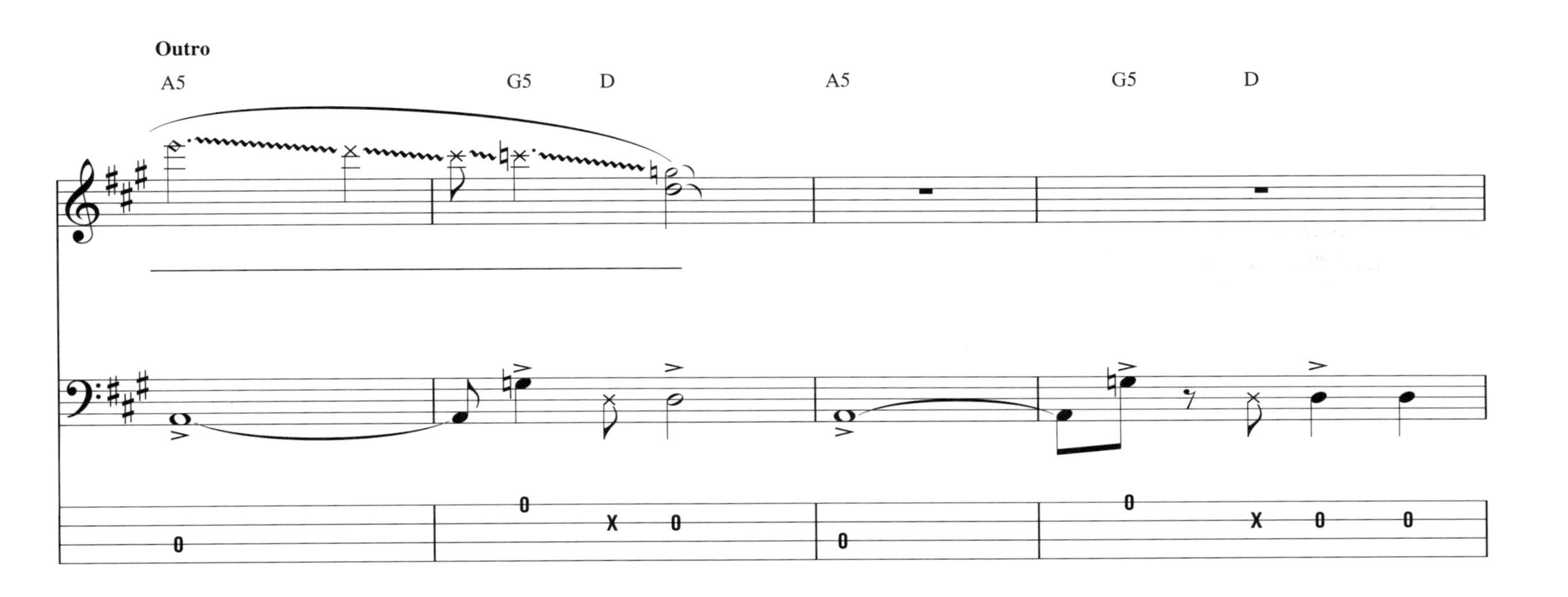
Outro
A5
G5
D
A5
G5
D

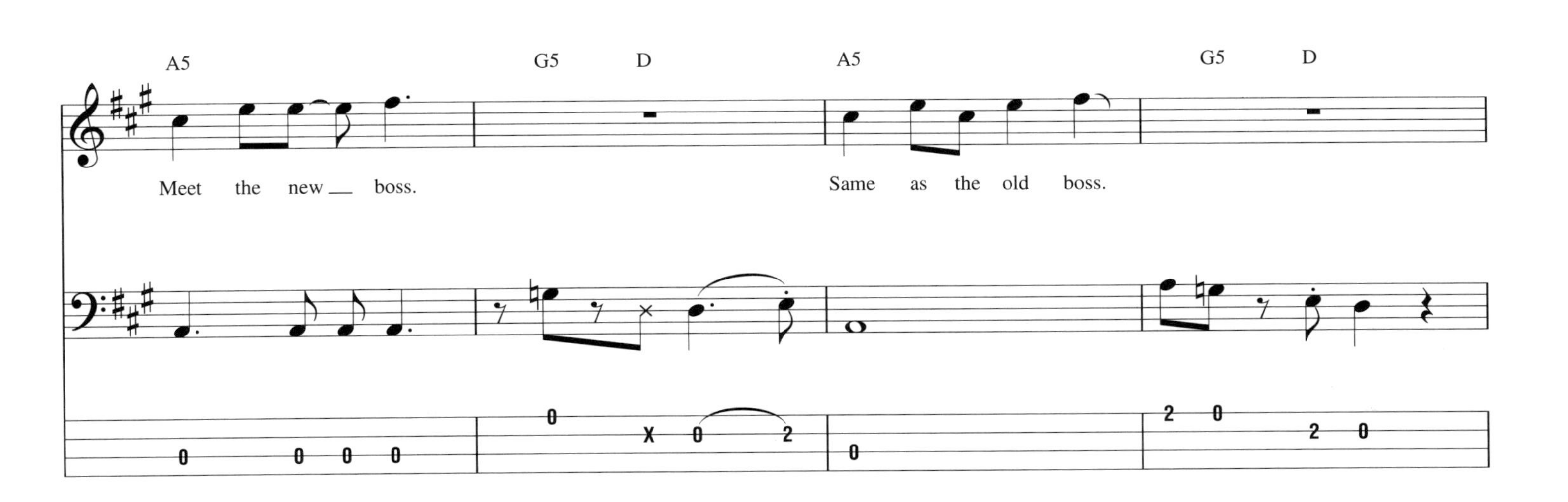
A5
G5
D
A5
G5
D
Meet the new boss.
Same as the old boss.

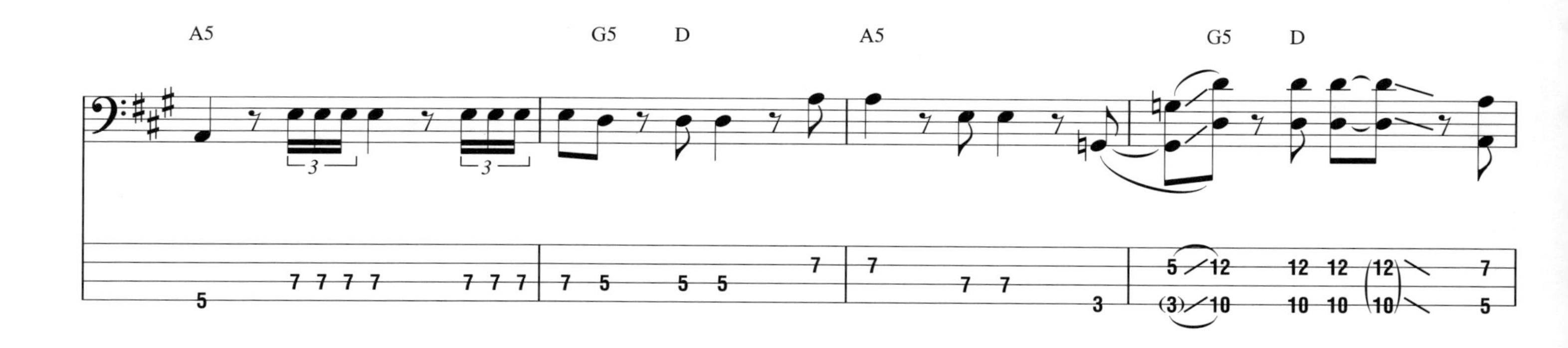
A5
G5
D
A5
G5
D

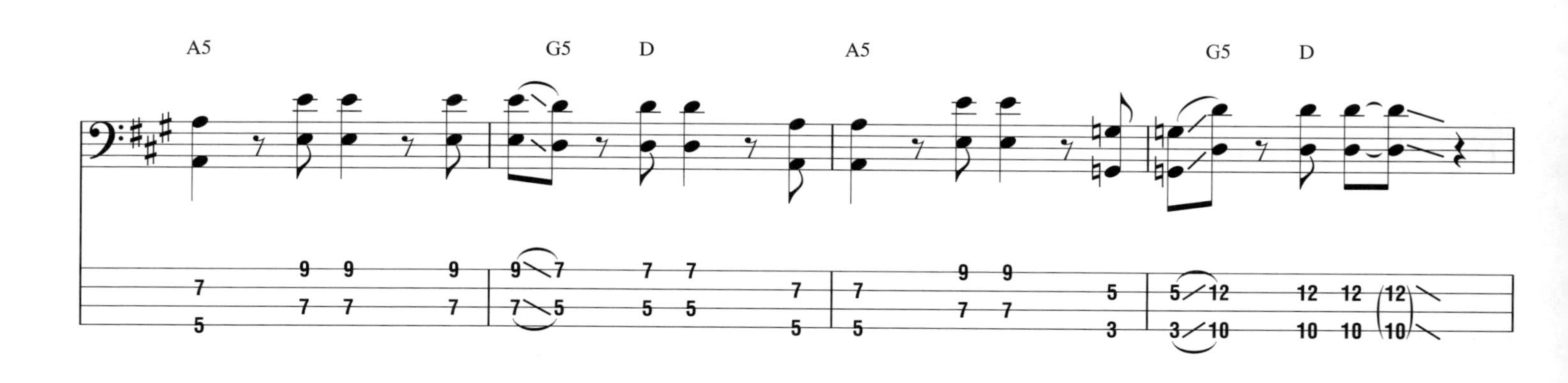
A5
G5
D
A5
G5
D

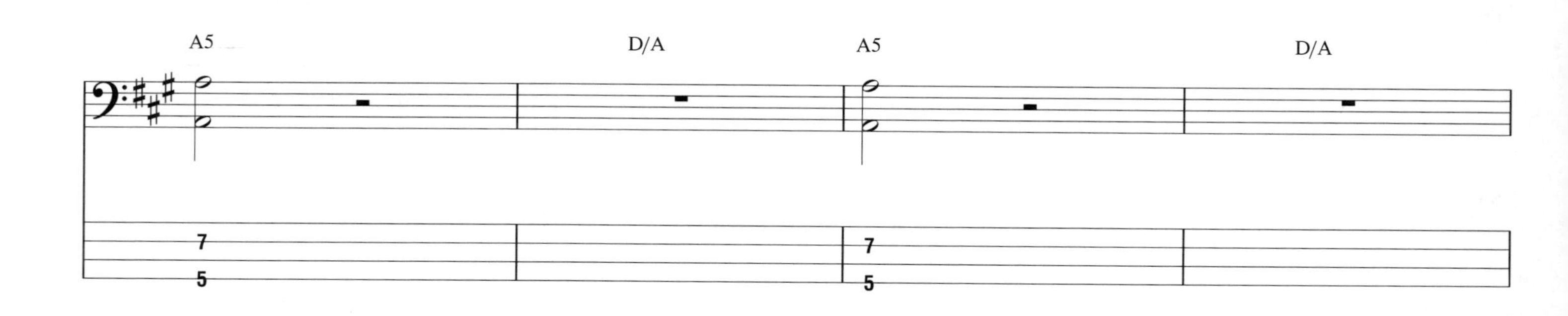
A5
D/A
A5
D/A

A5
Free time
(Townshend:) Hey!

Would?

Written by Jerry Cantrell

F#5
G
on child of love here - af - ter.
not yet quite the no - tion.

Chorus
B5
G5
In - to the flood a - gain.
The same old trip it was

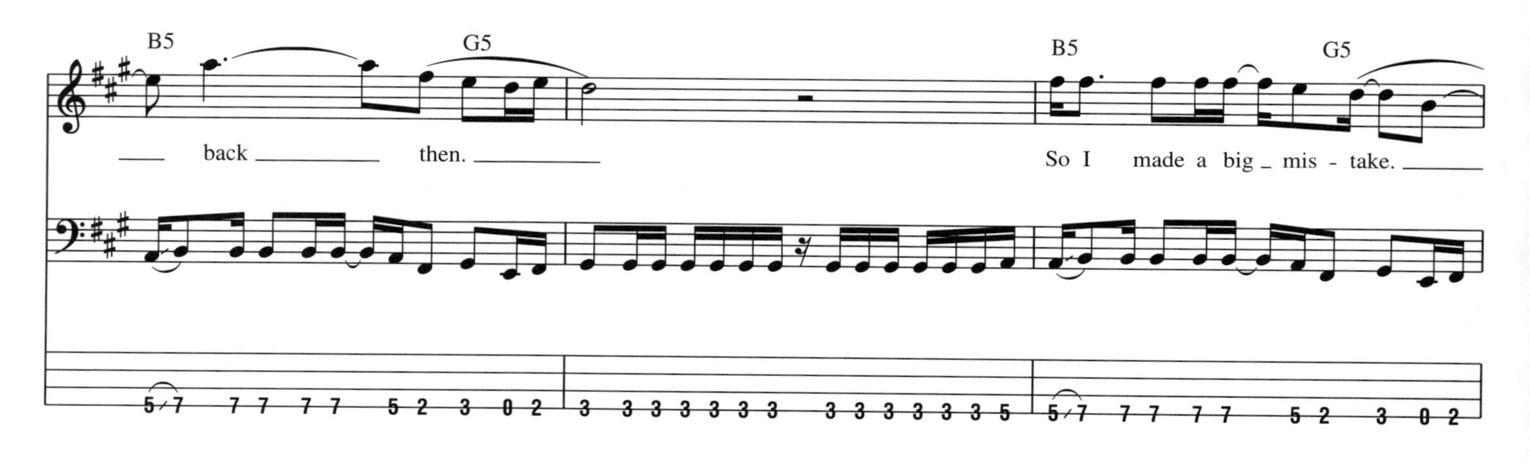
B5
G5
back then.
B5
G5
So I made a big mis - take.

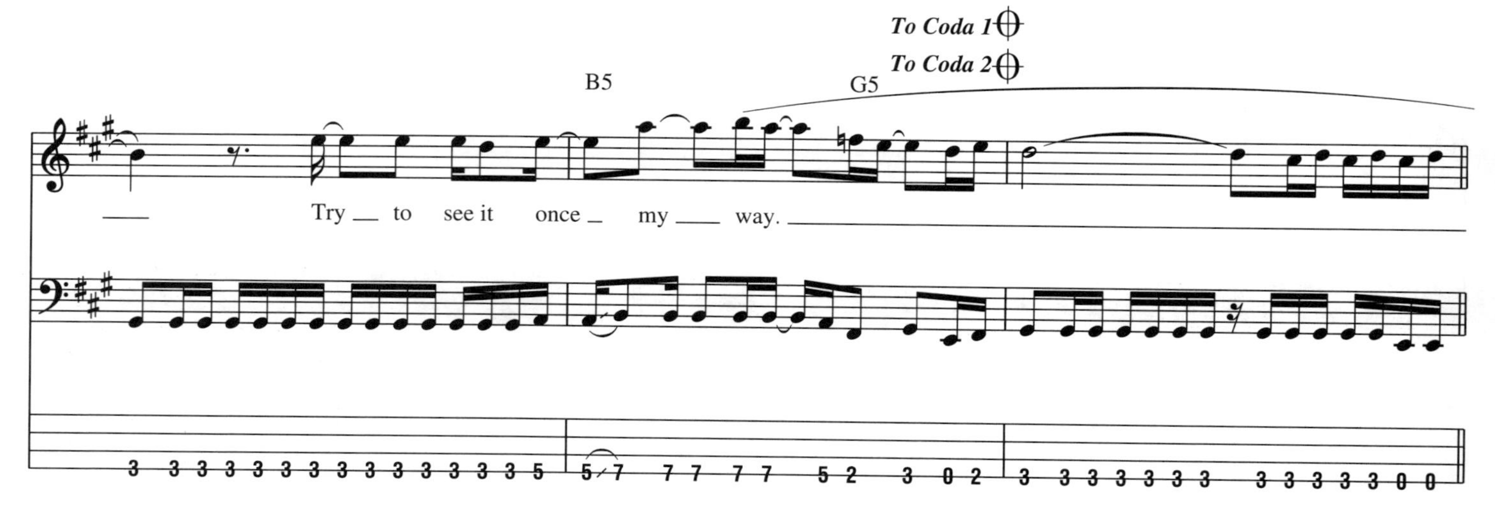
To Coda 1
To Coda 2
B5
G5
Try to see it once my way.

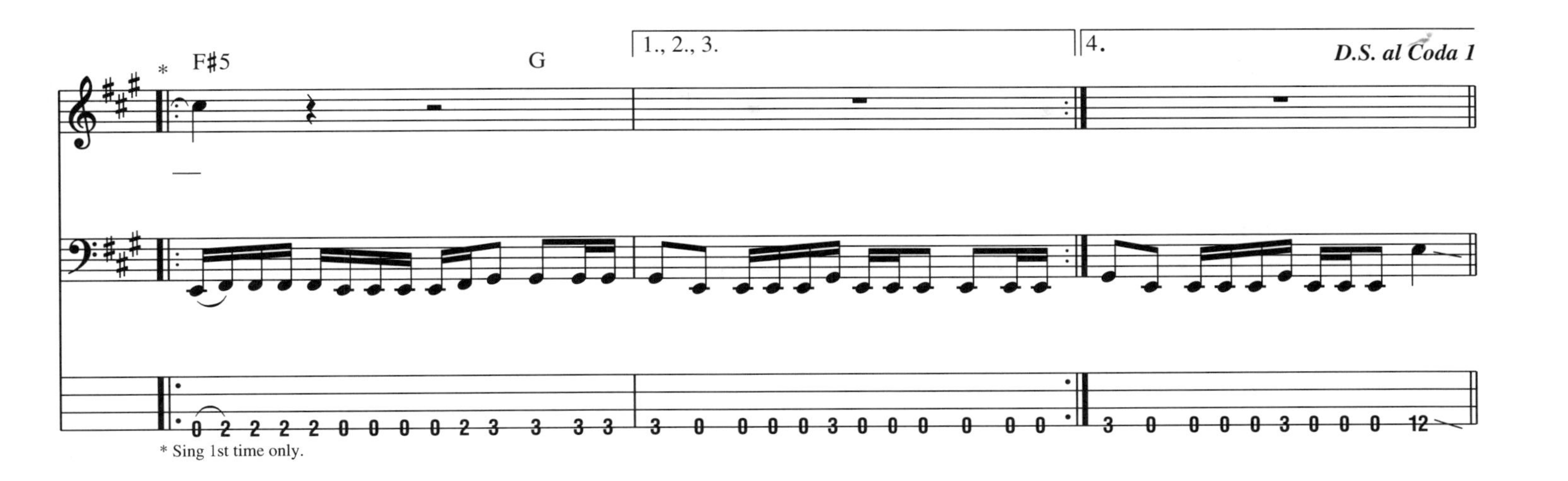
F#5
G
1., 2., 3.
4.
D.S. al Coda 1
* Sing 1st time only.

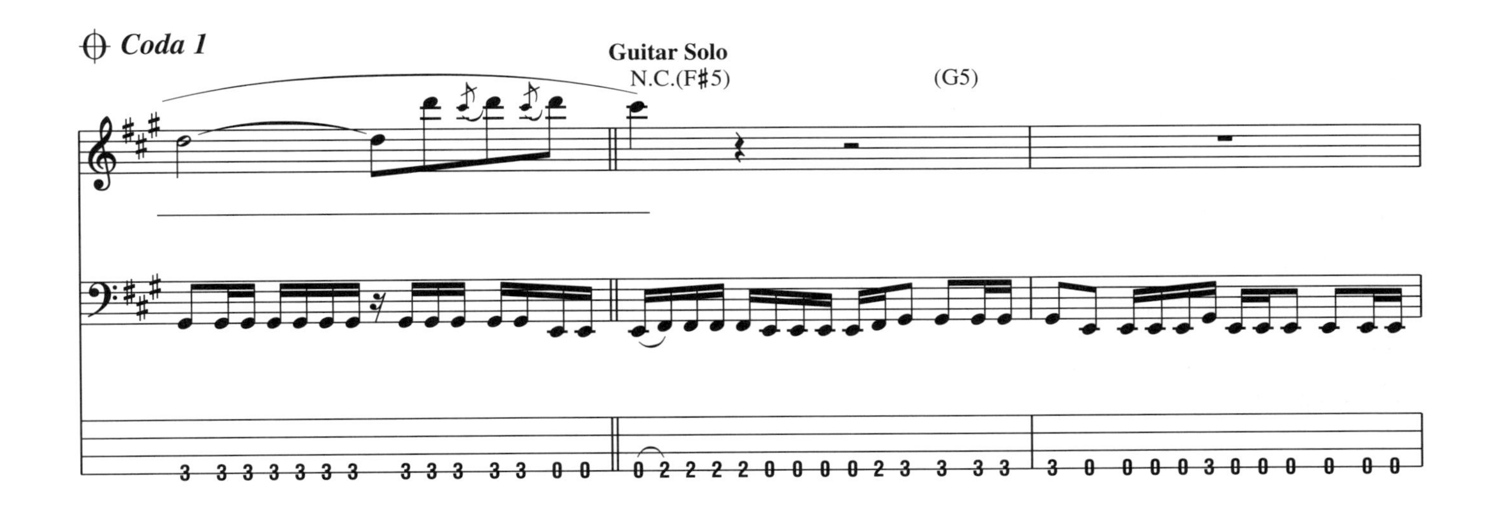
Coda 1
Guitar Solo
N.C.(F#5)
(G5)

(F#5)
(G)
(F#5)
(G)

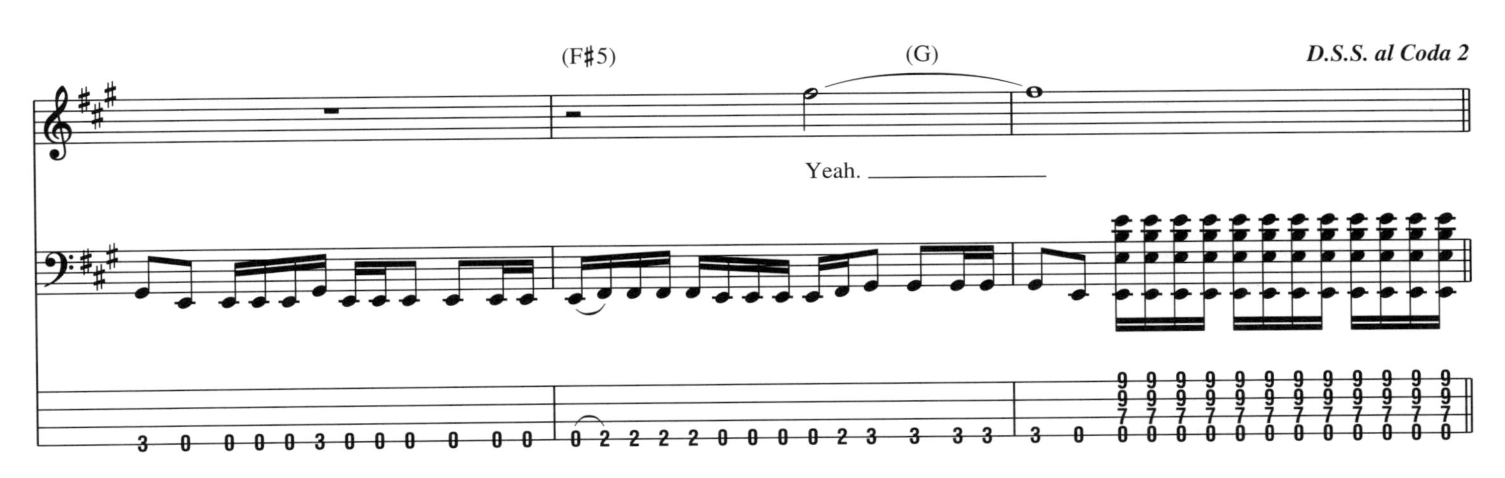
(F#5)
(G)
D.S.S. al Coda 2
Yeah.

Coda 2
Outro
D5
D7(no 3rd)
Yeah.
Am I wrong?
Bass Fig. 1
G#5
G5
E5
N.C.
Have I run too far to get home?
End Bass Fig. 1
Bass: w/ Bass Fig. 1, 3 times
D5
D7(no 3rd)
G#5
G5
E5
N.C.
Have I gone,
left you here a - lone?
D5
D7(no 3rd)
G#5
G5
E5
N.C.
Am I wrong?
Have I run too far to get home? Yeah.
D
D7(no 3rd)
G#5
G5
E5
Have I gone,
left you here a - lone?
Freely
D7#9
If I would, could you?
Bass
rit.

Yankee Rose

Words by David Lee Roth
Music by Steve Vai

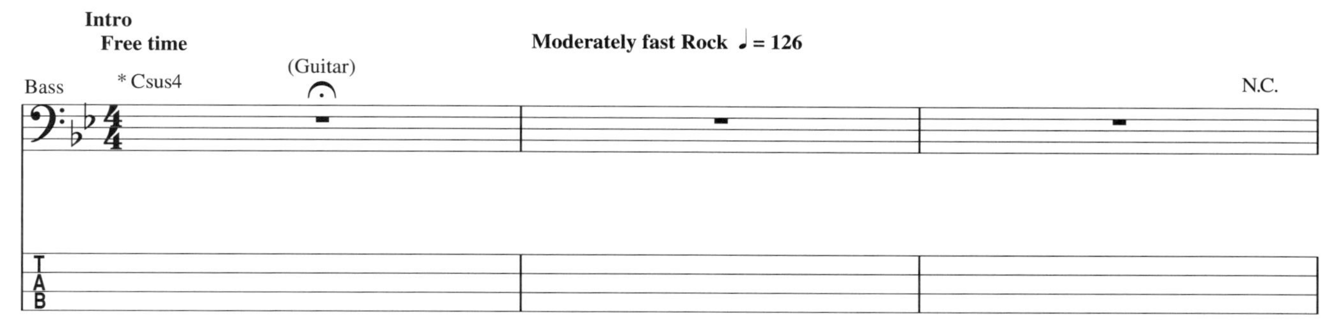

*Chord symbols reflect overall harmony.

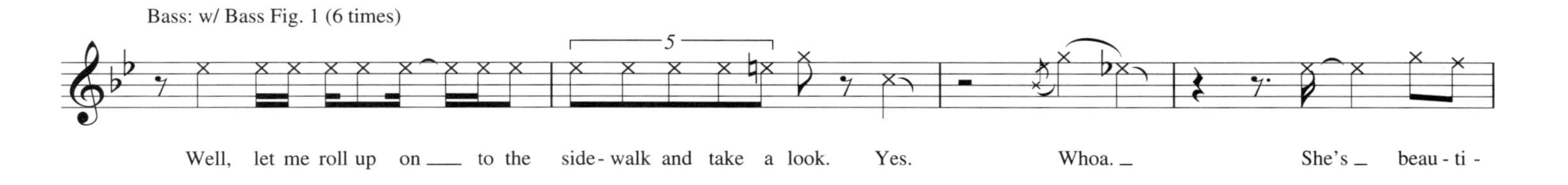

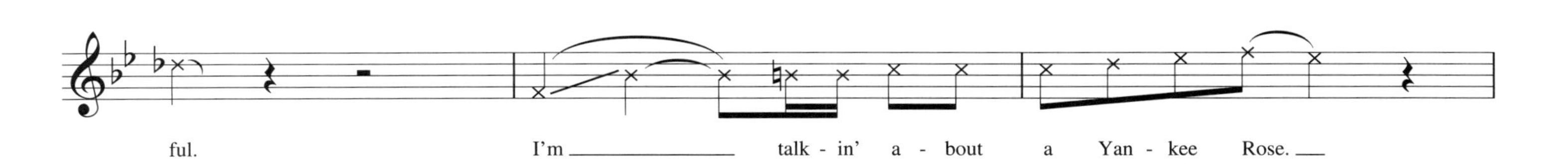

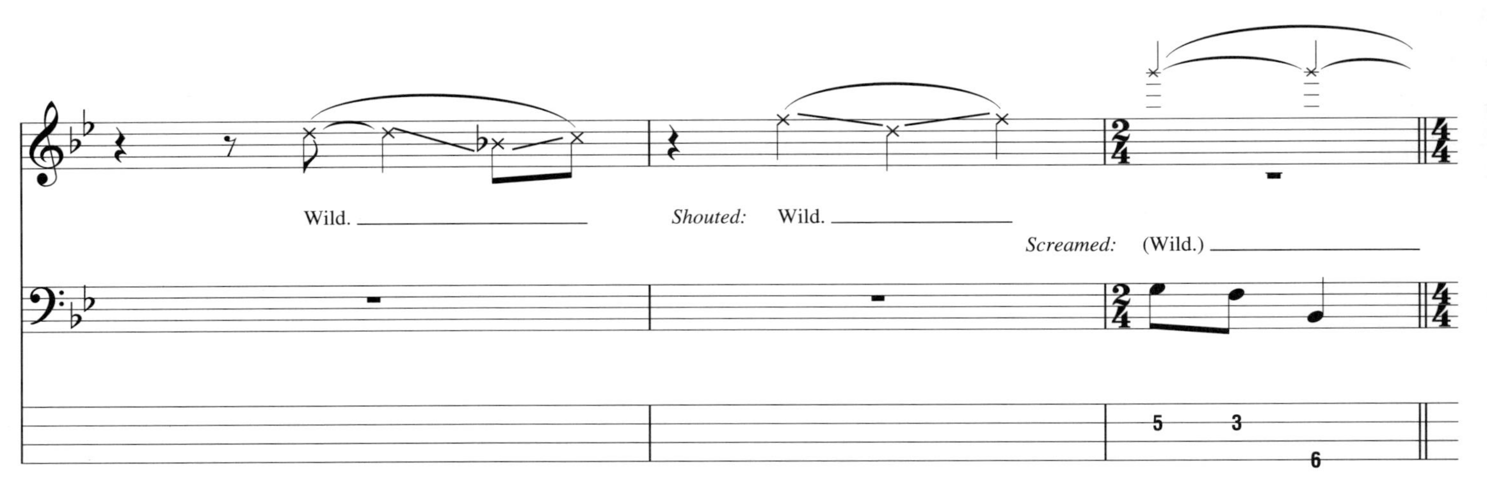
Wild.
Shouted: Wild.
Screamed: (Wild.)

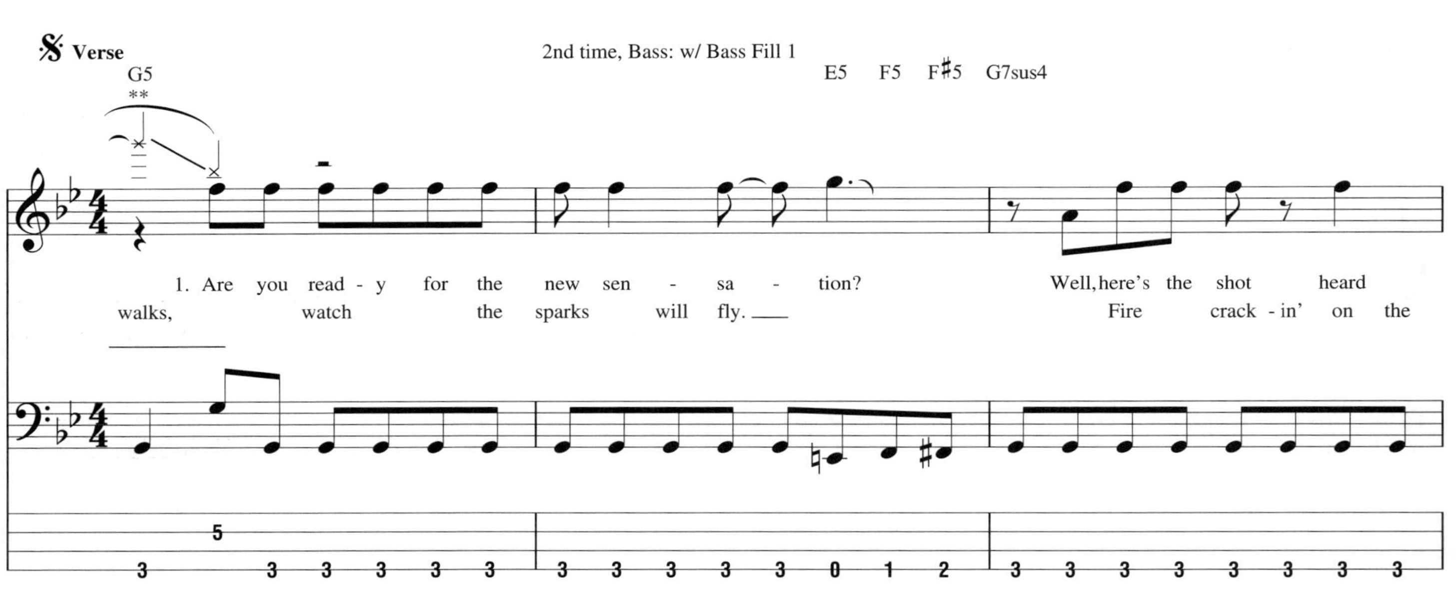
Verse
2nd time, Bass: w/ Bass Fill 1
G5
E5 F5 F♯5 G7sus4
1. Are you read - y for the new sen - sa - tion? Well, here's the shot heard
walks, watch the sparks will fly. Fire crack - in' on the

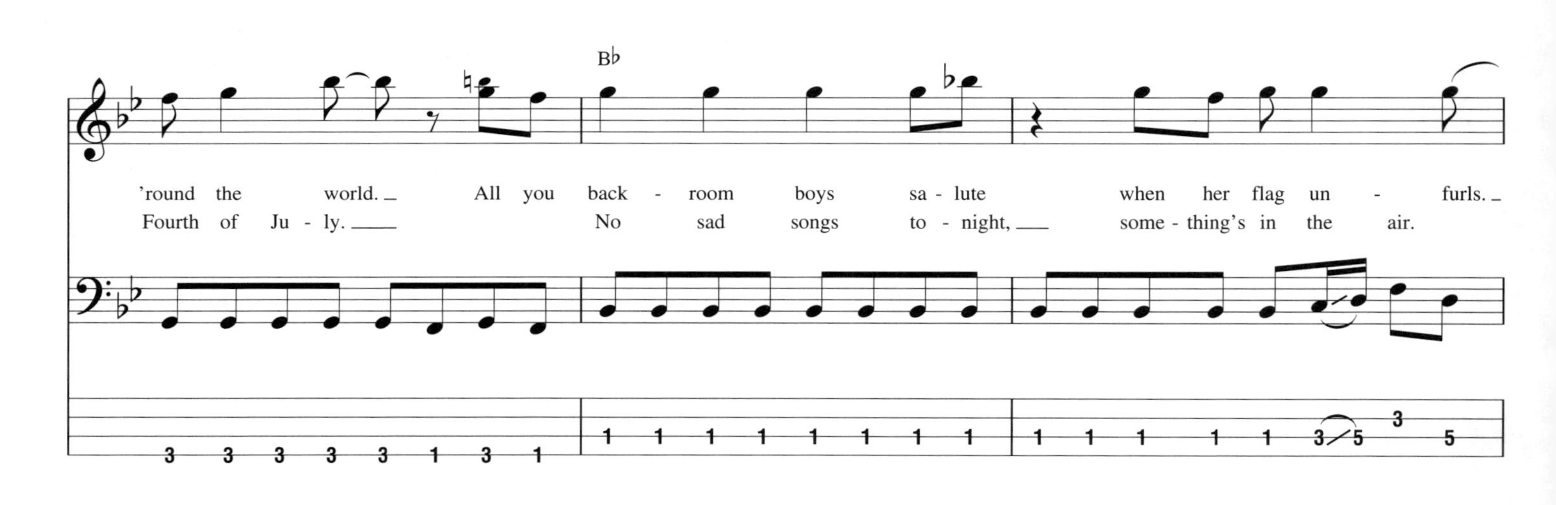
B♭
'round the world. All you back - room boys sa - lute when her flag un - furls.
Fourth of Ju - ly. No sad songs to - night, some - thing's in the air.

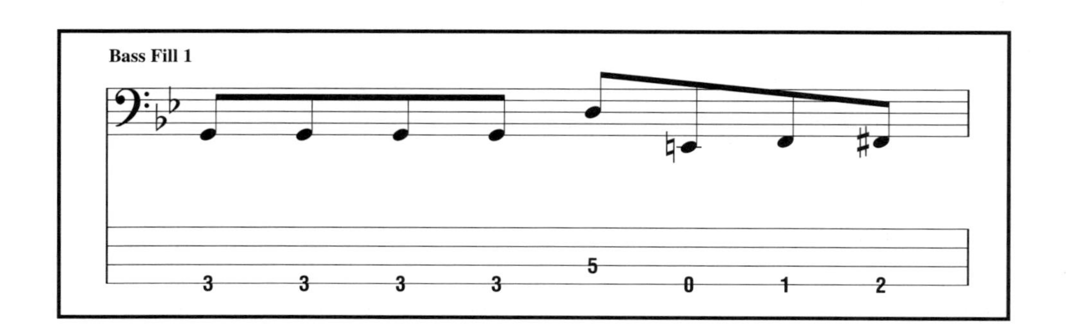
Bass Fill 1

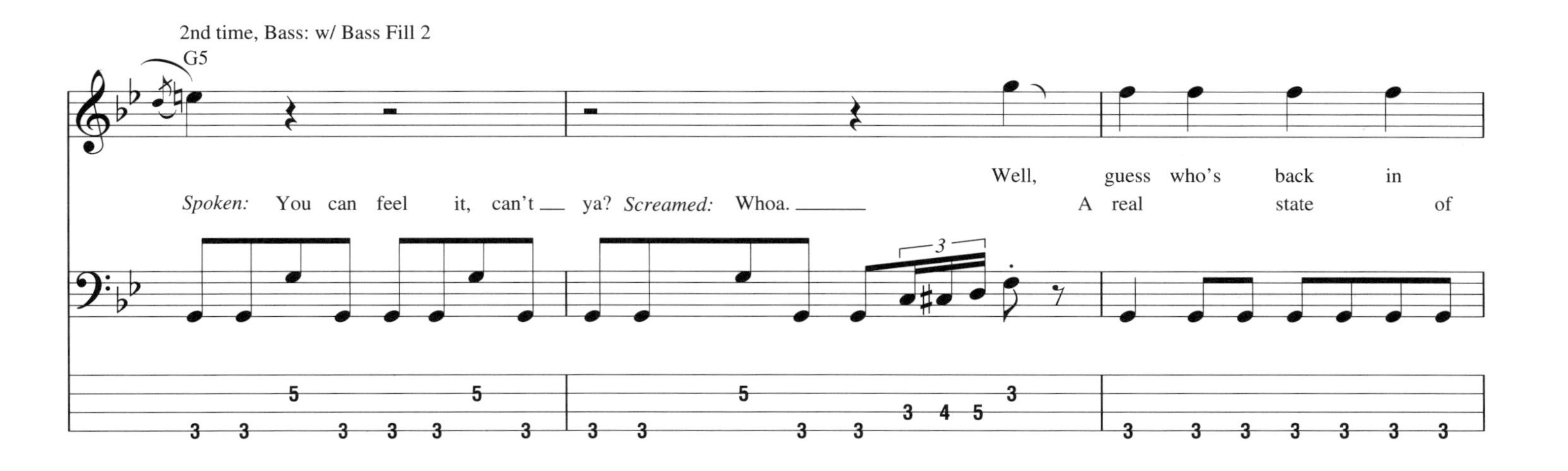
2nd time, Bass: w/ Bass Fill 2
G5
Well, guess who's back in
Spoken: You can feel it, can't ya? Screamed: Whoa. A real state of

2nd time, Bass: w/ Bass Fill 1
E5 F5 F♯5 G7sus4
cir - cu - la - tion? Now I don't know what you may have heard, but what I
in - de - pen - dence. So pret - ty when her rock - ets glare

B♭
G5
need right now is the o - rig - i - nal good time girl.
Still prov - in' an - y night that her flag's still there.

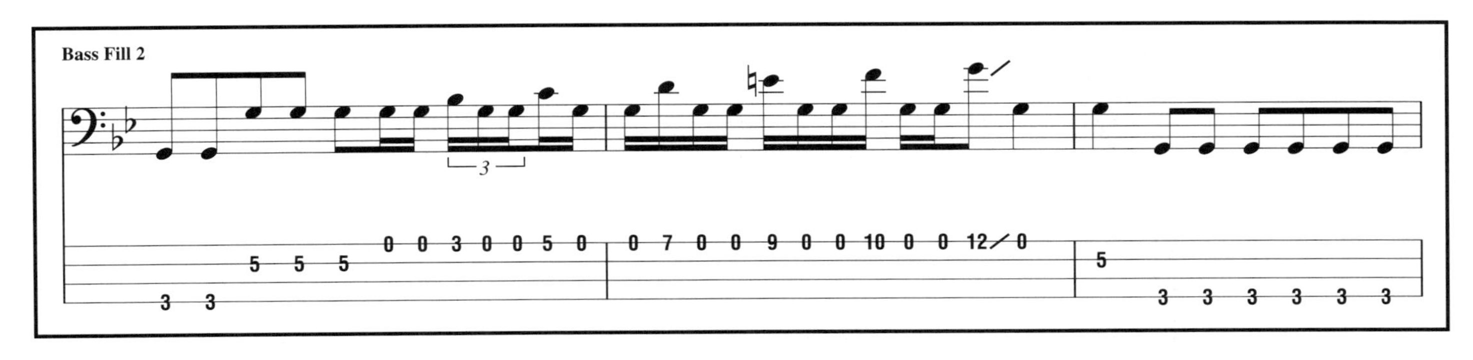
Bass Fill 2

Pre-Chorus
2nd time, Bass: w/ Bass Fill 3
C5
Dm7
Spoken: Whoa.
Coast to coast
Coast to
(She's a vi - sion from coast to coast.
coast.
Sea to shin - ing sea.
Bbsus2
Sea to shin - ing sea.
Dm7
Hey, sis - ter you're the
per - fect toast.)
That's
Make
a
toast.
Bbsus2
E5
Bb5
F5
G5
Show me your.
Bass Fill 3

Chorus
Gm7
And your. Al - right. I'm talk - in' 'bout the
(Bright lights, your cit - y lights.
3 3 3 3 3 3 3 3 3 3 3 3 3 3 3 1 3 3 3 3 3 3 3 3
To Coda
D5 C5 B♭5 C5 B♭5 G5 E5 B♭5 Gm7
Yan - kee Rose. Your Bright lights, And your. cit - y lights.) Al - right.
3 3 5 3 6 3 6 3 0 6 3 3 3 3 3 3 3 3 3 3 3 3 3 3
D.S. al Coda
D5 C5 B♭5 C5 B♭5 G5 E5 B♭5 G5 N.C.
I'm talk - in' 'bout it. 2. When she
3 3 3 3 3 3 3 3 5 3 6 3 6 3 0 6 3
Coda
Al - right. I'm in love with a
cit - y lights.)
3 3 3 3 3 3 1 3 3 3 3 3 3 3 3 3

D5 C5 B♭5 C5 B♭5 G5 E5 B♭5 G5 N.C.
Yan - kee Rose.
Whispered: Ah.
Bridge
Half-time feel
B♭add#11/9
G6sus2
Spoken: Ah, she's beau - ti - ful al - right.
*Two handed tapping: Tap notes on 1st & 3rd strings w/ 1st & 3rd fingers of right hand; hammer on notes on 2nd & 4th strings w/ 1st & 3rd fingers of left hand.
B♭add#11/9
Mm, noth - in' like her in the whole world.
G6sus2
End half-time feel
Yeah!
She's right on

B♭5
C5
D5
C5
D5
C5
B♭5
time. I'm on the case.
Pick up the phone.
No time to

F5
waste. She got the beat
and here's a lit - tle bit com - ing your way.

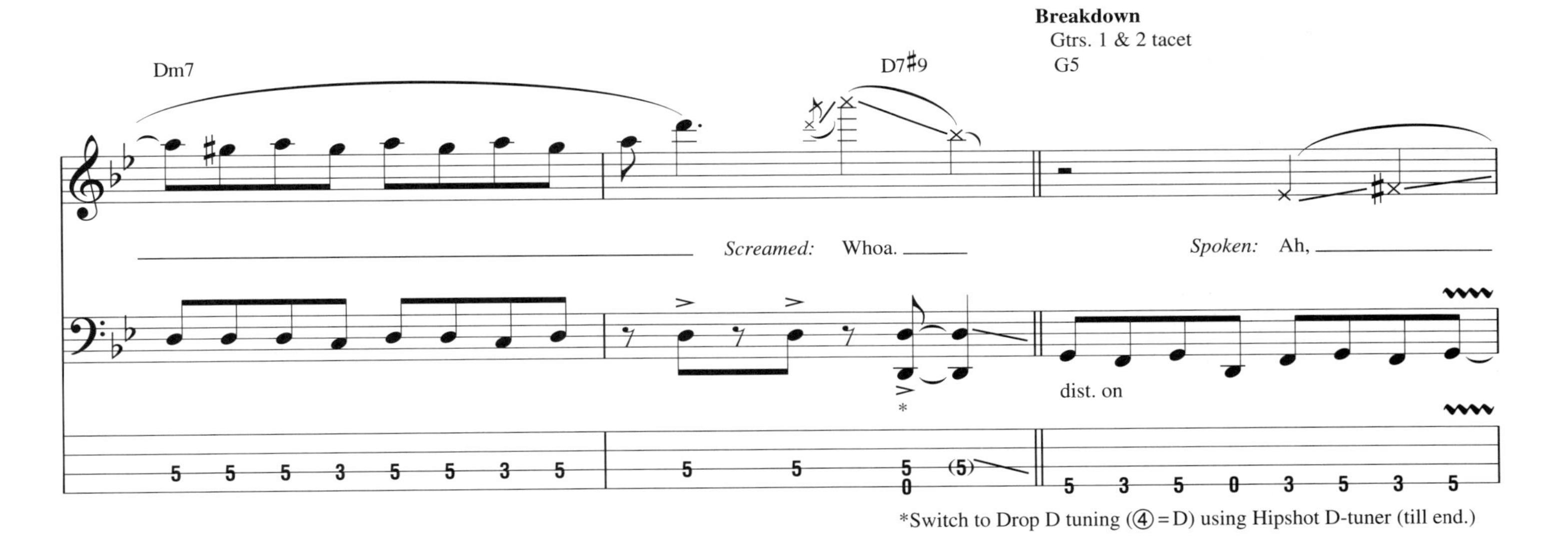
Breakdown
Gtrs. 1 & 2 tacet
Dm7
D7♯9
G5
Screamed: Whoa.
Spoken: Ah,
dist. on
*Switch to Drop D tuning (④ = D) using Hipshot D-tuner (till end.)

raise them up, now. Let's see who sa - lutes, ba - by.

Yeah. Yeah. Yeah. Yeah. Yeah. Lit-tle bit, lit-tle bit, lit-tle bit high-er.
(5) 3 5 0 3 5 3 5 | 3 5 0 3 5 3 5 | 3 5 0 3 5 3 5

Csus4 C Bb
Here's the na - tion - al an - them. Yeah, say. Come on!
(5) 3 5 0 3 5 3 4 | 5 3 5 0 3 5 3 5 | 3 5 0 3 5 3 4 5

A5 G5 F5 G5 Csus4 C
6
I wan-na get a lit-tle bit of ap - ple pie, man.
5 3 5 0 3 5 3 5 | 5 3 5 3 5 3 0 5 | 5 3 5 0 3 5 3 5

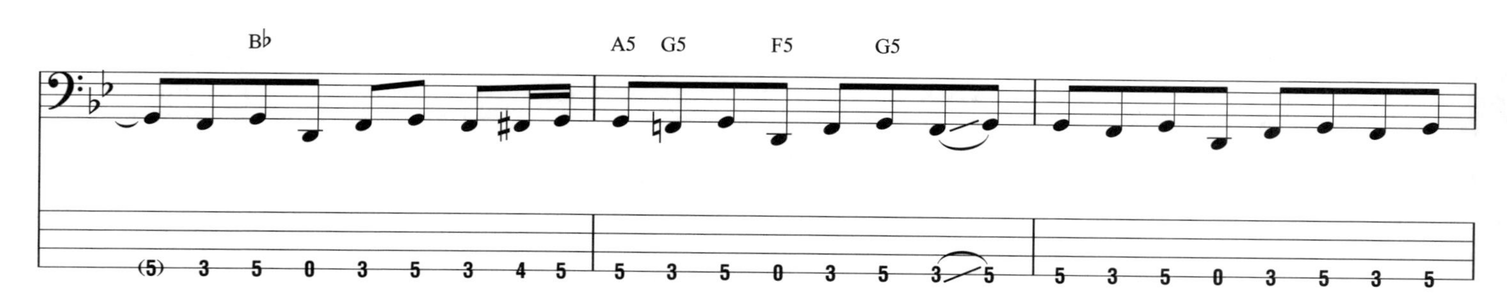
Bb A5 G5 F5 G5
(5) 3 5 0 3 5 3 4 5 | 5 3 5 0 3 5 3 5 | 5 3 5 0 3 5 3 5

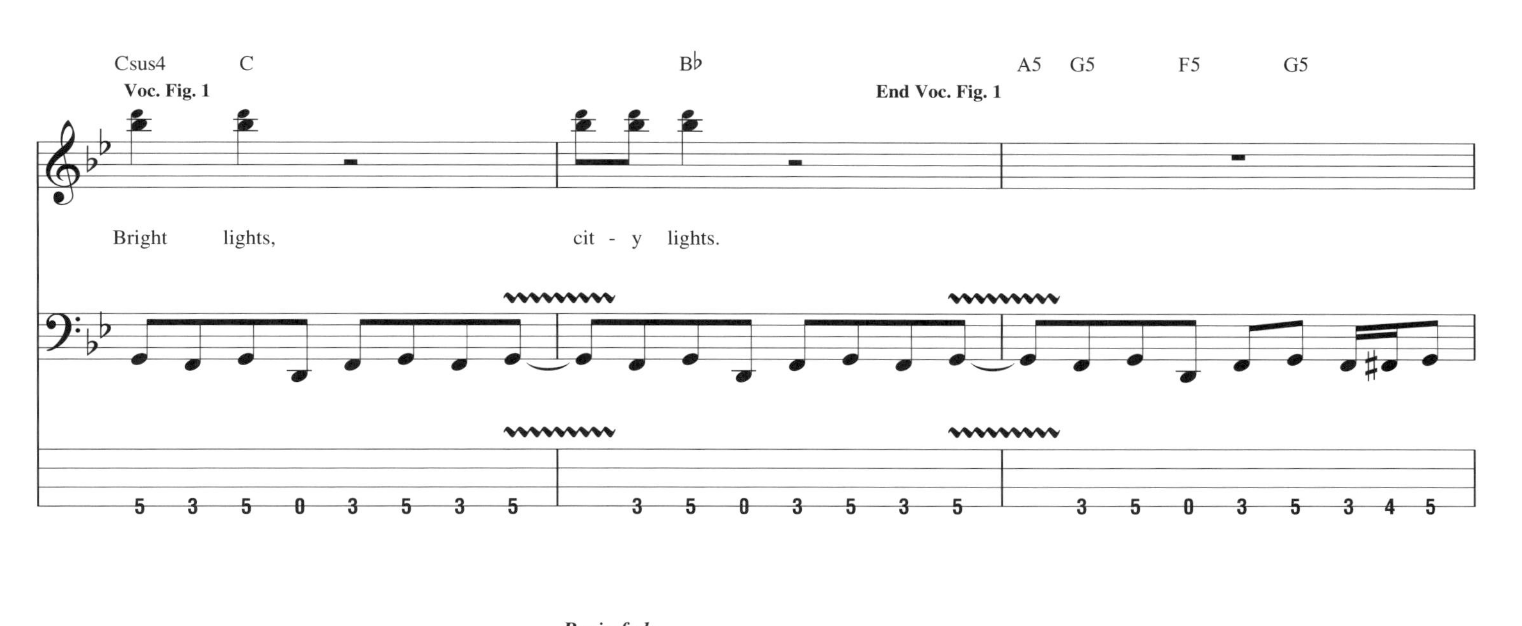
Csus4
C
B♭
A5
G5
F5
G5
Voc. Fig. 1
End Voc. Fig. 1
Bright lights, cit - y lights.
5 3 5 0 3 5 3 5
3 5 0 3 5 3 5
3 5 0 3 5 3 4 5

Begin fade
Voc.: w/ Voc. Fig. 1
Csus4
C
B♭
5 3 5 0 3 5 3 5
5 3 5 0 3 5 3 5
3 5 0 3 5 3 4 5

A5
G5
F5
G5
Voc.: w/ Voc. Fig. 1
Csus4
C
5 3 5 3 5 3 5 3
5 3 4 5 3 4 5 3 0 5
3 5 0 3 5 3 5

B♭
A5
G5
F5
G5
(5) 3 5 0 3 5 3 4 5
5 3 5 0 3 5 3 4 5
5 3 4 5 0 0 3 5 3 5

Fade out
Voc.: w/ Voc. Fig. 1
Csus4
C
B♭
5 3 5 0 3 5 3 5
3 5 0 3 5 3 4 5

You've Got Another Thing Comin'

Words and Music by Glenn Tipton, Rob Halford and K.K. Downing

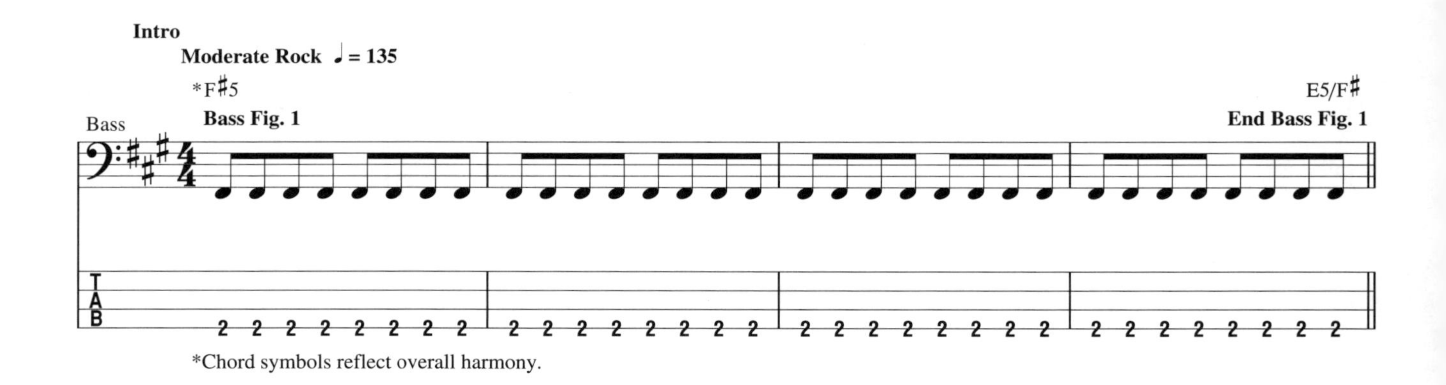

*Chord symbols reflect overall harmony.

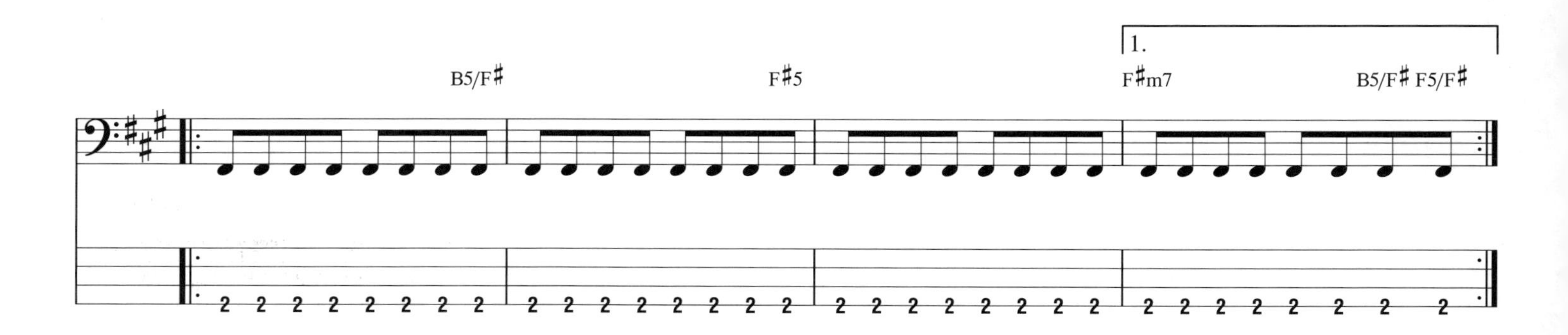

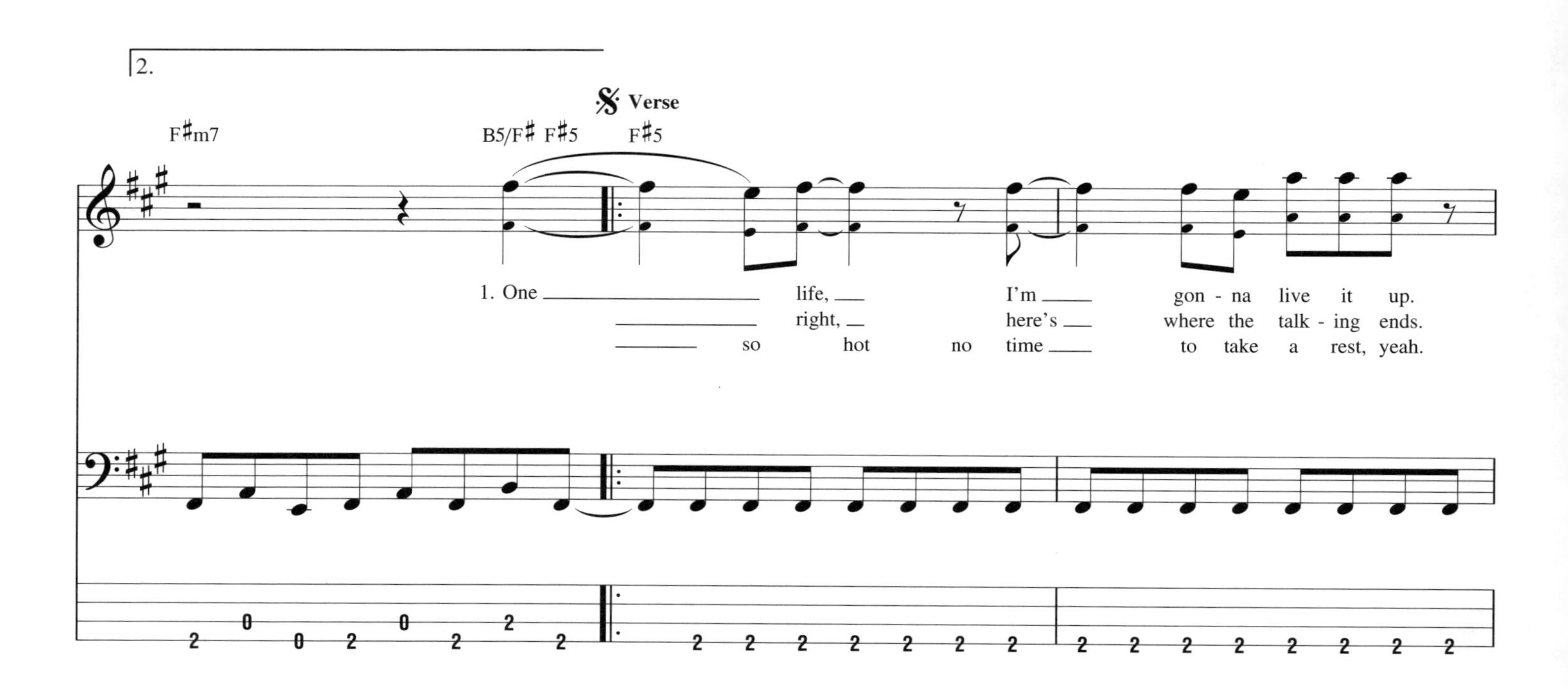

I'm talk - in' flight, I said I'll
Well lis - ten this a night there'll
Act tough, ain't room
Bass Fig. 2

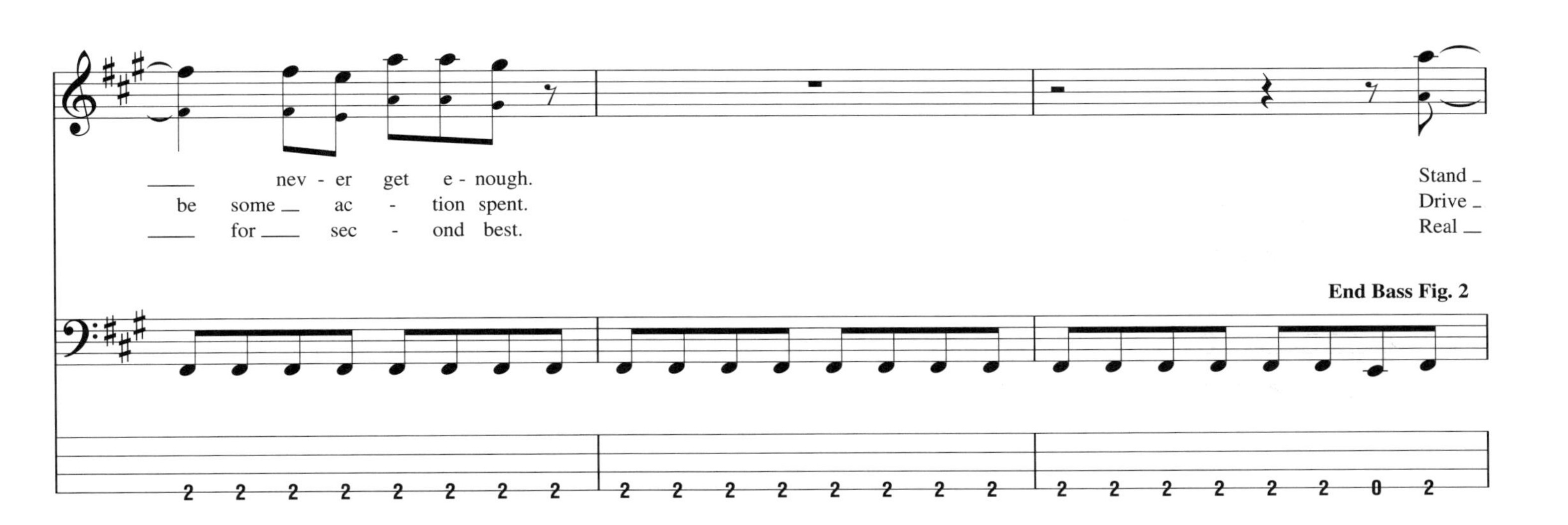
nev - er get e - nough.
be some ac - tion spent.
for sec - ond best.
Stand
Drive
Real
End Bass Fig. 2

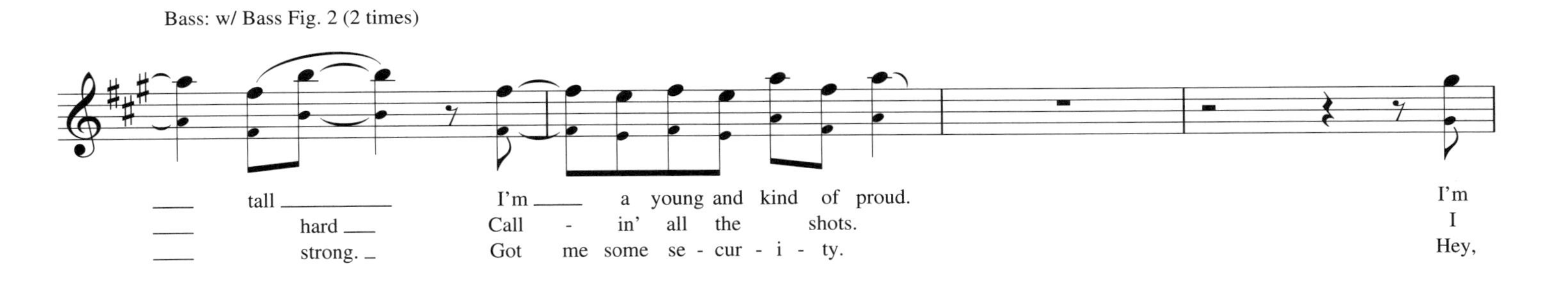
Bass: w/ Bass Fig. 2 (2 times)
tall I'm a young and kind of proud.
hard Call - in' all the shots.
strong. Got me some se - cur - i - ty.
I'm
I
Hey,

on the top, but as long as the mu - sic's loud.
got an ace card com - in' down the rocks.
I'm a big smash, I'm go - in' for in - fin - i - ty, yeah.

Pre-Chorus
F#5
D5
B5
F#5
1., 3. If you think I'll sit a - round as the world goes by, you're think - in' like a fool 'cause it's a case
2. If you think I'll sit a - round while you chip a - way my brain lis - ten I ain't fool - in' and you'd bet -
Bass Fig. 3
of do or die.
ter think a - gain.
Out there is a for - tune wait - ing to be had. If you
D5
B5
End Bass Fig. 3
1.
Chorus
C#5
F#m7
F#5
think I'll let it go you're mad. You've got a - no - ther thing com - in'.
F#m7
B5/F#
F#m7
F#5
F#m7
B5/F# F#5
You've got an - oth - er thing com - in'.
2. That's

2.
Chorus
F♯m7
F♯5
B5/F♯
com - in'.
You've got an - oth - er thing
com - in'.
Bass Fig. 4
End Bass Fig. 4
To Coda
Bridge
Bm7
In this world we're
Bm7/A
A5
liv - in' in we have our share of sor - row.
An -

Bm7
Bm7/A
A5
C♯5
- swer now is don't give in. Aim for a new to - mor - row.
Guitar Solo
Bass: w/ Bass Fig. 1 (2 times)
Bass: w/ Bass Fig. 3
F♯m7
F♯5
F♯m7
B5/F♯
F♯m7
F♯5
5
6
D.S. al Coda
(take 2nd ending)
C♯5
F♯m7
B5/F♯
F♯5
3. Oh,
Coda
Interlude
F♯m7
B5/F♯
F♯m7
F♯5
F♯m7
B5/F♯
6
You've got an - oth - er thing ah. Com - in' on down.
Outro
w/ Voc. ad lib. (till fade)
Bass: w/ Bass Fig. 4
Play 10 times and fade
E5/F♯
B5/F♯
F♯5
You've got an - oth - er thing com - in'.

Bass Notation Legend

Bass music can be notated two different ways: on a *musical staff*, and in *tablature*.

THE MUSICAL STAFF shows pitches and rhythms and is divided by bar lines into measures. Pitches are named after the first seven letters of the alphabet.

TABLATURE graphically represents the bass fingerboard. Each horizontal line represents a string, and each number represents a fret.

Notes:

Strings: high G D A low E

3rd string, open — 2nd string, 2nd fret — 1st & 2nd strings open, played together

HAMMER-ON: Strike the first (lower) note with one finger, then sound the higher note (on the same string) with another finger by fretting it without picking.

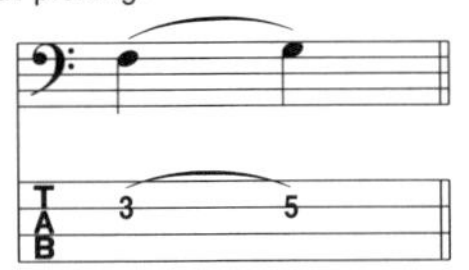

PULL-OFF: Place both fingers on the notes to be sounded. Strike the first note and without picking, pull the finger off to sound the second (lower) note.

LEGATO SLIDE: Strike the first note and then slide the same fret-hand finger up or down to the second note. The second note is not struck.

SHIFT SLIDE: Same as legato slide, except the second note is struck.

TRILL: Very rapidly alternate between the notes indicated by continuously hammering on and pulling off.

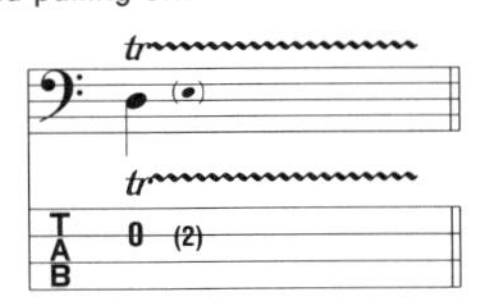

TREMOLO PICKING: The note is picked as rapidly and continuously as possible.

VIBRATO: The string is vibrated by rapidly bending and releasing the note with the fretting hand.

SHAKE: Using one finger, rapidly alternate between two notes on one string by sliding either a half-step above or below.

NATURAL HARMONIC: Strike the note while the fret hand lightly touches the string directly over the fret indicated.

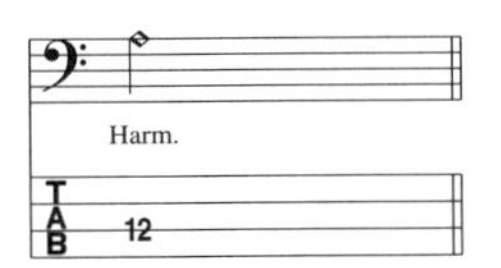

MUFFLED STRINGS: A percussive sound is produced by laying the fret hand across the string(s) without depressing them and striking them with the pick hand.

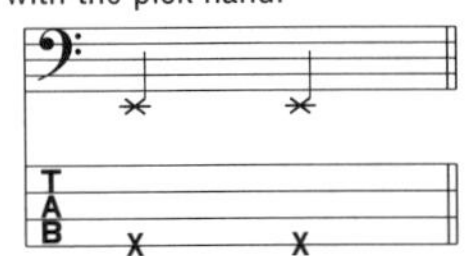

BEND: Strike the note and bend up the interval shown.

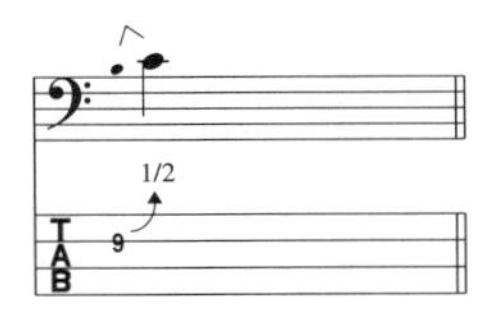

BEND AND RELEASE: Strike the note and bend up as indicated, then release back to the original note. Only the first note is struck.

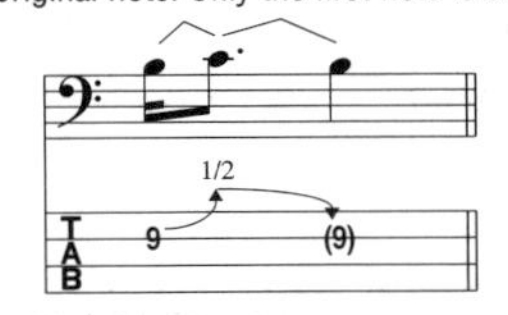

RIGHT-HAND TAP: Hammer ("tap") the fret indicated with the "pick-hand" index or middle finger and pull off to the note fretted by the fret hand.

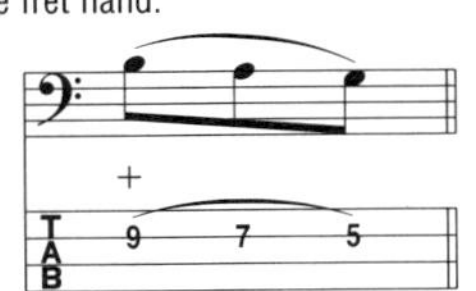

LEFT-HAND TAP: Hammer ("tap") the fret indicated with the "fret-hand" index or middle finger.

SLAP: Strike ("slap") string with right-hand thumb.

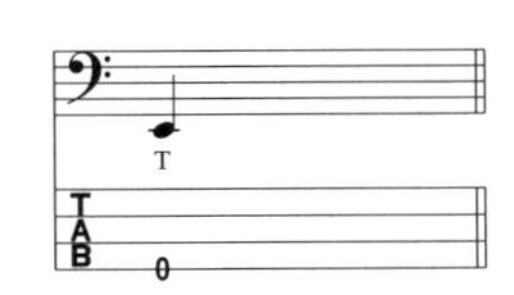

POP: Snap ("pop") string with right-hand index or middle finger.

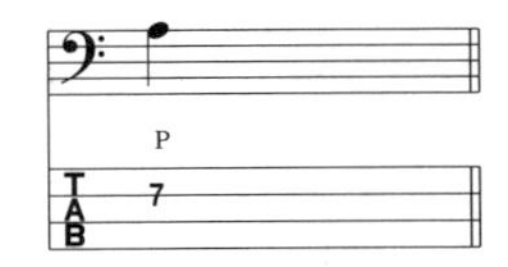

Additional Musical Definitions

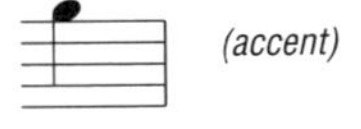
(accent) • Accentuate note (play it louder)

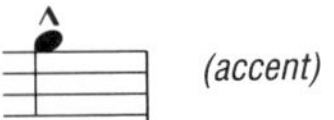
(accent) • Accentuate note with great intensity

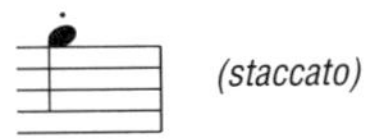
(staccato) • Play the note short

⊓ • Downstroke

V • Upstroke

D.S. al Coda • Go back to the sign (𝄋), then play until the measure marked "***To Coda***," then skip to the section labelled "**Coda**."

D.C. al Fine • Go back to the beginning of the song and play until the measure marked "***Fine***" (end).

Bass Fig. • Label used to recall a recurring pattern.

Fill • Label used to identify a brief pattern which is to be inserted into the arrangement.

tacet • Instrument is silent (drops out).

• Repeat measures between signs.

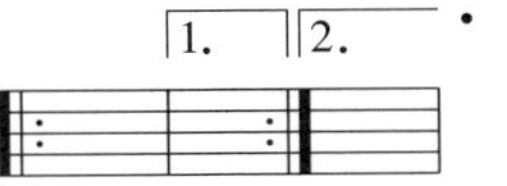

• When a repeated section has different endings, play the first ending only the first time and the second ending only the second time.

NOTE: Tablature numbers in parentheses mean:
1. The note is being sustained over a system (note in standard notation is tied), or
2. The note is sustained, but a new articulation (such as a hammer-on, pull-off, slide or vibrato begins), or
3. The note is a barely audible "ghost" note (note in standard notation is also in parentheses).

Bass Recorded Versions® feature authentic transcriptions written in standard notation and tablature for bass guitar. This series features complete bass lines from the classics to contemporary superstars.

25 All-Time Rock Bass Classics
00690445 / $14.95

25 Essential Rock Bass Classics
00690210 / $14.95

Bass Tab 1990-1999
00690400 / $16.95

Bass Tab 1999-2000
00690404 / $14.95

Bass Tab 2000
00690434 / $14.95

Bass Tab 2001
00690522 / $14.95

Bass Tab White Pages
00690508 / $29.95

The Beatles Bass Lines
00690170 / $12.95

The Beatles 1962-1966
00690556 / $17.95

The Beatles 1966-1970
00690557 / $16.95

Best Bass Rock Hits
00694803 / $12.95

Black Sabbath – We Sold Our Soul For Rock 'N' Roll
00660116 / $17.95

The Best of Blink 182
00690549 / $17.95

Blues Bass Classics
00690291 / $14.95

Chart Hits for Bass
00690729 / $14.95

The Best of Eric Clapton
00660187 / $16.95

Stanley Clarke Collection
00672307 / $19.95

Hard Rock Bass Bible
00690746 / $17.95

Jimi Hendrix – Are You Experienced?
00690371 / $14.95

Jimi Hendrix – Axis Bold As Love
00690373 / $14.95

Jimi Hendrix – Electric Ladyland
00690375 / $14.95

The Buddy Holly Bass Book
00660132 / $12.95

Incubus – Morning View
00690639 / $17.95

Best of Kiss for Bass
00690080 / $19.95

Bob Marley Bass Collection
00690568 / $17.95

Motown Bass Classics
00690253 / $14.95

Nirvana Bass Collection
00690066 / $19.95

No Doubt – Tragic Kingdom
00120112 / $22.95

Jaco Pastorius – Greatest Jazz Fusion Bass Player
00690421 / $17.95

The Essential Jaco Pastorius
00690420 / $17.95

Pearl Jam – Ten
00694882 / $14.95

Pink Floyd – Dark Side of the Moon
00660172 / $14.95

The Best of Police
00660207 / $14.95

Queen – The Bass Collection
00690065 / $17.95

Rage Against the Machine
00690248 / $16.95

Rage Against the Machine – Evil Empire
00690249 / $14.95

Red Hot Chili Peppers – Blood Sugar Sex Magik
00690064 / $19.95

Red Hot Chili Peppers - By the Way
00690585 / $19.95

Red Hot Chili Peppers – Californication
00690390 / $19.95

Red Hot Chili Peppers – Greatest Hits
00690675 / $17.95

Red Hot Chili Peppers – One Hot Minute
00690091 / $18.95

Rock Bass Bible
00690446 / $18.95

Rolling Stones
00690256 / $14.95

System of a Down – Toxicity
00690592 / $19.95

Top Hits for Bass
00690677 / $14.95

Stevie Ray Vaughan – In Step
00694777 / $14.95

Stevie Ray Vaughan – Lightnin' Blues 1983-1987
00694778 / $19.95

FOR MORE INFORMATION, SEE YOUR LOCAL MUSIC DEALER, OR WRITE TO:

7777 W. BLUEMOUND RD. P.O. BOX 13819 MILWAUKEE, WI 53213

Visit Hal Leonard Online at
www.halleonard.com

Prices, contents & availability subject to change without notice. Some products may not be available outside the U.S.A.

0205